AF531375

Philosophical and Sociological Foundations of Education

Philosophical and Sociological Foundations of Education

Sunanda Chopra

Publishing House

4735/22, Prakash Deep Building,
Ansari Road, Daryaganj,
New Delhi-110002

Published by :
SAURABH PUBLISHING HOUSE

Distributed by :
LOTUS PRESS PUBLISHERS & DISTRIBUTORS
Unit No. 220, Second Floor, 4735/22, Prakash Deep Building,
Ansari Road, Daryaganj, New Delhi - 110002
Ph : 011-23280047, 32903912, 098118-38000
E-mail : lotus_press@sify.com

Saurabh Publishing is an imprint of
Lotus Press Publishers & Distributors

Philosophical and Sociological Foundations of Education

ISBN : 978-93-83045-02-0 (H/B)

Printed at : Bharat Offset Works, Delhi

Preface

Every educational system must have some goals, aims or objectives. These act as guides for the educator in educating the child. In fact, we cannot think of any process of education without specific aims and objectives. Bode says, "Unless we have some guiding philosophy in the determination of objectives, we get nowhere at all." These aims of education, in different countries, are determined by the aims and ideals of life which the people of those countries have at that particular time. The aims and ideals of life, in their turn, are determined by the philosophy of the time. It is, therefore, that aims and ideals of education vary with the different philosophers. It is the philosophy of the time which determines whether the aim of education should be moral, vocational, intellectual, liberal or spiritual. In the words of Rusk, "Every system of education must have an aim and the aim of education is relative to the aim of life. Philosophy formulates what should be the end of life while education offers suggestions how this end is to be achieved." The philosopher struggles hard with the mysteries of life and arrives at their solution after mature reflection and thinking. He then suggests ways and means of dealing with them. Thus, he lays down ultimate values and explains their significance to the community. In this way, he tries to convert people to his own beliefs and philosophy. These ultimate values, as formulated by the philosopher, become the aims of education for that community. The training of the younger generation, according to those aims and values, then lies on the shoulders of the educator in the field. He selects the material for instruction and determines the methods of procedure for the attainment of those aims. In this way, the entire educational programme proceeds with its foundations on sound philosophy.

This book deals with the topics of—*Significance of Philosophy of Education; Philosophy of Education in Different Ages; Philosophy of Idealism in Education; Philosophy of Realism in Education; Philosophy of Naturalism in Education; Philosophy of Pragmatism and Humanism in Education; Contribution of Indian Educational Thinkers; Contribution of Western Educational Thinkers; Socialisation and Social Change; Social System and Family; Social and Culture; Social and Mobility; Social Caste and Class System; Nature and Aims of Democratic Education; Religion in Education; Women Education in Society;* etc.

I hope that students and those in the education field will find it useful for academic and competitive examinations. I owe a deep sense of gratitude to my publisher for materializing my present endeavour.

Sunanda Chopra

Contents

1

Significance of Philosophy of Education

The traditional view of philosophy is that its business or aim in knowledge of Being or Reality, which is more comprehensive, fundamental and ultimate than the knowledge which can be provided by the organs and methods at the disposal of the special science, for according to this view, with the possible exception of matter; Science deal with what is temporal, changing and contingent while philosophy aims at knowledge of that which is eternal and inherently necessary. Its (Philosophy) knowings are so primary and final that it alone can give sure support to the claims of truth put forward by the lesser form of knowledge.

Since the business of philosophy is with ultimate reality behind and beyond the phenomenal world, the possibility of knowledge, the conditions of knowing before knowing, takes place, becomes the chief problems of philosophy.

Dewey's conception of philosophy widely differs from this. He does not believe in two levels of beings: The phenomenal level and the ultimate level, 'Dewey is out to abolish all dualism in ontology and epistemology, science and philosophy.

Dewey's conception is that philosophy is not outside of and above all other human pursuits, cultivating in secrecy and silence a remote, stacked-off pressure of its own.

Philosophy is and works within the open and public domain of all human activities, one among others, differentiated by its scope and function, but in no way set apart.

The scope of subject-matter of Philosophy, as described by Dewey can be represented in the form of three concentric circles. The first area, bounded by the innermost circle, is occupied by reflective thought, by logic or what logic or Dewey now calls Inquiry. In the second area are the typical modes of human experience, such as the practical or utilitarian, the aesthetic, religious, socioethical, scientific. Philosophic inquiry here concerns itself with analysing what these modes of experience are and particularly, with discovering their inter-relations, how the practical or utilitarian developes with scientific, the scientific into aesthetic and *vice versa*.

The third area is that of the socio-cultural world. The social world raises such questions as "the Value of research for social progress : The bearing of psychology upon educational procedures: The mutual relation of fine and industrial arts; the adjustment of religious aspirations to scientific statements, the relation of organization to individuality."

The significance of Dewey: Conception is not, to be found in the mere extension of the range, significant as that is. It is to be found in the inter-relations of the three areas, that they are functional distinctions, discriminable divisions within one inclusive field of experience, the boundary lines being neither fixed nor impermeable, marking off, but not insulating any one from any of the rest.

Philosophy is an enterprise of reflective thought and can only deal with problems in a reflective or intellectual way. But when each bundle of actualised problems labelled with its own bag of epistemology, ethics, logic, aesthetics, social philosophy, are treated as if each constituted a separate and distinct substantive realm, as being the original and primary subject-matter of inquiry, philosophy instead of prospering as a reflective enterprise, degenerate into a mere process of untying each bundle in some way and tying it again in another.

Reflective inquiry, philosophic or otherwise can handle and actual condition that is a problem only transforming it into an intellectual form. An architect engaged on the problem of remodelling a house uses a blue print. The blue print is an intellectualised form of the actual house. An architect does not substitute his blue print for the house; he does not consider the blue print as constituting the original and primary subject-matter of his inquiry and he does not think that he changes the house when he changes the blue print although changing the blue print may be all that he professionally contributes towards the consummation of that final end.

In philosophy blue prints have taken the place of the actual house. This substitutions in philosophy has resulted in vain disputes and arid verbal jugglery. It has led to a diseased formulation of philosophic problems. Dewey distinguishes between problems in 'General' and the 'General Problem'. The problem of *e.g.,* knowledge in General, *i.e.,* 'Is knowledge prossible'? Is a disceased formulation of the problem of developing a general theory of knowledge. It is just as intelligent for a philosopher ask 'Is knowledge possible' as it would be for a scientist to ask 'Is motion possible'. There are specific cases of motion and scientific inquiry experiments with these specific cases. There is no 'motion in general' and hence no 'problem in general'. But there is a general problem of theory of motion, which for the scientist consists in Central laws of motion. The general laws are not proved valid by evaporating out of scientific existence, specific cases of motion, but their validity rests on their ability to explain or account for the specific cases. Similarly there are specific cases of knowing. There is no knoweldge in general and hence no problems of knowledge in general. But there is the general problem of knowledge, which consists in finding general conditions in knowledge.

Thus, a philosophic generalisation must satisfy the same requirements as a scientific generalisation. The philosophic task is to reach generalisations that meet specific conditions. It is true that generalisation of the nature of the reflections process certainly involves elimination of much of the specific material and contents of the thought situations of daily life and of critical science. Quite compatible with this, however, is the notion that it seizes upon certain specific conditions and factors and aims to bring them to clear consciousness not to abolish them while eliminating the particular materials of particular practical and scientific pursuits, *(i)* it may strive to hit upon the common denominator in the various situations which are antecendent or primary to thought and which evoke, *(ii)* It may attempt to show how typical features in the specific antecedents of thought call out diverse typical modes of thought-reaction; It may attempt to state the nature of the specific consequences in which thought fulfils it careers.

There is thus, no conflict between the philosophic concern with the general or generic and interest in the specific. Where philosophic activity eliminates the specific entirely, it gets into insoluable problems.

Philosophy if it is to escape being confined to the futile world of blue prints must adopt empirical method so that its activity is in continuous functional connection with socio-cultural and scientific world. All philosophic problems have empirical fathers who can be empirically traced, located and identified. An insoluable problem in philosophy is an intellectual disease which can be caused by tracing back the problem as it appears in philosophy backs to its origins in the primary subject method of experience and finding out how, in the course of its intellectual genetic history, it got that way. Again the prevention against a insoluable problem and futile and frustrated philosophic activity consists in working back and forth between the narrow and large fields of the technical study of the intellectualised problems in philosophy and the socio-cultural and scientific world that generate those problems. A working back and forward between the three areas of problems called by Dewey 'double movements'. This "double movements" is both corrective and cummulative. It tests the increment in our field by transferring into method of work in another field. Again it functions to uncover new clues for different fields.

Philosophy has at various times been set-up as a separate and peculiar science, sin genesis. This according to Dewey, is not true. Philosophic problems arise out of the common matrix of experience. For philosophy to solve its own intellectualised problem it must move into the common field of problematic situations. The solution of problems in philosophy can be reached only by working back and forth between the technical or private domain of philosophy and the final or public domain of socio-cultural experience.

RELATION OF PHILOSOPHY WITH EDUCATION

Philosophy as a field of knowledge deals with three things *(i)* reality (metaphysics), *(ii)* knowledge (epistemology) and *(iii)* problems related to values (axiology). What is reality? What is the purpose of creation? What are time and space? These are some of the questions that are answered by metaphysics. It is the main branch of philosophy. It discusses three aspects of reality *e.g.,* the world, the self and the God. Epistemology examines different methods to achieve different types of knowledge. Axiology is mainly concerned with value. It is a science of value. It concerns itself with problems such as what is value, what is good, what are fundamental values? and so on.

Reality, knowledge and values are very much the concern of education. All problems of education, finally get concerned with these. What knowledge should be imparted to pupils, what values should be learnt by them, exactly is the reality to which education should be made to conform are questions which can be answered in several ways depending upon the kind of philosophy one believes in. Different views about reality, knowledge values etc., have been expressed by different philosophers. There is no philosophy. There are several schools of philosophy. Within each school there are several philosophers who have contributed to the thoughts on that philosophy. These have influenced the theory and practice of education also.

1. Philosophy of Education. Education is said to be the dynamic side of philosophy. It means philosophy tells what education should be and what it should aim at, but education implements that or practices that. Education is the purposive influence to be brought upon the pupils. But what kind of influence this ought to be has to be decided prior to any atempt on making it real. Who should do this? How should it be done? Philosophy of education helps in solving these problems.

2. Different Philosophy of Education have described the content and methods of education in different ways. This is so because each one of them makes different assumptions about human nature, knowledge, ethics, morals and values. *For example*, idealists consider man a spiritual being, a supreme creation of God who is regarded by them as the source of all knowledge. So they consider values of life absolute and unchanging and recommend that education should make all-out effort on teaching these values. To the naturalists material world alone is real and so all values exist in nature, in living close to nature. So they recommend that goals of education and methods of education should be determined by the nature of the child. Like that other philosophies of education also differ in their philosophical views and corresponding aims and methods of education. Thus, philosophy of education means a specific point of view on aspects of education. Dewey, for that reason, said that "philosophy is the theory of education in its most general phases". It is philosophy applied to education. There are several aspects of education like the aims, the curriculum, the methods, the discipline, the values to be taught, etc. Philosophies of education present specific ideas about each of these. Thus, it may be said that they constitute different foundations on which the superstructures called education are raised.

3. Philosophy of education is a rational way to taking decisions in the field of education, a rational process to solving problems. Instead of taking decisions about what to teach, how to teach on *ad hoc* basis without any rationale underlying them, philosophy of education makes it possible to provide sound and reasonable basis.

4. Philosophy of education is a critical method of approaching education and its various elements. It is true that there are certain well-defined philosophies of education but apart from these views, underlying them is essentially a spirit or method of approach to education, the philosophical way of thinking and appraising educational matters. Thus, philosophy of education is a way of looking at various aspects of education. In other words it may be regarded as a general theory of criticism of education. It is a reflective approach to education leading to "wisdom".

5. The main problems of philosophy of education are aims and ideals of education, analysis of pupil's nature, relations of education and state, analysis of knowledge and curriculum, methods of teaching, place of the school in the society, relationship of education to social system, education of religions, etc. Critical evaluation of these from philosophical point of view constitutes the subject-matter of philosophy of education.

Determination of educational values of largely, a function of philosophy of education.

How Does It Influence the Field of Education

Philosophy of education influences almost all the aspects of a country's educational system. Particularly, it influences the following aspects:

1. Relationship between the State and Education. Depending upon the philosophy a country believes in there are rigidly controlled and free schools. In the totalitarian states the schools have to teach what the state wants with strict discipline and rigid schedule enforced in them. In democratic countries there is ample freedom for the schools.

2. Philosophy of Education Influences the Aims of Education. The aims and ideals of education, too, are determined by the philosophy of education a country believes in. Different philosophies of education have different views on education. A country that tends to believe in the philosophy of idealism will stress on creating a spiritual environment in the school as that pupils develop spiritual values and attain self-realization. Naturalism will like to see that the child is made to learn from nature in a natural way and realizes his potentialities. Pragmatism does not accept any universal or eternal and preconceived aim of education. Like that aims of education are necessarily influenced by the philosophy of education.

3. Philosophy of Education Influences the Curriculum. What should be taught in the schools is also influenced by the kind of philosophy of education a society supports. Various philosophies of education advocate differing views on curriculum. Naturalism, *for example,* lays stress on subjects that help in self-expression and self-preservation. It advocates teaching of basic sciences, physical and health education. Idealism emphasizes teaching of higher values through ethics, religion, art and subjects of humanities. Pragmatism focusses on child-centered curriculum consisting of activities and based on child's experience.

4. Philosophy of Education Influences Theory and Practice of Discipline Also. The concept of discipline and its practice also are influenced by the philosophy of education. To naturalists discipline is to be learnt by natural consequences. The child enjoys maximum freedom. Self-discipline is preferred to external control. The idealists on the other hand wish to enforce discipline through cultivation of higher values, moral and religious teachings and strict control over the child. In the scheme of the pragmatists, there is no place for punishment and discipline is learnt through moral training which is based child's experience gained through various kinds of school activities and programmes.

5. Philosophy of Education Influences Teaching Methods. Methods of teaching, too, are influenced by the philosophy of education a society adopts. A system of education based on naturalism stresses learning by doing, learning through experience and learning through observation. Societies which tend towards idealism prefer to have a system of education which prescribes rigid methods of teaching such as lecturing and prefer learning through imitation, memorization and discussion. Pragmatism stresses problem solving and project methods of teaching.

In the same way several other aspects such as the place of the child in education, the importance of the teacher, preparation of textbooks, etc., are influenced by the philosophy of education adopted by a system of education.

Influence of Philosophy on Different Aspects of Education

1. Philosophy and Aims of Education. Every educational system must have some goals, aims or objectives. These act as guides for the educator in educating the child. In fact, we cannot think of any process of education without specific aims and objectives. Bode says, "Unless we have some guiding philosophy in the determination of objectives, we get nowhere at all." These aims of education, in different countries, are determined by the aims and ideals of life which the people of those countries have at that particular time. The aims and ideals of life, in their turn, are determined by the philosophy of the time. It is, therefore, that aims and ideals of education vary with the different philosophers. It is the philosophy of the time which determines whether the aim of education should be moral, vocational, intellectual, liberal or spiritual. In the words of Rusk, "Every system of education must have an aim and the aim of education is relative to the aim of life. Philosophy formulates what should be the end of life while education offers suggestions how this end is to be achieved." The philosopher struggles hard with the mysteries of life and arrives at their solution after mature reflection and thinking. He then suggests ways and means of dealing with them. Thus, he lays down ultimate values and explains their significance to the community. In this way, he tries to convert people to his own beliefs and philosophy. These ultimate values, as formulated by the philosopher, become the aims of education for that community. The training of the younger generation, according to those aims and values, then lies on the shoulders of the educator in the field. He selects the material for instruction and determines the methods of procedure for the attainment of those aims. In this way, the entire educational programme proceeds with its foundations on sound philosophy.

2. Philosophy and Curriculum. Curriculum is the means through which we realise the aims of education. Naturally, therefore, our educational aims determine the curriculum of studies. But aims of education, in their own turn, are determined by philosophy, as we have noted above just now. So we can say that philosophy also determines the curriculum. As is the philosophy so will be the aims of all education and courses of study. Thus, they are closely inter-related. It is philosophy and courses of study. Thus, they are closely inter-related. It is philosophy which will decide why a particular subject should be included in the curriculum and what particular discipline that subject will promote. Thus, as Briggs has put it, "It is here (in curriculum) that education seriously needs leaders—leaders who hold a sound comprehensive philosophy, of which they can convince others and who can direct its consistent application to the formulation of appropriate curricula."

It should be clearly noted that curriculum is not fixed for all times. It changes in accordance with the aims of education determined by philosophy. It is, therefore, that curriculum differs with different schools of philosophy, according to their own beliefs. The naturalists advocate the selection of subjects according to the present needs, interests and activities of the child. They insist that adult interference should be reduced to the minimum and that the child should grow up in a free atmosphere. They are, therefore, of the opinion that curriculum should include subjects which are useful for the present life situations, experience and interests of the child. Those subjects must, in no case, be included in which the child is not interested at all. The idealists, on the other hand, approach the problem of curriculum from the point of higher values in life rather than from that of the child or his present needs. Their emphasis is on the experience of human race as a whole. They, therefore, advocate that curriculum should be graded in such a way as may enable that child to march gradually towards self-realization. The pragmatists emphasise the principle of utility in the choice of subjects. They are of the opinion that only such functional subjects should be included in the curriculum as are useful to the child in the present day world. The curriculum should give knowledge and skills which the child requires for his present as well as future life as an adult. Only that bookish knowledge which stuffs the mind with abstract ideas, is condemned as it does not equip children to face the real problems of life. Instead, curriculum should consist of subjects which may improve the health, vocational efficiency and social fitness of the child. Realists also put greater premium upon the vocational education.

Thus, we conclude that philosophy not only influences the curriculum, it also determines the subjects of study that meet its requirements.

3. Philosophy and Textbooks. Textbooks are important instruments, through which the aims of education are realised.

In the selection of Textbooks, therefore, there is as much need of ideals and principles as in the choice of subjects. Those who select textbooks, must have a standard of judgement, which should enable them to select the right type of books. This standard is supplied by philosophy.

Again, a good textbook must reflect the prevailing values of life, fixed by philosophy. If it does not, it is out-of-date and inappropriate. An appropriate textbook, therefore, must be according to the accepted ideals of the society as a whole. Then and only then its will be able to serve its desired purpose.

In the case of Textbooks also, there is difference of opinion among the different schools of philosophy. While the naturalists are in favour of illustrations, pictures and diagrams for capturing the interest of children, the pragmatists are satisfied only with the objective statement of generalization in a logical order. The idealists, on the other hand with the Textbooks should reflect the individuality of the author. They are in favour of the subjective presentation of the subject-matter so that there may be interaction of the prosonalities of the author and the reader.

4. Philosophy and Discipline. Like curriculum, Textbooks and methods, discipline, too, reflects the philosophy of life, accepted at a particular time. It is mainly governed by the aim of education. In ancient India when salvation was the chief aim of education, stress was laid on a strict type of discipline. The student was required to lead a life of austerity and self-denial. In medieval ages when despotic system of government was established, a very harsh and strict discipline was advocated and practised. "Spare the rod and spoil the child" was the maxim for the guidance of teachers. In the present age of democracy, however, the concept of discipline is totally different. Whereas in the past, perfect order and silence prevailed in the educational institutions, now we insist on self-government of students and free discipline.

Different schools of philosophy also differ in their concept of discipline. While the idealists are in favour of punishment for maintaining order in the class, the naturalists advocate perfect freedom to the child. They believe in discipline by natural consequences. The pragmatists, on the other hand, emphasise social discipline, which is maintained by the proper direction of the pupil's natural impulses through cooperative activities.

5. Philosophy and Methods. Method is the procedure through which the aims of education are realised. And as we have already noted, aims of education are subject to the philosophy of life. It is, therefore, that there is close relationship between philosophy and methodology of teaching.

Every philosopher formulates his own methods of teaching, according to his own philosophy. It is, therefore, that different schools of philosophy have laid down their own methods of teaching. The naturalists emphasise the child-centred methods of teaching. They recommend proper motivation and effective use of illustrative aids to capture and maintain the child's interest in the lesson. The idealists believe that teaching is essentially an impact of the teacher's personality on that of the pupil. They recommend discussion method, rote-learning and a meditation in a cordial atmosphere. The pupil is expected to obey his teacher and have full faith in him. The pragmatists advocate that teaching is possible only in a social medium. So they recommend project and problem methods of teaching in which the pupils are engaged in a useful activity of their own choice and interest. Thus, we can say that all the methods of education that have come into vogue, have been the result of one philosophy or the other.

6. Philosophy and Teacher. Teacher is the back-bone of the entire process of education. It is, therefore, essential that the teacher's philosophy of life should be in perfect consonance with the philosophy on which the educational system is based. To be a successful teacher, he must know his subject, his pupil, the society and the philosophy of education. A teacher in a Basic school, who has no faith in and no regard for the Gandhian way of life, will never prove to be a successful teacher.

The naturalists insist that the teacher should never interfere with the free activities of children. He is simply to set the educational environment and that is all he is expected to do. Then his role is a negative one. The idealists advocate that the teacher's role should be that of the head of a family. Pupils should be inspired by his personality and develop full faith in him. According to pragmatists, the teacher is not to impose anything on the pupil. He is simply to provide opportunity to his pupils for activity and learning.

7. General Impact of Modern Philosophies on Education. The nineteenth and the twentieth centuries have witnessed a radical change in the educational practices as a result of some common elements in all the modern philosophies. *Firstly,* education has been psychologised. Instructions have become paedo-centric or child-centred rather than book-centred. Individual differences have been recognised. *Secondly,* the principles of activity has gained ground. Learning by doing has been the common watchword. *Thirdly,* the social discipline has been recognised as a potent factor of educational development. The child is to be trained for community life. *Fourthly,* democracy has been recognised in most of the developed or developing countries as the guiding factor of educational practices. Fifthly, there has been a metamorphis in the social structure of each country. There is shift of emphasis from rural to urban, joint family to individualism, capitalism to socialism and spiritualism to materialism. New concepts of citizenship, social life and political life have emerged. Westernization has taken place rapidly and there is a scientific outlook on all matters of life. There are new business and professional practices. Hence there is need for a new type of education which can meet the existing demands of life. Man is a socialised being and so the current social philosophies have their bearing or education. To cite one example, the restless adolescents of today cannot be treated in the same nanner as they were treated during the last century. The concept of discipline in education has undergone a radical change.

8. Philosophy and Evaluation. Evaluation is the pivot of educational system. Goals or aims are only cherished desires which decorate the reports of education commission. Curriculum also remain confined to booklets on syllabus. It is evaluation alone which gives an exact idea of what has actually been achieved at the end of a particular period or stage as a result of the teaching-learning experiences, provided in the classroom. Evaluation is also the process of determining the extent to which the aims and objectives are being attained. Again, the maintenance of good educational programmes and the improvement of techniques and procedures of education also require good evaluation. It is, therefore, that there is a close relationship between objectives, learning experiences and evaluation. Object-ship between objectives, learning experiences and evaluation. It is, therefore, legitimate to ascertain how far our evaluation programme is in conformity with the philosophy that has determined the aims and objectives of education, its curriculum and its methodology. It was this judgement that led the educationists in many progressive countries to search for the philosophical analysis which proved very helpful in thrashing out the issue and in overhauling the entire system of examination. The term 'examination' which was mainly based on essay and which measured only the factual knowledge retained by the pupils, was replaced by the new term 'evaluation' which takes into account the growth of the child as a whole individual and in his total environment. It is also this philosophical analysis which is responsible for the movement of objectivity in the field of relationship between philosophy and valuation.

For the successful harnessing of education, for the good of life, for the good of individual and for the good of society, it stands in need of direction. This direction is provided exclusively by philosophy, which is the mother of all sciences and to which education is very intimately related. In fact, philosophy and education are two sides of the same coin. While philosophy is the contemplative side, education represents the dynamic side. In the words of Rusk, "From every angle comes a demand for a philosophic basis of education. There is no escape from a philosophy of life and philosophy of education." Education, therefore, is the dynamic side of philosophy. It is an active aspect of philosophical beliefs and a practical means of realising the ideals of life. Without wisdom and philosophy, education is irrelevant. In the words of Whitehead, "Wisdom is the fruit of balanced development. It is this balanced growth of individuality which should be the aim of education to secure....when you understand all about the sun and all about the atmosphere and all about the rotation of the earth, you may still miss the radiance of the sunset."

❋❋❋

2

Philosophy of Education in Different Ages

PHILOSOPHY OF VEDIC EDUCATION

What are the Vedas? What have been their objectives? Why were they written? These questions are being debated since long. Many commentators have expressed their views on these issues. But the commentary written by *Sayan* is accepted as most authentic. He has explained the meaning of Veda in his book entitled Krishna Yajurveda. According to *Sayan* Veda in his book entitied Krishna Yajurveda. According to *Sayan* Veda is a symbol of that thing through which one attains his objective and protects oneself against bad traits, undesirable things and behaviours. Vedas have their own characteristic features. Through them we are able to know about the culture, civilization, life and philosophy of people in ancient India. Vedas symbolise the chief objective of human life which has been deliberance from this world of births and deaths. This objective has always been unchangeable. The Indian philosophy of life has never accepted life as purposeless. The deliberance of soul has been the chief objective of this philosophy of life from time immemorial. This fact is very clear from the study of the Rigveda.

Yajna (Sacred offering or religious sacrifice to Fire) occupied a very important place in human life during the Vedic period. In each and every sacred work some Yajna was performed. It will be wrong to regard Yajna as a tradition of ancient Indians. In fact, they were purposeful as experimental laboratories of great thinkers, teachers, philosophers, Rishis and Munis of the period. Through these Yajnas the learned saints used to realise the truth of human life. The great saints like Vashistha, Vishwamitra, Kanva, Narad, Atri and Gautam etc. realised the truth through their penances of which Yajnas were essential parts. The Rigveda, the chief of all the Vedas is the essence of their basic teachings and realizations.

Yajnas were not only experimental laboratories. They may be compared with those successful experiments through which man may obtain knowledge of even many practical spheres of life. The Yajnas were performed under the headship of Brahma.

Equal Right for Education to All. During the Vedic period educational right was given to all without any distinction of class and colour. There was no caste system then. According to one's capacity each one was free to receive education.

Method of Teaching. Two methods of teaching were being practised during the Vedic period. The first method was Muakhik (Oral) and the second was based on Chintan (Thinking or reflection). In the oral method the students were to memories the Mantras (Vedic hymns) and Richayas (Verses of Rigveda) in order that they might not be changed wrongly and they might not be changed wrongly and they might remain preserved in their original forms. Under the oral methods those prosodies were thoroughly taught on which Richayas happened to be based. Special emphasis was laid on the various lines of a particular verse, their pronunciations and meanings. In the oral method correct pronunciation was specially emphasised. For this instruction in grammar and pronunciation was compulsory for all. The success of the oral method of the Vedic age lies in the fact that it could preserve the Richayas (Vedic verses) in their original forms down the ages.

Thinking method was another part of the teaching method. Through this an attempt was made to preserve the Veda Mantras (Vedic hymns) and Richayas (Vedic verses).

Manan was a higher method of teaching than thinking. Through Manan the meanings of Vedic Mantras were developed and preserved in one's own mind. This method was used to encourage the highly intelligent students. Just as in modern days teachers encourage intelligent students by guiding them to make research, similarly in ancient days 'Manan' (Reflection) was a method specially for highly intelligent students. During the Vedic age the oral education was started in the family. The Rishis (Sage or ascetic) used to educate their children in the family through the oral method. They used to emphasise the learning of correct pronunciation. No new word was taught unless it was ascertained that the previously taught word was correctly learnt with correct pronunciation. The teachers were very particular about the correct learning of all vowels, consonants, rules of Sandhis (*i.e.,* joining of words) and compound word (Samasas). Through the oral method one had to learn through hearing and the Veda Mantras (hymns) were learnt through hearing. Therefore, the Vedas were also called Shruti (that which is heard). It was after learning the correct pronunciation through hearing that the student was advised to follow the method (Chintan-Manan). From the above it is clear that there were two methods of teaching. The oral method meant for students of average intelligence and the thinking (Chintan-Manan) method was for those who were highly endowed.

The Curriculum of Vedic Education. Various subjects were incorporated in the curriculum of Vedic education. Grammar, rhetoric, astrology, logic, Nirukti (etymological interpretation of words) Manan the meanings of Vedic Mantras were developed and preserved were the main subjects. Vedang was the synonym of all these subjects taken together. The study of logic occupied a special place, because knowledge of any other subject was tested on its basis. Debates and discussions were organised for training in logic. Logic was regarded as the criterion for finding out truth and untruth. Logical discussion was usually organised between two scholars or two groups of learned persons. The main purpose of this discussion was to find out the truth and untruth and to make as assessment of the same.

Women Education. During the Vedic age women were given full status with men. They were honoured and respected in society. Therefore, women education was at its peak at the time. Women were regarded as a great source of power, peace and knowledge for men. It was thought that without women, men could not progress. Therefore, girls during the Vedic period were taught like boys. No distinction was made between the two. The importance of women has been explained in the Vedas days 'Manan' (Reflection) was a method specially for highly intelligent who due to their deep scholarship and penance were regarded as Women-sages. Lopamudra, Apala, Ghosh and Vishwavara were some of the great women-sages who were held in high esteem.

Characteristics of Education

Such terms as knowledge, awakening, humility, modesty, etc., are often used to characterise education in the Vedic period. Ancient texts refer to the uneducated person as an ignorant beast. Education is regarded as the source of light. The main features of Vedic education can be briefly enumerated as follows:

1. Knowledge. Education is knowledge. It is man's third eye. This aphorism means that knowledge opens man's inner eye, flooding him with spiritual and divine light, which forms the provision for man's journey through life. Through education, the development of every aspect of human life becomes possible. Knowledge protects an individual like a mother, inspires him to follow the path of good conduct as a father does and gives the pleasure that one's wife provides.

Education leads to the development of personality. The word 'Veda' originates from the root 'vid' which bears the meaning of knowledge. Sayana declares that the Veda is a means to the obtaining of the adorced that which is worthy of worship, as well as a means to the banishment of the underised, the evil. Knowledge of the four Vedas (Rigveda, Yajurveda, Samaveda and Atharvaveda), along with the knowledge of Shruti, Smriti, etc., provided an individual, with new knowledge which broadened his inteclletual horizon.

2. Aims of Education. In the Vedic period, education had an idealistic form, in which the teachers (acharyas) laid stress upon worship of God, religiousness, spirituality, formation of character, development of personality, creation of an aptitude for the development of culture, nation and society. It is in this context that Dr. Altekar said that the objectives of education in ancient India were worship of God, a feeling for religion, formation of character, fulfilment of public and civic duties, an increase in social efficiency or skill and the protection the propagation of national culture. These objectives and ideals took an individual along the path of spiritual development. In their fundamental form, these objectives and ideals were:

(i) ***Emphasis upon Knowledge and Experience.*** The Gurukuls laid emphasis upon knowledge and obtaining of experience. During the Vedic period, the practice of distributing degrees did not exist. Students exhibited the knowledge obtained through discourses and discussions conducted in a concourse of scholars.

(ii) ***Spirituality.*** In the Vedic period, Nature was regarded as divine and worshipped. During this period, many hypotheses concerning spirituality took birth. Knowledge came to be seen as the instrument of salvation. Fire sacrifices, fasting and taking of vows became a part of life. Education was given the objective of inculcating control over these aspects and learning right conduct based on them.

(iii) ***Sublimation of Instincts.*** Man is the virtual slave of the instinctive drives embedded in his psyche and when he is obsessed by his senses, he often adopts the wrong path. The objective of education was to sublimate these instinctive tendencies, to turn the mind away from material knowledge and centre it upon the spiritual world, thus, establishing control over materialistic and base tendencies.

(iv) ***Fulfilment of Duty.*** Great importance was attached to developing such qualities as discipline, obedience, performance of hostly duties, rendering help to others, fulfilment of social responsibilities, etc. Through such education social skills were developed in the students. In addition, education was also provided for earning a livelihood and for this, one or more skills were taught. Dr. Mukerjee says that this education was not exclusively theortical or literary. It was related to one or the other manual skill.

(v) ***Growth of Character and Personality.*** The objective of education was the formation of character and personality of children. It was achieved through an appropriate environment, lessons on right conduct and teachings based on the life, character and ideals of great persons. Education aimed at developing the virtues of self-control, self-respect, love, cooperation, sympathy, etc., in the students.

3. The 'Upnayana' Ritual. The word 'Upnayana' means to take close to, or to bring in touch with. A ceremony called the Uphayana ceremony was performed before the child was taken to his teacher. This ceremony was performed at the ages of 8, 11 and 12 for the brahmins, kshatriyas and vaishyas, respectively. The ceremony signalled the childs's transition from infancy to childhood and his initiation into educational life. In this context, the term 'Upnayana' means putting the student in touch with his teacher. With the passage of time, the ceremony came to be confined to the brahmin class only.

4. Celibacy or Brahmacharya. Every student was required to observe celibacy in his specific path of life. Purity of conduct was regarded as of supreme importance. Only the unmarried could become students in a Gurukul. On entering student life, the student was made to wear a special girdle called a 'makhla'. Its quality depended on the caste of the student. Brahmins wore a girdle of moonj grass, the kshatriyas of string gut-taanta-and the vaishyas a girdle made of wool. The clothes worn by them were also accordingly of silk, wool, etc. The students were not allowed to make use of fragrant, cosometic or intoxicating things.

5. The Method of Education. During the Vedic period, the Gurukul method prevailed, in which the student lived in the house of the Guru, instead of living with his parents. Along with his colleagues, he led a celibate life and obtained education in the house of the Guru. Initially, in the Vedic period, it was the teacher who occupied the primary place, but in the later period, it was the student who occupied the central place in education, the process of education passed through the three stages of comprehension, meditation, memory and nidhi-dhyaasana. The Gurukuls were the centres of education, in which education was imparted only by individuals of character and ability. The student remained with his Guru for 12 years. There were parishads or committees to satisfy the student's thirst for knowledge.

6. Service of the Teacher. Every student was required, while residing in the Gurukul, to serve his teacher compulsorily. Any violation of the Guru's instructions was regarded as a sin and subject to stern punishment. The student's duties included obtaining such daily necessities as water, a twig for brushing the teeth, etc., for his guru. The teachers also ensured that the students should not be distracted from their studies while performing such duties. During the vacations in which the student returned home he was not required to perform any service for the teacher.

7. Alms System. The student had to bear the responsibility of feeding both himself and his teacher, this was done through begging for alms, which was not considered bad, since every domestic knew that his own son must be begging for alms in the same way at some other place. The reason behind the introduction of such a practice was that accepting alms induces humility. The student realised that both education and subsequent earning of livelihood were made possible for him only through society's service and its sympathy. For the poor students, begging for alms was compulsory and unavoidable, but even among the prosperous, it was a generally accepted practice.

The work of teaching began early in the morning. After performing their ablutions, students participated in some religious rituals, such as havans. Subsequently, they were put to the task of studying. In the afternoon, after partaking of lunch, the students returned to their studies. At sunset, some more religious rituals were performed. They denoted the end of the day's routine.

8. Practicality. The education of that period encompassed the necessary activities of life. Students were given education about animal-husbandry, agriculture and other professions. In addition education in medicine was also imparted. According to Dr. Alteker, the purpose of education was not to provide general knowledge about a variety of subjects, but to produce specialists of the best kind in various spheres.

9. Education for the Individual. In the Vedic period, every teacher devoted himself to the integral development of each student. He aimed at the physical and intellectual development of his wards. The maximum attention was devoted to the individual development of every student, but there was no provision for the education of the incapable and the handicapped, especially those who were lacking in mental and moral qualities or were known for moral turpitude.

10. Duration of Education. In the house of the teacher, the student was required to obtain education upto the age of 24, after which he was expected to enter domestic life. Students were divided into three categories:

(*a*) Those obtaining education upto the age of 24—Vasu.

(*b*) Those obtaining education upto the age of 36—Rudra.

(*c*) Those obtaining education upto the age of 48—Aaditya.

11. Curriculum. Although the education of this period was dominated by the study of Vedic literature, historical study, stories of heroic lives and discourses on the Puranas also formed a part of the syllabus. Students had necessarily to obtain knowledge of metrics. Arithmetic was supplemented by a knowledge of geometry. Students were given knowledge of the four Vedas—Rigveda, Yajurveda, Samaveda and Atharvaveda. The syllabus took with in its compass such subjects as spiritual as well as meterialistic knowledge, Vedas, Vedic grammar, arithmetic, knowledge of gods, knowledge of the absolute, knowledge of ghosts, astronomy, logic, philosophy, ethics, conduct, etc. The richness of the syllabus was responsible for the creation of Brahman literature in this period.

Objectives of the Post-Vedic Education

To attain salvation by realising the truth has been the aim of education, during this period. Only that education was regarded true which helped one to realise this supreme truth. According to the Upanishads 'truth' alone is the knowledge and the other worldly knowledge is untruth. The worldly knowledge was regarded as ignorance. Upanishads maintain that one cannot attain salvation through worldly knowledge because through this one becomes involved in illusion (Maya).

Upanayan Sanskar. Upanayan Sanskar was considered important both in the Vedic and Post-Vedic periods. This is evident at several piaces in the Rigveda. But different values were adhered to in the two periods. It was not necessary during the Vedic period to have the Upanayan ceremony before starting education. But during the Post-Vedic period Upanayan ceremony was considered necessary for starting education.

The word 'Upanayan' means to come near. In the context of education this word signifies that the student should come near the teacher for receiving education. The Upanayan ceremony became so important during the Post-Vedic period that it was usually regarded as second birth of the individual. For the Brahmans this became very important. Brahmans began to be called as Dvij (the twice born or born again). It was after the Upanayan that a Brahman boy could be called a Dvij.

Two births signify the worldly and the spiritual births. On the Upanayan occasion the Guru (preceptor) used to give him his Mantra (Advice). His spiritual life used to begin from this point. That is, from this day his education was started which ultimately led to his spiritual development in due course of time. The Upanayan ceremony is still in vogue in certain religious groups in the world, though in different forms.

The Important Place of the Teacher. During this period the teacher (Guru) enjoyed a pre-dominant place not only in his Gurukul (seat of learning) but in the entire society. He was regarded as a great guide for all. To his pupils he showered all love and affection and used to teach them whatever he knew, but before doing this he always tested the deservingness of a particular pupil. The pupils were free to discuss points freely with the Guru. We find many examples of free discussion between the teacher and his taught. We may cite here an example from Brahma and his son Bhrigu. Brahma gave the Brahma-gyan, *i.e.,* the knowledge of the ultimate or God in an outline form and advised him to perceive the same through thinking (*Manan*) and meditation. Bhrigu accepted this advice and realised God (*Brahma*) on the basis of the same.

Curriculum During the Post-Vedic Period. During this period the curriculum included more subjects than during the Vedic age. Veda mantras (Vedic hymns and verses) were principally taught in the Vedic period. During the Post-Vedic period various types of literatures were produced pertaining to the different Vedas. In addition to religious subjects many worldly subjects were also included in the curriculum. This may be verified in the conversation between Narrad and Sanat Kuman which is incorporated in the Chhandogya Upanishad. During the Post-Vedic period the curriculum consisted of Vedas, History, Puranas, Grammar, Mathematics, Brahma-Vidya, Nirukti (etymological interpretation of words), astronomy, dance, music, etc., etc.

In addition to the above three methods we find a mention of another method—Question-Answer System in the Upanishad literature. In fact, the entire Upanished literature is on the question-answer system. We do not find its practice in the Rigvedic period. Through this system difficult and abstract ideas were made simple. The terse-spiritual elements were explained through this system. Examples, strories and help of certain biographies were also taken in the system for elucidating certain points. This question-answer method was also successfully used by Socrates in Greece to explain abstract ideas.

Daily Routine of Students. During the Post-Vedic period the Ashramas (Schools) were generally organised and run by Guru (preceptors). It was compulsory to adhere to laid down rules of discipline and conduct. No distinction was made between students in this respect. Everyone was required to observe celibacy. Rules of conduct were enforced keeping in view the physical, mental and moral development of students. Strict adherence to rules of conduct and discipline was an inseparable aspect of education in those days.

(a) ***Practical Education.*** Practical education consisted of three parts : 1. to beg alms, 2. to prepare fire for the Yajna-kund and 3. to look after the animals and other fellow-beings of the Ashrama (School). Besides, the students were also expected to do some agricultural work.

There were varying aims of all these three aspects of practical education. Begging of alms was meant to teach politeness. Preparing of fire for the Yajna-kund signified mental development of students. Rearing up Ashrama animals and doing agricultural work were meant to make the students self-dependent.

(b) ***Moral Education.*** Leading a disciplined and controlled life is the real basis of moral education. Moral education affects the conduct of the individual. Only oral instruction cannot improve one's conduct. Therefore, observance of celibacy was considered necessary for good conduct.

(c) ***Mental Development.*** Hearing, thinking and meditation were the three parts of mental education. For full mental development all these three aspects were considered necessary. Thinking over the heard things and perception through meditation were the accepted methods of mental development. This is true even today.

Duration of Education. Duration of education during the Post-Vedic period was almost the same as in the Vedic age. This duration was of about twelve years, although the number of subjects of study were increased. However, there was no uniform rule for the duration of education. We find examples in which students continued to stay longer than twelve years for keeping the fire of the Yajna or looking after the animals and inmates of the Ashrama. Satyakam Jawal may be cited as an example in this respect.

Teacher's Place in the Ancient Indian Society. In the ancient Indian society the teacher always enjoyed a dignified place. During the Vedic and Post-Vedic periods the teacher's place was second to that of God only. He was more respected than the king in society. The Guru-Ashrama was known as the Gurukul (the family of the teacher) and the Guru was regarded as a Rishi (Sage) or Acharya (the one who practises what he professes). The Guru was given this significant place, because without him it was impossible to attain knowledge. The Guru was the guide and could help anyone to carve out his course of action. He used to bring light wherever there was darkness. Thus, the people always felt his necessity whenever there was a difficulty in solving any issue or problem.

During the Upanishadic period as well, when self-study was considered as dignified the place of Guru in society remained intact. It was believed that no knowledge could come without the assistance from the Guru. In other words, it was believed that the attainment of salvation was not possible without the help of the Guru.

Restriction on Teachers. The teacher was expected to lead a life of penance free of worldly things. He, too, was required to follow all the rules of strict discipline, thinking and meditation which were prescribed for the students. We find many references to such a position in the Maitrayan Upanishad. After the demise of the Guru even one of his disciples could succeed him if his son was not considered worthy of the same.

Women's Education. Many changes were introduced in women education during the Post-Vedic period. This led to the fall of women education. During the Vedic age the women enjoyed equal educational rights. During the Post-Vedic period they were deprived of the social and religious rights. They were not allowed to participate in social functions. Now they did not enjoy the same status as before. Thus, the path of their social and mental development was blocked. Ultimately the position of women in society fell down so low that the birth of a girl was regarded as a curse on the family.

But an upward trend again appeared in the status of women during the Upanishadic period. Now they were given social and educational rights again. Once again they were given equal status with men and many women bacame as learned as men. Many women became Acharya (Principal teacher-Guru) in Ashramas. The name of Gargi may be cited as an example.

Convocation Address. After receiving education for twelve years students used to assemble near their teacher (*Acharya*) for blessings before going home. The Acharya on this occasion used to give some places of advice for happy and smooth running of their future life. The teacher used to tell them how to lead a life of householder (*Grihastha*), how to take care of the society and the nation and how to serve the humanity as a whole. The teacher used to tell all these in a ceremony which was known as Samavartan Samaroha like the modern convocation address.

Varna System and Education in Society. The Varna system in the Vedic age was based on one's work or duty (Karma). Members of a family used to engage themselves in different types of work (profession) and their work decided their varna. During the Vedic period one could choose a particular profession as he liked and accordingly his Varna was determined. But during the Post-Vedic period Varna came to be determined by birth. Consequently, the whole society was divided into four Varnas—Brahman, Kshatriya, Vaishya and Shudra.

Out of these four Varnas, the Brahmans occupied the supreme position and enjoyed more rights. Kshatriyas resented this superiority and a clash ensued between the two. Kshatriya were the winners in the clash and the administrative powers came into their hands. Gradually they established their kingdoms and principalities. Thus, in the Varna system the Brahmans and the Kshatriyas became predominant. The Vaishyas and Shudras came into the lower groups. In this hierarchy Shudras were kept at the lowest order of society. In course of time the condition of Shudras fell down further and they came to be regarded as untouchables and they were denied all social and religious rights. Vaishyas remained superior to Shudras and they divided themselves into professional groups such as—goldsmith, blacksmith, potter, fowler, milkman and sweet-seller etc., etc.

However, the position of Varnas during the Post-Vedic period had not degenerated so much as it is found today. Than, its was possible to change one's Varna. One could marry a girl from a different Varna. The Vaishyas were permitted in the Rajya Surya Yajna upto some extent. Then, Brahmans also did not control the Yajnas. The marriages of Chyavan Rishi and king Shantanu and the religious rites performed by Vishwamitra (A Kshatriya) and other Kshatriyas bear a testimony to the above.

The Post-Vedic literature does not contain much about the education of Vaishyas and Shudras. Agriculture was the main occupation of Vaishyas during this period.

Shudras were given education by Brahmans. But the number of educated Shudras fell down day by day. According to Shatpaths, fisherman, snake-charmers and other alike professionals were some of the other students of Brahmans. Shudras were mostly engaged in manual labour in agricultural fields, grazing cattle and pottery. Some of them knew music and dance as well as we find even today.

PHILOSOPHY OF BUDDHIST

The history of education in Buddha period is inter-related with the history of monasteries and 'Vihars' because there were no independent educational institutions or centres, other than those religious centres. Only monks and shramanas were authorised to impart education to the people. Thus, the monasteries and 'Vihars' took the place of sacrificial altars and as a result, these places became the centres of cultural life. Thus, the methods of these monasteries and 'Vihars' were the educational methods of that time. Rules and regulations of Buddhist monasteries and 'Vihars' were not framed by Lord Buddha. They had been taken from Hinduism and the various sects of Sadhus and nuns so they resembled 'vedic' systems.

Admissions into Buddhist monasteries were based more or less on the rules and regulations observed by Gurukula as in Vedic period. Like the students of 'Vedic' period, here also the students had to present themselves before the teacher to ask for the admission. Like the 'Upanayan', 'Pabbaja or pravrajya' is to go out. The boys went out of their families and joined the monasteries. Every one had the opportunity to undergo 'Pabbaja' and become a 'Buddhist' monk. After admission into 'Sangh' they could remain a monk. They had to change the former caste, dress, character, etc. Though theoretically, all the castes were allowed to get admitted into the monastery but practically and mostly the people of higher classes were admitted there. However, it is also true that some of the monks were derived from the lower castes. At the time of entering into the 'Sangh' the disciple must have attained the age of 8 years and during this period the new monk made his preparation for the sangh-life. Afterwards at the age of 20 years, he accepted 'Upsampada' and became full-fledged member of the 'Sangh'.

The System of Pabbaja. At 8 years of age, one could go to any 'Vihar' or 'Sangh' according to his own will. With head shaved and a yellow cloth in hand he went to the principal monk and requested him for admission in 'Sangh'. He thus, surrendered himself fully. The monk caused him to put the yellow clothes on and surrendered to the three words of shelter in a loud voice:

I go into the shelter of Buddha.

I seek the shelter of Dharma.

I enter the shelter of Sangh.

After taking the above three vows, one became entitled to admission. No one could get admission into the 'Sangh' without the consent of his parents. Patients of infectious diseases like Leprosy. T.B., Eczema, etc., and Government servants, slaves and soldiers were not allowed to be admitted into 'Sanghs'. However, there was no discrimination of any kind on the basis of caste or creed.

Rules for the Students. Now the admitted student was called "Samner". He had to follow the following rules:

1. Not to kill any living being.
2. Live free from the impurity of character.
3. Not to speak ill of any body.
4. Not to take any interest in music, dance, playshow, etc.
5. Not to accept anything given to him.
6. Not to use any intoxicating thing.
7. Not to tell a lie.
8. Not to take food at improper time.
9. Not to use luxurious and scented things.
10. Not to accept the gifts of gold or silver, etc.

The ten rules were essentially observed by the new monk. The 'Upajsata' *i.e.,* the teacher took all responsibilities up to the age of 20 years when he became mature and capable for accepting 'Upsampada'. For the teacher, he was 'Sadvi Biharak'. Lord Buddha himself taught that teacher should recognise his taught (*Sadvi Biharak*) as his son and the taught (*Sadvi Biharak*) should recognise the teacher (*Upajsaya*) as his own father.

Upasampada. After completing the education for twelve years, the 'Monk' had to undergo the 'Upasampada' ritual at the age of 20 years and then he became the permanent member of the 'Sangh'. There is also evidence that only such monks who had enough of spiritual knowledge were taken in sangh. They were directly given 'Upsampada'. Their 'Pabbaja' and 'Upsampada' both the rituals were performed simultaneously.

The method of performing 'Upsampada' was slightly different from 'Pabbaja'. It was similar to Vedic 'Samavartan' ritual with some difference. After 'Samavartan' the Brahamchari entered into family life but after 'Upsampada' he became a full-fledged monk, having no concern with family life. While Pabbaja was a ritual for a limited period, 'Upsampada' was permanent. It was for the whole life. Celibacy or chastity was considered essential for Brahmanic education. While among Hindus those observing celibacy for the whole life were; in 'Buddhistic' education it was a common feature. In this respect, Buddhistic education was more austere than Brahmanic education.

At the time of 'Pabbaja' the new monk of 8 years would go to the teacher and say with folded hands, "You are my teacher (*Guru*)". Thus, their relationship was established. The 'Upsampada' was performed before the entire 'Sangh'. Therefore, 'Upsampada' was given unanimously or on the decision of the majority.

Restrictions on Admission. In 'Buddhist' education also, like 'Vedic' education, the eligibility and the competence of the entrant was taken into account. A candidate could not be admitted into 'Sangh' in the following conditions:

1. Without the permission of his parents.
2. Convict of any serious moral sin.
3. Patient of any infections or serious disease.
4. Not found generous and laborious during the probation period, which sometimes was four or five days.
5. Under any legal responsibility and who was not free from legal bondage.

Thus, Buddhist Sanghs did not intend to destroy the family system. No one was admitted into 'Sangh' without the due permission of his parents. Similarly those who wanted to get rid of their social, moral and economic obligations were not admitted. Moreover, only those were allowed admittance who were healthy both mentally and bodily. Hence Buddhism spread rapidly and in an organised manner, in so many countries of the world.

The Qualifications of the Teacher. In Buddhist educational system much stress was laid on the efficiency of the teachers. This has been described as follows:

(a) ***High Moral Order.*** The teacher himself, must have spent at least ten years as monk. He must have the purity of character, purity of thoughts and generosity, etc.

(b) ***High Mental Order.*** Essentially the teachers was expected to be of a high mental order, so that he might teach his disciple the religion and nobleness and he may also successfully combat the wrong religious notions.

Daily Routine of the Disciple. Regular service of the 'Guru' (teacher), was essential in the Buddhist system. In morning the student would arrange for water, duetonic, etc. for the teacher. He would also look after his meal. He would cook the food, feed the teacher and clean the utensils. He would go out for alms with the teacher. After bath the students would get ready for the education. The teacher would impart education according to the system of the day.

Thus, the disciple had to serve the teacher and keep the place tidy. His daily routine depended on the orders of the teacher. He was not bound to obey anyone else except his teacher. He could not take any service from any other person. nor could he go any where without the permission of the teacher. Thus, the disciples used to live under the disciplinary control of their teacher.

Levels of Education

During the Buddhist period, education had two levels—primary and higher levels.

1. Primary Level. The Jatakas stories indicate that during the Buddhist period, primary education took the form of worldly or materialistic education. Fa-Hien has also mentioned the existence of a system so general education. Children of six were admitted to this level of education.

2. Higher Level. Dr. Altekar opines that the Buddhists raised Indian's international stature considerably by the high level of education in their monastries since students from as far as Korea, Tibet, Java and other distant countries were attracted to them.

Centres of Education

During this period, some prominent centres of education sprang up. Their characteristics were their collective nature and their association with Buddhist Viharas or monasteries. There was no discrimination between students on any basis, some of these centres possessed an international reputation, proved by the fact that Chinese, Japanese, Tibetan and other sudents came there to receive education.

As already pointed out, th e were many universities in India during the Buddhist eriod. It was a time when democratic feelings were evolving and hence many famous educational centres came into existence. Wherever Buddhist monasteries or viharas were established, educational centres too emerged. Among the most notable universities to develop during this period were the universities at:

1. Taxila. Taxila was an important centre of education during the Buddhist period. It was then the capital of Gandhar. It had been founded by King Bharata after the name of his son Taxa. Being situated on the borders of this subcontinent, the kingdom was subject to frequent external aggressions. Because of this, the university in this kingdom developed on the basis of the family. Students started their education at the age of 16. The university provided education in numerous subjects, such as the three Vedas, Vedanta, Grammar, Ayurveda, the eighteen Sippas, military science, astrology, agriculture, commerce, treatment of snake-bite, (Sarpa-dansha chikitsa), magical charius (Tantra Vidya) etc.

2. Nalanda. The Nalanda University was situated in the State of Bihar, 40 miles south west of Patna and 7 miles north of Rajgraha. It was an internationally famed Buddhist centre of education. It became famous because it was the birth place of Sariputra the disciple of Lord Buddha. Emperor Ashok had a monastry constructed here. By the 4th century B.C. it had become a famous centre of education and by the 7th century it became the foremost centre of education.

Kings of the Gupta dynasty took interest in the growth of the university. Buddhist monastries were constructed here by Kumar Gupta, Narsingh Gupta, Baladitya, Buddha, Gupta, Vajra and Harsha. Because of these monastries, the university continued to grow and expand. Its land was surrounded by a rampart at the entrance to which lived a profound scholar who administered an entrance test to the students desirous of joining the university. The university had eight large assembly halls and 300 rooms for study. It had been stated in Epigraphic India that the highest point of Viharavali kissed the clouds. The buildings of the university are a fine example of the engineering skill existing in that age. The remains of these buildings are sufficient to prove that the art of construction had reached a peak during this period. In addition to the buildings, the university had beautiful lakes, numbering 10, according to It-Sing. The university also had a massive nine-storied library which was divided into three parts, called Ratna Sagar, Ratnodadhi and Ratna Ranjaka.

In Bihar, the Buddhist monks, teachers and students led a balanced, regulated and spiritualistic life, far removed from leisure and luxury. Students of this university carned great respect in many foreign countries. Students came from Java, Sumatra, Japan, China, Ceylon and other countries to receive education here. The staff of the university consisted of 1500 teachers. Huen Sang, in his travellouge, mentions the names of such renowned teachers as Chandrapal, Dharampal, Gunamati, Sthirmati, Prabhamitra, Gyanchandra, Sheelbhadra, etc.

3. Mithila. Mithila had been a centre of Brahman education in ancient times and when the Buddhist period came, it became an important centre of Buddhist education. It was here that a scholar named Jagdwara composed his renowned commentaries on such famous compositions as the Gita, Devi Mahatamaya, Meghdoot, Gita Govinda, Malati Madhava, etc. Vidyapati was born here. Apart from other subjects, Nyaya philosophy was also taught here. A student was deemed to have passed only after he had taken a difficult examination in Nyaya and Logic.

4. Vikramshila. Vikramshila was located on the banks of the Ganga in Magadha, Bihar. It was surrounded by a strong rampart. The teachers of this university were among the finest scholars of the day. Many important religious texts were translated into the Tibetan language at this university. Its administration was in the hands of a committee. Students were granted admission only after a test was administered to them at the gates. Among the famous scholars of that time who administered this test were Ratankar Shanti, Baghiswara Kirti, Naroha, Pargyakamnti, Ratna Vajra and Gyana Srimitra. The university provided education in grammar, logic, philosophy, tantra, etc. It, too, was destroyed in the 12th century by Bakhtiar Khiji.

5. Odantpuri. Odantpuri had evolved as an educational centre before the Pal dynasty came into existence. The kings of this dynasty further developed this university. Its library was internationally known. 1000 monks received education here.

6. Ballabhi. From 475 A.D. to 755 A.D., Ballabhi, in Kathiavar, was a famous centre of Buddhist education. Heun Sang visited Ballabhi also in his travels. At that time, there were a hundred Sangaramas here. This university imparted education in politics, diplomacy, medicine and various other disciplines apart from religious education. Its students obtained senior positions in the courts of kings after completing their education. This university, too became the unfortunate victim of foreign invasion in the 12th century.

7. Nadia. Nadia was established at the junction of the Bhaghirathi and Jalangi rivers in the 11th century by the Sen kings of Bengal. Jayaleva's Gita Govinda and Shoolapani's Smriti-viveka were composed here. It was a centre of teaching in Nyaya and Logic. It retained its reputation even during the middle ages.

8. Jagdalla. Rampal had the town of Ramvati established on the banks of the Ganges in Bengal in the 11th century. He also had a monastry named Jagdalla established here. This soon emerged as a centre of Buddhist education.

Vibhutichandra, Dansheela, Shubhkara and Mokshakara were some of the famous teachers of this university.

This period gave birth to distinctions of class and varna in the sphere of education and it was in reaction to this that the Buddhist and Jain religions came into existence. Their system of education changed from the method of teaching by gurus to an institutional method.

BRAHMANIC AGE

The educational structure in the Brahmanic Age was, to a very great extent, only a refined and developed form of Vedic education. However, during this age, various forms began to emerge in the institutions of education. Various institutions, such as shakha, charana, parishad, kul and gotra, began to emerge at the various levels of education. Besides the Upnishads, Aaranyaka, Brahman and other classical texts were created in this period. Famous ashramas or monasteries came to be established in the forests. It was in this period that the sutra literature was created, along with the development of the six systems of Indian philosophical thought—Samkhya, Yoga, Nyaya, Vaisheshika, Karma of Purva Mimansa and Vedanta or Uttara Mimansa. A significant characteristic of this period is the determination of the syllabus according to the Caste and Ashrama system. However, the education of the Shudras and women suffered a decline.

The best mirror of any country or society is the literature, it produces. From the Vedic to the Brahman period, literature and additional literature continued to be created. Even in the Brahman period, education continued to be looked upon as the means to knowledge. It has the same objectives that Vedic education had. However, with the passage of time and a change in the needs of society, the importance attached to them underwent a change. In this period, the following objectives were ascribed to education:

1. Self-control
2. Development of character
3. Generation of sociability or social awareness
4. Propagation of purity
5. Integral development of personality
6. Preservation of knowledge and culture.

Education in this age continued to proceed on the foundations given to it during the Vedic period, but a certain rigidity and narrowness now marked its implementation. Education now aimed at equipping the student for the struggle for existence. After the upnayana or introduction ceremony, teachers imparted education to their students according to the latter's interests, tendencies and nature. Celibacy was rigidly oberved. Teachers paid full attention to the psychological make-up of their students while teaching.

Students lived in close contact with their teacher or guru in the Gurukul. But, restrictions had now been placed upon the receiving of education by Shudras. For social reasons, they were not considered fit to receive education. After Vedic education, there was a gradual increase in ritualism. The result was that shudras and women began to lose their place in the educational sphere. But, on the other hand, education became more comprehensive in this period, as it was closely associated with every aspect of life. Some of its general characteristics are:

1. Dominance of Religion. As in the Vedic period, education in the Brahman period also was dominated by religion. Students were given knowledge of religious activities. Numerous religious and cultural activities were organised so as to acquaint students with them.

2. Individualism. Because of the absence of collective education, the emphasis was upon the individual. Teachers paid attention to the personal development of individual students.

3. Worldly and Other-worldly or Spiritual and Materialistic Education. During this period, education paid equal attention to spiritual as well as materialistic or worldly matters. Education comprehended the materialism of life.

4. Celibacy (Brahmcharya). Like the education in the Vedic period, education in this period also laid great emphasis upon celibacy. Students were expected to obey their teachers and indulge only in moral conduct.

5. Physical Punishment. In the Brahman age, the practice of giving physical punishment to students was not prevalent. Such famous acharyas as Manu, Gautum, Vishnu opposed physical punishment because they considered it inhuman.

6. Method of Education. In the Vedic period, education was primarily oral. Students were made to memorise aphorisms and then elaborate them. But, by the advent of the Brahman age, the art of writing had developed and so both oral and written education came into practice, though the emphasis was upon oral education. Bhojpatra, the bark of a tree, was used for writing. Teachers gave importance to purity in pronunciation. Education was conducted through discussion, answering of questions, removal of doubts, etc. Students were given continuous practice in the art of writing and for this they were required to copy manuscripts. Practical work was emphasized in such subjects as grammar, astrology, nyaya, medicine, etc. The students as well as the teachers themselves obtained informal education through the concourse of famed scholars.

7. Curriculum. In this age, too, primacy was given to the study of the Vedas. Among the subjects taught were grammar, arithmetic, geometry, astrology, economics, history, politics, agriculture, millitary science, nyaya philosophy, etc. A special feature of this period is that, as time progressed, two kinds of syllabi came to be prepared, one for the short-term and another for the long-term. In addition, clear and correct pronunciation of consonants and vowels was stressed. Students were also given knowledge of metrics and figures of speech. It was on this basis that learned commentaries on the Vedas came to be composed. The Pingal Shastra was composed for the teaching of matrics. Surgery had also developed by this time.

Merits of Education in the Brahman Period

Indian culture has developed through its system of education. This system was especially fruitful in propagating the ideas of love, truth, non-violence, religion, peace and world brotherhood. It also pointed out the path to salvation. It was also responsible for the creation and preservation of literature. F.E. Keay has expressed wonder at the fact that though divine texts were composed such a long time age and that though it seemed impossible to preserve them intact, this was done and is still being done today. The education of this period possessed the following features :

1. It paid the greatest attention to the child's physical and mental development.
2. The Gurukuls were situated at a distance from inhabited areas so as to prevent excessive contact between students and society.
3. In the teacher's house, there was an abundance of family feeling. Students did not suffer from the lack of any familial necessity.
4. It was conscious of the development of the child's character.
5. The teachers imparted education without any discrimiation.

Demerits of Education in the Brahman Age

Certain demerits stood, had crept into the educational system of the Brahman Age. They were:

1. Dominance of Religion. Since education was dominated by religion, less importance was attached to material or worldly development. This dominance also led to an increase in an anarchic attitude towards religion among the students and prevented the growth of rational thought.

2. Emphasis upon Philosophy. Education during this period laid excessive stress upon the study of philosophy, since the purpose was to put the student onto the path to salvation through a study of philosophy. The result was the growth of an escapist attitude towards life.

3. Faith in the Vedas. In this period, people came to have blined faith in the Vedas. They were convinced that only the Vedas were true. Consequently, the tendeney towards logical and rational thought was hampered.

4. Deprivation of the Shudras('s) Right to Education. During this period, the right to education became confined to the Brahmans, Kshatriyas and Vaishyas, because of the emergence of aristocracy. The Shudras were deprived of the right to education.

5. Women Education. There is some evidence of education of women during the Vedic period, but during the Brahman age, this was neglected. In addition, women became the victims of many restraints.

6. Lack of Handicrafts. During this age, the caste system became characterised by rigidity and narrowmindedness. Those engaged in handicrafts came to be regarded as inferior. The consequence to this was that handicrafts gradually vanished from educational curriculum.

7. Absence of Synthesis. The education of this period was taking in synthesis. Instead, it laid emphasis upon profound scholarship in any one subject.

Ancient Indian Universities

Seats of ancient Indian Universities were either holy places or capitals of great kings because the private teachers began to congregate in these place on account of facilities they received for educating pupils. To the holy places like Banaras, Kanchi, Karnataka and Gangasagar pilgrims flocked in large numbers and made huge gifts to the teachers there. In the capitals kings and princes patronised them. Hence, there rose up centres of high learning at Kailauj, Mithila, Dhara, Kalyani and Tanjore. Certain kings provided villages to a set of Brahman teachers and colonised them.

These seats of learning were simply centres of education where lived many famous teachers and to which flocked students from all parts of the country. They did not possess colleges in the modern sense of the term nor university campuses. Nor were the teachers members of anyone single institution like the professors in a modern university. Every teacher with his Pittiacharyas formed an institution. He admitted as many students as he liked. He taught them what they liked. Such was the form of the Taxila university, the most important seat of learning in Ancient India. It was founded by Bharata and named after his son Taksha.

Banaras was a seat of learning situated at a holy place. In the 7th country B.C., Banaras was the most important centre of Hindu learning. With the patronage of Ashoka, Sarnath in the outskirts of Banaras became the seat of Buddhist learning. It did not organise any public institutions like the Nalanda University. In the 17th century A.D., Bernier says, "Banaras is a kind of University, but it has no colleges or regular classes as in our Universities: but it looks like the school of the ancients, the masters being spread over the different parts of the town in private houses.

The universities and monasteries which belonged to the Buddhist order were Nalanda and Vikramshila. From the 10th century onwards, Hindu Temple colleges became prominent as seats of higher education. They were a natural reaction to the Buddhistic monastic universities. The Mathas of Acharyas continued the same tradition. Salotgi Temple College in Bijapur district in the 10th century A. D. was a centre of Vedic learning. Ennayiram Temple College in South Areot was an educational institution of the modern type with 16 teachers on its staff teaching a pre-determined curriculum.

Nalanda University. Nalanda was the seat of Buddhist learning. It was built largely by Buddhist disciples, but Guptas, the orthodox Hindus also patronised it. The University had a plan of its own. Monastic buildings and stupas were arranged in a regular fashion round the central college which had 7 halls. It had 300 smaller rooms for lecturing work. The building were exceptionally high. The very name Nalanda has been derived from the word Na-alam-da, insatiable in giving, implying that the university education in those days did not cram the mind with knowledge but created an insatiable thirst for it.

Rise and Fall. The date of its foundation is not known for certain. Though as a monastic seat it was founded long ago, as a seat of learning it rose into prominence about 450 A. D. General Cunningham assigns the probable date of the founding of university from 425 to 625A. D. The University began to decline during the 11th and 12th centuries when it was suppressed by Vikramshila and was finally destroyed by Muslim rulers in the beginning of the 13th century.

Library Facilities. Library facilities for self-study were abundant. A monastery without a library was like a castle without an armoury. From the Tibetan accounts mentioned by S. C. Vidya-bhushan in Medieval School of Indian Logic we learn that Nalanda had a fine library situated in Dharmganj and was housed in three splendid buildings; Ratansagara, Ratnadadhi, Ratnarayaka, Ratna-dadhi was nine-storied. Such spacious libraries met the needs of hundreds of teachers and thousands of students.

Student Body. Throughout these seven centuries of its existence Nalanda attracted students from all parts of India as well as from abroad. Students from China, Tibet, Bokhara and Korea came to Nalanda. *For example,* Fa Hien, Yuan, Chwang, Itsing were Chinese and Hwni Lun, Hwuii Viah were Koreans. Budhdharma was from Bokhara. The standard of admission to the university was naturally very high Watters says, "Of those from Abroad who wished to enter the schools of discussion, the majority beaten by the difficulty of problems, withdrew: and those who were deeply versed in old and modern learning were admitted: Only two or three out of ten succeeded."

Teachers. The standards of scholarship among the teachers were very high. They were not only famous for their piety, but were renowned for scholarship also. They were eminent for 'conspicuous talent, solid learning, great ability and illustrious virtues.' Saraha, the tutor of Nagarjun, Nagarjuna the founder of the school of Madhya-mika Philosophy, Aryadeva the pupil of Nagarjuna, Arya Asanga and his younger brother Vasubhandu, Dharampala the famous logician and grammarian and Silbhadra were some of the illustrious pundits of the University.

Administration. The university was controlled and administered well. At the head was the Abbot-Principal who was assisted by two councils, one academic and the other administrative. The chief abbot was elected by the members of the Sangha on the basis of his scholarship, seniority and character. Local and provincial jealousies did not influence the election. The academic council regulated admissions, determined courses and assigned work to different teachers. The administrative council boked after general administration and finance. The officials of this council were in-charges of construction of buildings and distribution of rations, superintendents of hostels and revenue officers. The head (chancellor) in Hiuen Tsang's time was Silbhadra. In the middle of the 8th century A. D. Kamalshila was its head. Besides the Dwarpandit and the Abbot Principal there were two other important officers. The Karmadana was the sub-director of the university and the Stavira, the presiding priest. Karmadana or Viharswami or Viharpal was the chief officer under the Chancellor and to him the utmost deference was paid.

Teaching Methods. The methods of teaching at the Nalanda University were tutorial as well as professional.

Beal says, "They arrange every day about 100 pupils for preaching and the students attend these discourses without fail even for a minute." There was a close touch between students and professors. Itsing says, "I have always been very glad that I had the opportunity of acquiring knowledge from teacher personally." A great importance was laid on discussion and debate. "The brethren are often assembled for discussion to test intellectual capacity, to reject the worthless and to advance the intellect", says Watters, "the day is not sufficient for asking and answering profound questions. From morning till night they engage in discussion; the old and the young mutually help one another."

Subjects of Study. The curriculum at Nalanda was catholic; *for example,* the works of Hinayana and Mahayana schools of Buddhistic philosophy both were studied. It was not sectarian because it was not confined to Buddhism alone. Subjects like Hindu religion and philosophy, were also thought there. Vedas, Vedanta and Sankhya philosophy were taught at the university with miscellaneous works. Subjects like grammar, logic, literature, astronomy and astrology, medicine which were of common interest were taught profusely.

Hostel Arrangements. Hostel arrangements were adequate. Satras were free-boarding hostels where students were supplied with necessaries out of the endowments to the university. Students were so abundantly supplied with clothes, food, bedding and medicine that they engaged themselves wholeheartedly in studies. *For example,* it is learnt that Hiuen Tsang received each day 120 fruits, 20 arecanuts, 20 nutmegs, an ounce of tack and peck of Mahasali rice. He was supplied with butter daily and other things that he needed.

GURUKULS AND VIHARS

In the Sixth Century B. C. and thereafter for a hundred years more, a section of people rose in revolt against the priestly class especially against their religious and social ideology. The revolt was headed by the Buddhists. The educational system was also opposed and in its place developed a system which had some elements in common and others quite different. The monastic system of education had the same spirit that prevailed in the Brahminic system. But the external forms became divergent.

The Brahminic system centred round sacrificial arrangements. The Buddhist system was born and grew up in the monasteries where the monks became the custodians of cultures and sources of learning. The Buddhist system was practically that of the Buddhist order (*Sangha*) and the Brahminic system belonged to the priestly class in the Brahmins.

The Buddhist Vihars ran counter to the Hindu Gurukuls. Whereas the Gurukuls centred round the hermitages of the saints and remained independent seats of learning throughout the Vedic period, the Vihars were organised on federal basis. The smallest link of the federation was a school—a small group of novices under a Uppajjhaya (*Acharya*). The group worked like a guild-a society for mutual aid and promotion of the common good. In a Vihar a number of such units were organised. Each units was expected to come forward to help the other. The entire Vihar was run by a body of officials with their functions well-defined.

Religious Rites. Both systems admitted students only after observing certain religious rites. The auspicious ceremony of Upnayan was replaced by Pabbajja, which literally meant going out of home or previous state and presenting oneself for admission into a Sangha. Upnayan also implied nearly the same thing. Literally, it meant a process of being 'taken near the teacher', but since after Upnayan the boy had to go out of his house and live with his teacher it practically meant going out. In Brahminic system the student was called a Brahmachari and in the Buddhist one he was named as Samanera. The regulations governing the life of a Brahmachari or that of a Pabbajja were ready alike. The Pabbajja had to obey the ten commandments as strictly as the Brahmachari had to abide by the ten qualities of a student. The only difference was in the manner of asking for alms. Whereas the Brahmachari could beg by words and could beg more food than was needed to feed himself the Pabbajja was not permitted to speak when he went a begging nor could he accept more than was needed for his upkeep. A Bhikshu as he was, he lived by alms. The Brahmachari also was to live by alms for begging was the first duty of a Brahmachari to be observed in Gurukul. The more dominant principles and manners of the life of Brahmacharya were adopted in the Buddhist system; *for example,* the modes of begging, eating, sitting, sleeping, cutting hair, clothing, were nearly alike.

Admission Policies. The Brahminic system of education was meant for the three castes the Brahmin, the Kshatriya and the Vaishya. The low-born were forbidden to study the Vedas because of a special sanctity that enveloped them. To Vihars persons of all classes of society, all castes and ranks (except the chandals) were admitted. No one was debarred entrance. Brahmins, Kshatriyas, Vaishyas, sons of merchants, tailors fishermen could get admittance. A common school system appears to have developed in the Buddhist period. The Buddhist monasteries did not however, admit a debtor, a slave, a crippled, a robber, an employee of the state, a person affected with leprosy, boils, fits and consumption.

Teacher Pupil Relationship. The teacher-taught relationships in the two systems were identical in nature. Every pupil had to perform domestic services for the teacher; *for example,* he was required to sweep the hermitage or the Vihar, beg for the teacher, wait upon and nurse him when he happened to be sick.

Teacher System. Domesticity was the prevailing note in the Gurukul system. The teacher's hermitage was the school. His personal impact was the potent factor in the education of the pupil. A striking difference became perceptible in the Buddhist monasteries. In the monasteries we had groups of novices under one Acharya. The novices were received in the religious house—the Sangha—on probation for taking a vow. The Acharya was required to work as their guardian. The fullfledged Achara or monk had a right to vote. The monks who had equal voting rights met usually and expressed their opinions. The resolutions of the Sangha were passed democratically. The Gurukul system favoured one-teacher, one-school whereas the Buddhist system had a large federation controlled by a collective assembly of teachers. The one-teacher-one-school system worked quite independently of other schools. The federated system of schools in the Buddhist period did not work in isolation.

The teacher in the latter system did not and could not wield supreme power over his pupil because there are evidences of the novices having been punished by the Vihar without any consultation with their Uppajjhaya.

The caste of teachers in the Brahminic system was only the priestly one. Instructions could be given only by Brahmans. There was a sort of Brahminic monopoly. But the teachers in Vihars were not necessarily Brahmans unless those who had become converted to Buddhistic order. The exclusive monopoly of the Brahmans was destroyed once for all. Different categories of teachers emerged. The main categories were those of the Dahara (Small Teacher), the sthara (settled teacher) and the Acharya.

In the Brahminic system the succession of teachers was not broken and individual schools were controlled by individual teachers only. But in the Buddhist system we have confederations of school. In the larger monastic institutions a number of teachers and students took a share of a wider, collective, academic life.

Discipline. The Brahmachari was not permitted to walk over ploughed land or through fields where corn was growing up. Every care had to be taken not to destroy life in any form. The prevailing note of Ahimsa in the Bundhist system of education was perhaps borrowed from there. The Brahmachari and the Bhikshu both had to abandon society, disclaim relationship with home and renounce homely pleasures if they wanted to seek education and acquire learning. Physical as well as mental purity was aimed at. Fasting was necessary. The eighth, the fourteenth and the fifteenth days of each fortnight were fasting days for students in Vihars.

Nature of Curriculum. The subjects of study in the Brahminic system were spiritual as well as worldly (*Para* and *Apart Vidyas*). The para Vidyas included the study of the Vedas, Chhandas, Kalp, Pitryas, Upanishads, Shiksha. The Apara Vidyas consisted of Sutras, Medicine, Surgery, Mathematics, Economics, Logic, Ethics, Physics, Chemistry, Astronomy, Biology, Bhu Vidya, Dharm Vidya, Sarp Vidya, dancing, sining, fine arts. The subjects of study in the Buddhist Vihars were Theology, Philosophy, Logic, Metaphysics, Sanskrit, Pali, Astrology, Medicine, Law, Politics, Administration but no technical subjects were taught.

The Buddhist system attached little significance to vocational training. Professional education was utterly neglected. In the Brahminic system importance was given not only to the cultivation of the mind and the spirit but also to the preparation for worldly life. It was the education for life. It was on the basis of professional education that ancient Indians could build up prosperity and fame in the comity of nations. Dr. R.K. Mukherjee holds that the professional education led to India's supremacy in export trade. Ancient India was the chief exporting country of the world, which supplied foreign lands with articles turned out by her cottage industries and handicrafts.

PHILOSOPHY OF MUSLIM EDUCATION

Muslim education system was essentially religious in character. It was patronised by the Muslim rulers who held orthodox views regarding perpetuating Muslim faith in lands they invaded and settled.

With the emergence of Islam, the attention of Muslim kings turned towards India. Time was kind to them. It allowed them to settle themselves firmly in this country. After the Gulam, Khilji, Tuglak, Sayyed and Lodhi dynasties, Mogul kings established many educational institutions in India. This education, too, had its roots in religion. During this period, Indian art and culture came under the influence of Arab culture and civilization. It was only natural that the same political influence should also have made itself felt. In consequence, education too came under this influence. Islam had its origin between 570 A.D. and 632 A.D. Hazrat Mohammed collected his messages in the Holy Kuran and this text came to be an instrument of social direction for the Muslim kings. During this period, these kings made arrangements for education in order to serve their own interests. Mohammed Gauri started his aggressions on India, but at the same time, he also had mosques and schools constructed in Ajmer to make arrangements for education in Islam and Muslim law. His successor Kutubuddin also followed in his footsteps. The other rulers of his dynasty, Altamesh, Razia Begum, Nasiruddin, Balban and others also had mosques, maktabs and schools established with government aid.

Ferozshah Tuglak of the Tuglak dynasty made efforts for the propagation of education. One of the schools established by him in Delhi has been described as follows. The school was located in a large ground and a big building with massive towers. It was situated in a garden in which human skill harmonized with nature, thus, creating an environment most suitable for contemplation and thought. Near the school was a lake, whose water shone like silver. The grand building of the school was reflected in its waters. It was an enchanting sight to see hundreds of students crossing the polished and soomth floors and congregating round their teachers. According to N.N. Law there were provisions for governmental aid and scholarships in these schools.

During the reign of Sikander Lodi (1489-1519), Indians, too, had begun to learn Persian (*Pharsi*). After obtaining knowledge of this laguage, they began to work in government departments. The Muslim rulers themselves felt the need for Hindu workers in the administrative sphere and hence they made arrangements for the study of Indian languages. And, as a result of the contact between the Hindus and Muslims, Urdu, which was the spoken form of Persian mixed with Hindi, was evolved. The Mughal rulers who followed the earlier Muslim rulers had relatively greater interest in education and hence it was in this later period that education developed more adequately. Akbar authorised the translation of many important Indian texts, including the Mahabharata, the Ramayana, Atharvaveda and Lilawati, into Persian. Akbar's deep interest in education is high-lighted by Abul Fazal's comments in his famous work 'Aaiyene Akbari' to the effect that in every country and especially in India, boys were kept in school for years where they were taught about consonants and vowels. Since they had to read numberous books, a large part of the boys' time was wasted. Emperor Akbar declared that each student should be taught to write the alphabet in various ways. Each student was required to learn the name of every letter (varna) within two days. Emphasis was laid upon imparting education in moral values, arithmetic, political arithmetic, agriculture, medicine, logic and physical, mathematical and divine philosophy to every student.

Jehangir went so far as to enact a law that the property and wealth of any person dying without an heir would be utilized for the repair of schools and religious buildings. Shahjahan had a university established near the Jama Masjid. Auraugzeb did propagate Muslim education, but at the same time he destroyed Hindu schools and temples. He granted excessive facilities for Muslim students, but he accorded a low status to teachers.

After the collapse of the Mughal Empire, schools suffered a severe blow. Many such institutions closed down due to anarchy and lack of finances. According to Vakil and Natrajan—"It must be noted that while mosques, maktabs and madrassas sprang up with the spread of Mohammadan power and provided facilities for Islamic learning in different parts of the country, the Hindu system of education continued to prevail in pathashalas, maths and temples except where their work was disturbed or dislocated by Mohammadan inroads or invasions." One finds a lack of organization in Muslim education. In the Muslim period, education was founded on community basis. Hence, it is illogical to claim that the Muslim ruler sought to propagate education liberally. Whatever the extent to which they propagated education, it was motivated by their own objectives, selfish interests and ambitions.

Bernier, the famous French traveller who visited India during this period, observed that during the period which he had described, it was only natural to find deep and universal ignorance. Was it possible to establish suitably financially aided schools and colleges or other centres of education in India? Where would the organisers be found? And, even if they were found, from where would the students be obtained? He also observed the absence of individuals whose wealth was adequate for providing suitable aid to colleges. And, even if such individuals existed, he felt that no one had the courage to compel them to bring out their wealth for such an investment. He felt that even some individual did venture on such a foolish act, there was an absence of religious places, enterprises and offices with employment potential which could utilize the ability and science imparted to students and thus, serve as an inspiration for youth to be hopeful and to compete for future success.

Characteristics of Muslim Education

During the Muslim period, education developed so slowly that no notable characteristic of it ever emerged. Minor rulers had educational institutions established for the satisfaction of their interests. However, the following features can be noted:

1. Encouragement by the State. Muslim rulers took an interest in education and so they provided aid to maktabs and madrassas. There were granted jagirs or landed property. Scholars were given places of eminence in the courts of kings. The rulers started giving aid to madrassas and maktabs being run in or along with mospues. Hence, their propagation of education was communal.

2. Arabic and Persian. During this period, special stress was laid on the teaching of Arabic and Persian, which were made the media of education by Muslim rulers. Knowledge of these two languages was essential for securing employment in government offices. Consequently, Hindus too began to learn Arabic and Persian.

3. Materialism. Muslim education sought the spread of education only from the practical and materialistic viewpoints. Education in manual skills, sculpture, agriculture, medicine, etc., is proof of this. In addition to religious education, teachers tried to ensure that after receiving education, the child should become capable of earning his livelihood. Consequently, knowledge of military science, painting, sculpture, housing construction, manufacture of weapons, etc., was also imparted. Knowledge of such subjects was given to students directly and individually by experts through a system of apprenticeship.

4. Religious Influence. The education of this period was profoundly influenced by Islam. Every Muslim sought education for the purpose of searching for knowledge and for religious purposes. There is direct evidence of the influence of Islam on the education of this period. Students were required to memorise the Koran. Importance was attached to study of Islam. This religious influence upon education was positive proof of the communal attitude of Muslim rulers.

5. Emergence of Urdu. The evolution of the new language 'Urdu' which emerged from the inter-mixing of Arabic and Persian, is the greatest contribution of the Mughal period. The importance that this language enjoys today is due entirely to the Muslim period.

6. Development of History-Writing. By initiating the writing of the history of their period, Muslim rulers helped to develop the art of writing history. Both Mughal and Muslim rulers commissioned the writing of the histories of their period or reigns. Among the most famous of these are Babar Nama, Akbar Nama, etc.

Centres of Education

The political organization of the Muslim rulers was decentralised. The Mansabdars, kings, zamindars or landlords, etc., became dependent rulers of their individual areas after paying the requisite tax to royal treasury. These rulers had mosques constructed and soon the mosques changed into maktabs and madrassas. During the Muslim period, Agra, Delhi, Jaunpur, Lahore, Ajmer, Bidar, Lucknow, Ferozabad, Jullundur, Multan, Bijapur, etc., became important centres of education.

1. Agra. Agra was founded by Sikandar Lodi. He had the town established as a centre of Islamic education and it soon took the form of a university. Hundreds of madrassas in this town provided education in literature, mathematics, philosophy, medicine, etc. Later on, Akbar, Jehangir and Shahjahan also contributed to the development of education in this town.

2. Bidar. Bidar, too, was an important educational centre. Mahmood Gawan had a huge madrassas and a library established here. Later, Alauddin Ahmed contributed to the development of education.

3. Delhi. Delhi was renowned far and wide as a centre of Muslim education. Nasiruddin established the Nasaria

Madrassas here. The Gulam dynasty also helped the spread of education in Delhi. During the reign of Alauddin Khilji, 34 famous scholars of Islam lived in Delhi. Feroz Tuglak had 30 madrassas established. Humayun opened madrassas for imparting knowledge of astrology and geography. Akbar, Jehangir, Shahjahan and Aurangazeb also established various madrassas for imparting knowledge of various specific fields.

4. Jaunpur. During the reign of Feroz, Jaunpur was a prominent centre of Muslim education. It had many schools imparting education in the arts, literature and other spheres of knowledge. The Sharkias made valuable contributions to the development of education. Sher Shah Suri himself was a student here.

In addition to the above centres, there were at least one maktab and one madrash in every village of Bijapur, Golkunda, Malwa, Khandesh, Multan, Gujrat, Lucknow, Sialkot and Bengal.

Organization and System of Education

During the Muslim period, the system of education was organised in the following manner:

1. Bismillah. Education began with the performance of the ritual known as 'Bismillah', which was performed at the age of 4 years, 4 months and 4 days. It was similar to the Upnayan ceremony of the Vedic period and the Pabbaja ritual of the Buddhist period. On this day, the child was adorned with a new crown and sent to his teacher, the Maulvi, where the latter inaugurated the child's education with a recitation from the Koran. Affluent people had this ritual performed at home.

2. Maktab. Education began in the maktab, *i.e.,* a primary school. The teachers called Maulvis taught the alphabet along with verses from the Koran. The child's primary education took place in these schools. Generally, most such maktabs were appendages of mosques. The child was taught writing, the Koran, namaz or prayer, azaan, arithmetic, drafting, conversation, letter-writing, etc.

3. Madrassa. Madrassas provided higher education to the students. They were aided by the Government. Here higher education was imparted through lectures. There were arrangements for hostels in the madrassas. They were owned privately as well as by the state.

4. Syllabus. The syllabus of education in the Muslim period included such subjects as the holy Koran, the biography of Hazrat Mohammed Sahib, the history and the laws of Islam, Arabic and Persian, grammar, literature, logic, philosophy, law, astrology, history, geography, agriculture, Unani system of medicine, etc. There were provisions for teaching Sanskrit to Hindu children. Madrassas provided both religious and material or worldly education. Subjects of religious education included Koran, Islamic laws, history and Sufi philosophy, while worldly or material education consisted of grammar, language, literature, etc. There were some specialized centres for education in particular subjects.

5. Method of Teaching. Emphasis was placed on memorisation in addition to reading, writing and arithmetic. The most prevalent method was the oral. Individual attention was paid to students, The monitor system had been used in maktabs and madrassas.

6. Student-Teacher Relationship. During this period, relations between students and teachers were not marked by intimacy, but there were no doubts about sincerity and purity. Though teachers received a low salary, they had an important place in society. People respected them and bestowed faith on them. The teacher had a paternal attitude towards his wards. It was believed that the students who served their teachers made God happy. Despite this, there was nothing notable in this relationship. Aurangzeb is known to have insulted his teacher Mulla Shah Saleh.

7. Reward and Punishment. There was a system of severe punishment to maintain order and discipline, but brilliant scholars were also rewarded.

8. Medium of Education. During the Muslim period, Arabic and Persian were the media of education. However, after the growth of Urdu, education began to be imparted though this language.

Merits of Muslim Education

1. Compulsory. Education was compulsory, specially for boys.

2. Co-ordination. There was proper co-ordination between religious values and material or worldly needs and well-being.

3. Character. Great stress was laid on character building.

4. Incentives. There was arrangement for rewards and scholarships for meritorious and intelligent students. This provided an incentive to learning and education.

5. Literature. Under Muslim rulers, through educational system, a good deal of development of literature took place.

6. Practical. Great stress was laid on practical utility.

7. Free. The education during the Muslim rule was mostly free.

8. Institutions. During this period, great attention was paid towards establishment of educational institutions. Prospersous people were encouraged to establish institutions.

9. Personal Touch. There was a personal touch between the teacher and the taught.

10. Curriculum. Curriculum included arrangement for the teaching of various subjects.

11. Writing of History. During this period, the tendency to write history was developed. This tendency was different from the tendency of the ancient India. It helped preservation of record.

12. Special Centres. There were centres of specialized education.

Demerits of Muslim Education

1. Unsuitable. Unsuitability was characteristic of the institution of education.

2. Material. There was predominance of material considerations.

3. Disbalance. Education of the Hindus was neglected. This brought about a disbalanced development of education.

4. One-sided Curricula. There was too much emphasis on teaching Arabic and Persian. This led to neglect of other subjects.

5. Lack of Co-ordination. There was no co-ordination between reading and writing.

6. Wrong Methods of Teachings. Oral or verbal method of teaching did not help the consolidation of the knowledge.

7. No Development of Reasoning. No encouragement to students to develop their power of reasoning.

8. Low Status of Teachers. The teacher-taught relationship was not ideal. The teacher did not occupy that position that he occupied during the Vedic period.

9. Lack of Psychological Basis. Muslim education lacked psychological incentives.

10. No Universal Education. There was no provision for universal education.

11. Defective Curriculum. Curriculum was defective.

12. Indifference Towards Women Education.

***

3

Philosophy of Idealism in Education

Man has two facts—Spiritual and Material. When the emphasis is on the realization of spiritual life, it is called idealism.

Idealism is the oldest theory of philosophy. It reflects in the complete history of philosophy. It is born out of Plato's 'Theory of Ideas'. According to this, the ultimate supermacy is of ideas. The word idealism has been derived from the word idea. It should be taken as that of ideas and not to be confused with philosophy of ideals. Plato and other idealism philosophers believed that only ideas are permanent. Idealism holds that the essential nature of man is spiritual which is revealed in mental, religious and aesthetic areas. To them spiritual world is more important than material world. This spiritual world is a world of ideas and feelings. To idealists 'Mind and Soul' are more important rather than Matter and Body. These ideas art eternal and unchanging.

The important definitions regarding idealism are as follows:

According to Ross, "To Idealistic Philosophy spirit is the essential world stuff and true reality is of a mental character."

According to Dutta, "Idealism holds that ultimate reality is spiritualism."

Supporters of Idealism—Protagonists of idealism are Plato, Socrates, Kant, Hegal, Green, Gentile, Vivekanand, Mahatma Gandhi and Dayanand.

Idealism and Philosophy

Metaphysics. Idealism is concerned with the Natue of Reality. For Idealist Ultimate Reality is of the Nature of Mind. Universe is the idea of the division of reality. The visible universe does not exist of itself, its existence depends upon the real world of mind or spirit. Spiritual world is the reality and true. Man is different from other creatures due to his spiritual power. Man is the grandest creation of God.

Axiology. Idealism believes in Truth, Goodness and Beauty. These values are eternal and permanent. To this philosophy God is truth, beautiful and good. It emphasises faith in God, character building, social responsibilities and other values.

Epistemology. For Idealists truth can exist only in the 'Real world of Ideas'. To arrive at truth man uses the methods of reasoning and intuition and through his mind trascends his physical impressions and gets some insight into the real world. Through logic and reason man discovers the pre-existent truths of the physical world and gains some insight into the ultimate truths of the world of ideas.

Fundamental Principles

Fundamental Priciples of Idealism are as follows:

(a) Idealists believe that spiritual world is real and the ultimate truth whereas the material world is transitory and mortal.

(b) They hold that the order of the world is due to the manifestation in space and time of an eternal and spiritual reality.

(c) To them, ideas are the ultimate reality. They are eternal and unchanging.

(*d*) To idealists man is more important than material nature. It is because man can think and experience about meterial objects.

(*e*) The spiritual or cultural environment is an environment of man's own making. It is a product of man's creative activity.

(*f*) Idealists give full support to the principle of unity in diversity.

(*g*) Idealism believes in spiritual values. They are Truth, Beauty and Goodness. The realization of these values is the realization of God.

(*h*) Idealists insist upon the fullest development of the personality of an individual. Human personality is of supreme value and constitutes the noblest work of God.

(*i*) To them God is the Supreme Force which is omnipotent and omnipresent.

Idealism and Aims of Education

The following are the aims of education according to the philosophy of Idealism:

Self Ralization. Idealism considers self-realization as an important aim of education. Self-realization involves full knowledge of the self. The aim of education is to enable man to become his truest self. Human personality is of supreme value and constitutes the noblest work of God. Every individual life has got the possibility of becoming a perfect pattern after his own self.

According to Ross, "The aim of education is the exhaltation of personality or self-realization, the making actual or real the highest potentialities of the self."

Spiritual Development. To idealism the aim of education is to develop the child mentally, morally and spiritually, Teacher should so organize education as to develop the child spiritually. To them truth, beauty and goodness should be encouraged more and more. The more an individual realizes these ideals the more spiritually enlightened he will be.

Preparation for Holy Life. To Froeblel "The object of education is the realization of a faithful, pure and holy life." Idealists uphold that education should create such conditions and provide an environment which are conducive to the development of spiritual values in a child. Good ideals will lead a child towards self-realization and prepare him for a holy life.

Preservation and Enrichment of Cultural Heritage. To idealists the aim of education is to acquaint the child with the cultural heritage so that he conserves, promotes and tansmits it to the next generation. Our cultural heritage is of great value and worth. This cultural treasure belongs to the whole humanity and it is the prupose of education to preserve, develop and transmit it in all corners of the world.

Character Formation. To develop morality in man is an important aim of education. Man is essentially a moral being. Idealism emphasises character building and character formation. The process of education must lead to the deepest spiritual insight to the highest moral and spiritual conduct.

Intellectual and Physical Development. The aim of education is to ensure the intellectual development and rationality of the child so that he may develop his innate and creative powers and thereby achieve his goal and seek adjustment with the environment. The aim of education is to ensure physical development of the child also. Sound mind lives in a sound body. Physically developed students can easily achieve their goals of life.

To develop the Feeling of Integrity. Idealists give full support to the principle of unity in diversity. They believe that implicit in all the diversities is an essential unity. This implicit unifying factor is of spiritual nature. The underlying divine force is God which is omnipotent and omnipresent. On the basis of caste, sex, colour and religion there are differences in the society, but God is present in all humanity. Feeling of unity is developed among the students through education.

Universalization of Education. Idealism is in favour of universalization is of education so that an ideal society may be established. Every child must have an access to education. In idealistic society, no exception should be made in the education of children. It should be universal because all human beings are equally the children of God.

Development of Moral Values. The aim of education is to develop morality in students. Education should develop the will power of the child so that he may be able to follow the good and avoid evil. This power can be developed by the correct appreciation of truth, goodness and beauty which are the highest moral values.

Idealism and Curriculum

Idealistic curriculum is thought-oriented and it stresses on those subjects which are related to the spiritual world. It provides for the training and cultivation of moral, intellectual and aesthetic activities.

For the asethetic and moral development Herbart gave prime importance to subjects like history, fine-art, music, poetry, ethics and religion.

For intellectual development of the child literature, language, science, social studies and mathematics are included in the curriculum.

Ross holds the view that man can develop spiritually only when he is physically fit and healthy. This philosophy insists on a sound mind in a sound body. It is essential to keep the body in a proper working order through physical activities. Hence this philosophy insists subjects related to care of body and skills, intellectual, moral, aesthetic and religious activities in the curriculum.

B.B. Bogoslovasky in his 'Ideal School' has given the new scheme of Idealistic curriculum construction as follows:

The first is the universe division an enlarged science department in which students study the inanimate forces of nature, the origin of our solar system, the development of life and the entire background of human drama, the second section deals with the civilization division which offers an inclusive study of social sciences. By civilization means all the activities, achievements and institutions of humanity which control our environment and provide the necessities of life. Security and comfort, food, clothing, shelter, technology, communication and government are all within the field of civilization. 'Culture Division' includes philosophy, art literature, religion etc. The fourth is the 'personality division' which offers study of physical, physiological, emotional and intellectual factors that shape and determine the human personality.

Nature of Idealistic Curriculum is cleared through the following diagram :

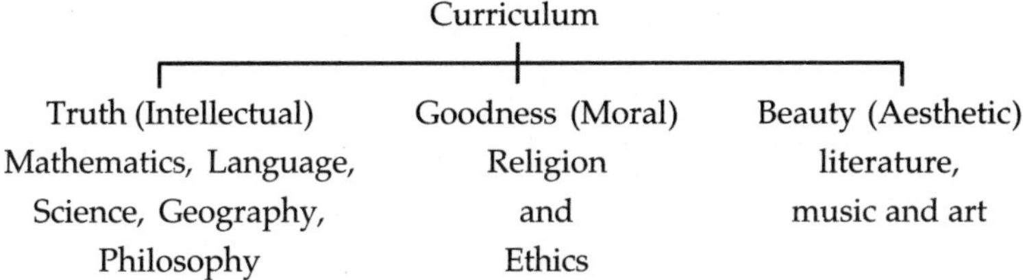

In nut shell we can say that idealistic curriculum insists on values and ideals.

(a) It gives more importance to religion, ethics music and art.

(b) This curriculum is thoughtful-centred curriculum. In this only those subjects have been emphasised which are helpful in the personality development.

(c) This curriculum lays more importance to those subjects which reflect the achievements of human culture and civilization.

(d) It includes the subjects relating to social, spiritual, intellectual, moral, religious and aesthetic activities.

(e) According to Horne "Information will become knowledge, books will become tools and best ideas will become ideals."

Idealism and Methods of Teaching

The ultimate goal of the teacher is the attainment of the aim(s) of education for his pupils. Therefore, whichever method is appropriate should be practised. After all, method is a means and not the end. Teaching methods should be chosen according to the nature of ends and means. The teachers have also to put their maximum efforts in formulating the aims. They should select any method keeping in view the content or nature of learner, or the educational objectives.

Idealists consider themselves creators and determinaters of method, not devoters of some one method. An idealist has adopted different methods according to the needs such as Socrates followed Question method, Plato developed Dialectic method, Aristotle initiated Deductive-Inductive method, Hegel followed Instruction method and so on.

Most of the idealists considered Lecture, Discussion and Questioning as the best methods of teaching.

Froebel developed the methodology of play which is known as kindergarten. He regards the school as garden and the teacher as a gardener, whose main function is to tend the little human plants under his charge, very carefully and thus, help them to grow to beauty and perfection.

There is a regulated and directed freedom for teachers in Idealistic methods of teaching. A teacher remains active, in teaching. To Butler, "An Idealist teacher is the creater and determinater of independent teaching method. He is not slave of any method." Idealism has advised the teacher to follow the method of teaching according to his convenience. To Horn, "The aim of teacher is to develop the personality of the child. For fulfilling this aim, the teacher should select the teaching method." Teaching methods followed by Idealistic philosophy are as follows:

Question Method. Socrates followed Question method. In this method effort is made to draw out right answer from the students by putting questions.

Deductive and Inductive Method. Aristotle initiated inductive and deductive method. Today this method occupies an important place in teaching learning.

Lecture Method. This method is followed to enrich the knowledge of the students.

Dialectic Method. Plato developed dialectic method to develop the knowledge of the students.

Kindergarten Method. Froebel developed this method. It is used for small children. It is known as Play Method. It is essential for the physical and spiritual development of the child.

Instruction Method. Hegel followed this method wherein teacher gives instructions to the students.

Drill and Repetition Method. Pestalozzi advocated practice and repetition method in order to evaluate the knowledge of the students.

Textbook Method. In this method more emphasis is given on the reading of textbooks.

Discussion Method. Teacher and students discover the truth through discussion method.

Imitation Method. This method is followed in Gurukul. In case of imitation the teacher sets before students some models and directs them to observe and try to reproduce them. The pupils are expected to follow the examples of great personalities and imbibe some of their good qualities.

Idealism and Student

Idealists have imagined an ideal student. To Bogoslovasky, "The student is a finite person, growing, when properly educated into the image of an infinite person." Idealists give more importance to thoughts and secondary place to student in the educational process. They consider a child under the control of the teacher. Teacher is the maker of his destiny. A student must obey his teacher. The order of his teacher is supreme for him and he must follow it. Other directions may be ignored. A student must have qualities like respect towards his teacher. The relationship between teacher and taught must be positive and congenial.

Idealism and Discipline

Idealism believe that there can be no spiritual development of the child without discipline. They give importance to impressionistic discipline in comparison to repressionistic discipline. They assert that the teacher should gain respect from the child by his affectionate and sympathetic behaviour and then motivate him by his praiseworthy ideals. Idealist believe in guided freedom and strict discipline. Children must endure a restraint on freedom. Self insight and self-analysis are the main disciplinary factors. Teacher's guidance is essential. The discipline is not to be imposed on pupils. The teacher has only to help them to develop self-discipline through that self knowledge. To them freedom is not means but it is an end. Idealists are the supporters of self discipline. They are not in favour of militant disciplne. They want to combine humility, courtesy, obedience and subordination in discipline. This approach signifies effective discipline.

Idealism and Teacher

According to Gentile, 'Teacher is a spiritual symbol of right conduct'. Teacher leads a child toward absolute perfection. That is why he is considered as pilot of God in perfecting man. He provides to the child the knowledge of his cultural heritage. He is the priest of man's spiritual heritage. He tells the child the way to reach God. He is a living ideal. Children imitate him. His personality therfore must be ideal. He acts as a friend, philosopher and guide.

According to Aurobindo, "The first principle of true teaching is that nothing can be taught. The teacher is not instructor or task master; he is helper and guide. His business is to suggest and guide and not to impose. He does not impart knowledge to him; he shows him how to acquire knowledge for himself. In idealistic philosophy the teacher has a very important role to play in education as he has to lead the pupil from darkness to light and he has to help him in development of his personality.

Idealism and School

School is a place where the capacities of logical thinking, reasoning and evaluating of the child are progessively sublimated and developed by the teacher. According to Idealism spiritual ideals and values are achieved through proper guidance of teacher given in school.

Idealists lay more emphasis on the inner aspect of the school and less on its building.

Such schools are based on ideal principles.

Idealism incorporates the principle of simple living and high thinking.

Idealism has imagined such an ideal school where a child is equipped with spiritual and human qualities.

They want to develop in child love for the nation, humanism, love of God and religion through school.

IDEALIST ROLE OF THE EUDCATOR

Idealistic pattern of education grants the highest place to the educator and conceives of the educator and educand as two parts of an organic plant. The educator creates a specific environment for the educand's development and provides guidance so that the later may progress towards perfection and a rounded personality. The most precise explanation of educator's role is manifested in Froebel's Kindergarten pattern of education, in which the school is treated as a garden, the educand as a delicate plant which requires nurturing and the educator as the cautious gardener. Although even in the absence of the gardener the plant will continue to grow and will inevitably follow the laws governing its nature, the gardener has a certain significance in that he has the skill to develop plants. He may be unable to change a rose into a cabbage, but he certainly can contribute his mite to the plant's development. His efforts help in achieving perfection in this development, a level of perfection which would otherwise have been impossible. The educand plays a parallel role in the school. He can guide the educand appropriately because he knows the rules which govern the latter's development into a process leading to perfection and beauty. Ross explains, "The naturalists may be content with briars, but the idealists want fine developing which may be denied to him." Clearly, the idealists attach much more value to the educator than do the naturalists. Adams opined that both the educator and educand are two parts of the intellectual universe both of which should be considered equally important.

Idealist Educational Methods

Turning to methodology in education, idealists suggest that the method must be oriented to achieving the complete development of all innate abilities of the child and to train him for self-realization. In Rivers' words, "The process of education in childhood consists, or should consist, in the direction of innate or instinctive tendencies towards an end in harmony with the highest good of society of which the child is an active member. Idealists believe in a harmony between individual and social objectives. The child must be provided with a liberal environment for his development and his education should be related to present experience. One finds, therefore, that many elements of the idealist methodology are common with those of the naturalist, realist and pragmatist methodology.

The idealist methodology in education lays special stress on the three following processes :

1. Instruction. The term instruction, as used here, implies educational instruction which is believed by Herbart to be essential to education. But instruction does not mean that the child mind should be stuffed with various scraps of information. It implies a modification and a refinement of the child's mind. For this it is essential that the educator must provide sympathetic guidance. The idealists believe that training of all kinds must be provided in the school.

2. Experience. Idealist methodology also lays considerable strees on experience. Every educand must base all his education on his own experience. The educator's task is not to stuff his own experience in the educand's mind but to provide the latter some insight into his own experience. The guidance given by the educator helps to manifest many frustrated and repressed tendencies and drives of the educand. Independence is an essential pre-requisite for experience. For this reason the idealist believes freedom to be an essential part of education but it must be remembered that this freedom is not absolute, but controlled and guided.

3. Activity. Like the naturalist methodology, the educational methods recommended by the idealists also are based on activity. The child must learn through doing. Although the child can learn much by asking questions after lectures in the school, creative activity is much more important. This creative activity should be natural, continuous and progressive. This helps in moving towards self-realization, because it encourages the child to manifest his innate tendencies. Through mental activity the child learns cheerfully and happily and this also helps in the development of his personality. Besides, by these means the child learns rapidly. Hence, the idealists also stress that instruction should be active.

❋❋❋

4

Philosophy of Realism in Education

Realism was born as a reaction to excessive idealism.

Characteristics of Realistic Education

The chief characteristics of realistic education are given below:

1. Based on Science. The supporters of Realism emphasized the importance of useful and purposive education. They advocated the inclusion of scientific subjects in the curriculum and in place of academic and artificial education, they laid stress on the natural education which gave birth to Naturalism. Thus, the emphasis on scientific education is the first characteristics of realistic education.

2. Emphasis on Present Life of Child. The second characteristic of realistic education is to make the present life of child as the focal point of educational system. As we know the fact that Realism was born as a reaction to excessively Idealism, it opposed the academic education of mere ideals and values and emphasized the immediate real and practical problems of day-to-day living which only can promote individual goods and welfare.

3. Emphasis on Experiment and Applied Life. The third characteristic of racialistic education is emphasis on experiments, experiences and application of knowledge learnt. It lays great stress on learning by doing, by developing creativity and urge of political work in children so that they are able to solve their immediate practical problems and lead a real successful life.

4. Opposition of Bookish Knowledge. Realists decry mere academic, theoretical and bookish knowledge which develops only rote memory and encourages cramming. It does not enable the child to understand the realities of external things and natural phenomena. According to Realists, education should inculcate in the child an understanding of both the thing and the environment. Thus, the slogan of realistic education is 'Not words but things'. Such type of education promotes intelligence and a sense of judgement which the bookish education does not do.

5. Limited Freedom of Child. Realistic education realizes the prime importance of child. Hence, according to Realists the child should be given full freedom to develop his self according to his innate tendencies. But this freedom should promote self-discipline and self-control. In other words, the child should procced from ignorance to knowledge slowly but surely through his own efforts and self-discipline.

6. Emphasis on Training of Senses. The sixth characteristic of realistic education is to train and develop the senses of child. Unlike Idealists who impose knowledge from above, Realists advocate self-learning through senses which ought to be trained. These senses are the gateways of knowledge and develop by use and experience.

7. Equal Importance of Individuality and Sociability. The seventh characteristic of realistic education is to emphasize equally the individuality and sociability of the child. Thus, the aim of realistic education is to develop both the individual self and the society of which he is an integral part. Bacon clearly asserts that realistic education develops the individual on the one hand and on the other hand tries to develop society through the development of social consciousness and sense of service of the individual.

AIMS OF EDUCATION

The following are the aims of realistic education:

1. Preparing the Child for a Happy and Successful Life. The first aim of realistic education is to prepare the child to lead a successful and happy life. Thus, education should be such that the child is able to love his problems of life successfully and lead a happy life promoting the welfare of society as well.

2. Preparing the Child for a Real Life. The second aim of realistic education is to prepare the child for a real and practical life. Realists believe in the reality of knowledge of external material world gained through senses. Thus, they wish to prepare the child for the real life of material world.

3. Developing the Physical and Mental Powers of Child. According to Realism, mind as well as the physical organs together constitute an organism composed of matter. Hence, according to this ideology, the third aim of education is to develop the physical and mental powers of the child so that with the help of his developed intelligence, discrimination and judgement, he is able to solve all the problems of life successfully.

4. Acquainting the Child with Nature and Social Environment. According to Realism, a child is related both to the external Nature and the social environment. Hence, the fifth aim of education is to provide the child full knowledge of both the society and the external Nature so that he is able to strike a balance between the two.

5. Imparting Vocational Education. According to Realism, education should be of practical utility of child. Since the problem of livelihood is main problem of life these days, so according to this ideology, the sixth aim of education is to provide vocational education to the child.

6. Developing and Training of Senses. Resists believe that unless the senses of the child are developed fully well, he will not be able to have full knowledge about the external world. Thus, the fourth aim of realistic education is to develop and train the senses of the child through varied experiences.

Curriculum

Realists insisted that only those subjects and activities should be included in the curriculum which prepare children for actual day to day living. Accordingly, considering the real situations, conditions and circumstances of the present day life of human beings, realists emphasized to give prime place to Nature, Science and vocational subjects whereas secondary place to Arts, Literature and Languages. It is to be noted that Realists have recommended about thirty subjects for the curriculum. They have also advocated free choosing by the children from among these subjects. At the same time they have made clear that teaching of mother-tongue is the foundation of all development and vocational subjects which are essential for livelihood. Hence, the essential subjects in the curriculum should be language and vocational subjects.

Methods of Teaching

Traditional system of education gave to the child only bookish knowledge which was purely academic and wordy. Hence, it failed to prepare the child for real life. Realists changed that system of teaching to gaining knowledge through senses according to the child's nature and capacity by way of observation and experience. Emphasizing that objects are real, the Realists insisted to impart knowledge of objects and external phenomena through senses. In their opinion, objects should be first shown and allowed to be handled if need be arise and then only they be interpreted and explained to the child.

Bacon, the famous Realist introduced the inductive method in the process of education. According to this method the object is shown to the child first and then its interpretation is done. In addition to this, the child does his own observation, experimentation and derives conclusions. In short, the child does self-learning to a great extent by employing inductive method.

Milton advocated learning by travelling. John Locke also spoke of tours, observation and learning by experience as powerful means of education. Some Realists also propounded many maxims of teaching which discourage rote memorization and prescribed instead learning by observation and experience.

Role of Teacher

The role of teacher according to Realists is neither as high and important as the Idealists advocate nor so negligible as the Naturalists speak out, it is fairly important. The teacher, according to Realists, is expected to have full knowledge of the content and the needs of children. Not only this, he must also be capable to present before children the content in a clear and intelligible way by employing psychological and scientific methods. It is the duty of teacher to tell children about scientific discoveries, researches and inventions by others in various fields of knowledge. He himself should also be engaged in some research work on experimentation. At the same time he must inspire children to undertake wide and close observation and experimentation themselves so that they are able to find out new facts. Not only this, the teacher must understand well the amount of knowledge to be provided to each child at a specific time.

Discipline

Realists emphasize moral and religious education of the child. For this type of education, discipline is essential and a pre-requisite condition. But what type of discipline? The upholders of this ideology decry repressibilities discipline. They advocate self-discipline to effect smooth adjustment of the child with external environment, the teacher only inspiring and encouraging sympathetically. According to Coummnis the school should be like the lap of mother full of affection, love and sympathy. In short, Realists advocate a synthetic form of impressionistic and emancipator forms of discipline.

School Management

Realists have different views about school. Some Realists do not feel any need of school at all. They prescribe wide travelling, tours and teaching by private tutors as the best means of education. On the contrary, other Realists emphasize the importance of school and class teaching. They regard school as a mirror of society reflecting its true state of affairs. As such, the school should not only include, in its work, all the activities going on in society, but it should also be well-furnished and equipped with all the necessary aids and device for effective observation and experimentations by children. According to them, the school is an agency which meets the needs of the child and the demands of society as well. Insert, it is school only which provides for the fullest development of the child according to his nature and needs.

PRINCIPLES OF REALISM

The principles of realism are as follows:

1. Material World is True. This philosophy considers materialistic world as true which we see directly. Moor has said, "Existence is perceiving." This world is a combination of matters. Matter is true. It is real. Therefore this world is also real. Spiritual world is thought-oriented, thus, it is unreal. Soul and God is a figment of imagination and mind is just a thing of the world.

2. Emphasis on Present Life. Realism lays emphasis on the present life and behavioural (practical) aspect of man. It opposes the ideals. It has no concern with the ideals and rules of past and future.

3. Man is Supreme. Realism considers man as the supreme creature of the material world. The ultimate aim of life is to live a peaceful life after acquiring the knowledge of things.

4. Universe is not External. Realists believe that universe is not external. There is law that governs the universe and the law is supreme since it is through this law and order that cohesion prevails.

5. Senses are the Gateway of Knowledge. According to realism whatever sensation we get while coming in contact with objects through our senses is the only reality. This philosophy considers senses as the gateway of knowledge. We receive knowledge by seeing, smelling, touching and tasting. This knowledge is real.

Realism and Philosophy

Metaphysics. This world is made of many materials. Material world is true and real. It is directly visible to us. Whatever is beyond this is unreal. Soul and God is a figment of imagination. Matter is dynamic. Mind is matter-oriented.

Axiology. Realism believes in the material-oriented world. Realists search for beauty in the natural beauty. They have no faith on eternal values, because they consider spiritual world as a figment of imagination. They believe that beauty is the reflection of nature. They stress on the practical aspect of the present. Man is the maker of his destiny. It does not believe in the pre-determined values.

Epistemology. Realists consider senses as the gateway of knowledge. This material world is real because it has existence, this existence is felt through senses. Therefore, it is real and true.

Realism and Aims of Education

Realism recommends the following aims of Education :

1. Preparation for Real Life. The aim of realistic education should be such that the child is able to solve his problems of life successfully and lead a happy life. Realists believe in the reality of knowledge of external material world gained through senses. They want to prepare the child for the real life of material world. Spencer recommends, 'complete living' as the aim of education.

2. Training of Senses. The aim of education is to develop and train the senses of the child through varied experiences. Realists believe that unless the senses of the child are developed fully well, he will not be able to have full knowledge about the external world.

3. Physical and Mental Development. Aim of education is to develop the physical and mental powers of the child so that with the help of his developed intelligence, discrimination and judgement, he is able to solve all the problems of life successfully.

4. Scientific Outlook. Realism considers the 'development of scientific attitude' as an important aim of education. It aims at the development of the habit of reasoning, independent thinking and judgement among the pupils.

5. Social Development. To ralism, a child is related both to the external nature and social environment. The aim of education is to provide the child full knowledge of both the society and the external nature so that he is able to keep a balance between the two. Aim of education is the social development of the child.

6. Vocational Development. Realism lays emphasis on material comforts and facilities. Attainment of material happiness is possible through a vocation. Therefore, we must make a child self-sufficient by developing vocational skills in him so that he may live a happy life by fulfilling his needs.

Realism and Curriculum

Curriculum is a means of realising the aims of education. Realists insisted that only those subjects and activities should be included in the curriculum which prepare children for actual day to day living. Accordingly, considering the real situations, conditions and circumstances of the present day life of human beings, realists emphasized to give prime place to Nature, Science and vocational subjects whereas secondary place to Arts, Literature and Languages. Knowledge must be given through the medium of mother tongue so that the child is in a position to solve his daily life problems and make his life happy. Hence, the essential subjects in the curriculum should be language and vocational subjects.

Realism and Teacher

Realism recognises the teacher but does not attach much importance to the personality of the teacher like Idealism. The teacher is supposed to put the facts as they are in their real form. He should present the knowledge in an effective and intelligible way. He should create opportunities for observation and experimentation. He should be well versed in the psychological methods, techinques and skills of teaching. Realists insist upon the training of teachers before they engage themselves in the teaching work in an effective way.

Realism and Methods of Teaching

The realism is opposed to the traditional methods of teaching. Realists stress the use of objective and scientific techniques. They support inductive-deductive experimenta-tion, tours, self-experiences, use of audio-visual aids and other methods of teaching. In their opinion objects should be first shown and allowed to be handled if need be and then only they be interpreted and explained to the child. This encouraged the use of audio-visual aids in education. They are the supporters of correlation method.

Realism and School

According to Comenius, 'schools are true foregoing places of men'. Realists emphasize the importance of school and class teaching. They regard school as a mirror of society reflecting its true state of affairs. School should also be well furnished and equipped with all the necessary aids and devices for effective observation and experimentations by children. According to them, the school is an agency which meets the needs to the child and the demand of society. It is school only which provides for the fullest development of the child according to his nature and needs. Not only this, school is the only agency to provide vocational education to prepare the child for some livelihood.

Realism and Discipline

Realism emphasizes moral and religious education of the child. For this type of education, discipline is essential condition. Realists advocate self-discipline to effect smooth adjustment of the child with external environment with the teacher only inspiring and encouraging sympathetically. To Comenius the school should be like the lap of mother full of affection, love and sympathy. They advocate a synthetic form of impressionistic and emancipatory discipline.

✸✸✸

5

Philosophy of Naturalism in Education

Although no system of education in the world may be found such as wholly operating according to the tenets of the philosophy of Naturalism, yet education in general throughout the world has been greatly influenced by it. In a sense the contributions made by naturalism to education are many. Some of the most important of these are as follows:

1. Paidocentric Movement. A natural consequence of the philosophy was that education was made paidocentric, *i.e.,* child-centred. It constantly emphasized the nature of the child as the focal point of all aspects of education. The child was put in the forefront and all other things such as the educator, the books, the curriculum, the school, etc., were thrown into the background. This tendency was called by John Adams as the paidocentric tendency in education. This conception emphasized that education is not preparation for life but life itself. Children should live like children and enjoy life. Education should be guided by the nature of the child. They take it for granted that the child is basically good. Rousseau himself said, "Eveything is good as it comes from the hands of the Author of Nature, but everything degenerates in the hands of men." The child is good, but he should be protected from a degrading environment. The child is desirable for his won sake. He should not be burdened with restrictions and made miserable. Allow him to develop naturally. These views constitute an important contribution of naturalism to education.

2. Education was Psychologized. This was another contribution made by the naturalists to education. When the naturalists stressed the nature and the natural development of the child, they immediately entered into the arena of psychology as it raised the question 'what is child's nature, what is natural development and so on'. Thus, a psychological tendency was developed in education which forced educators to view every aspect of education from psyschological point of view. It was emphasized that education must study the nature of the child and should adapt itself to this nature. Rousseau may be considered the pioneer for introducing the psychological tendency in education. He was the first person among the naturalists to say that education should follow the child's nature. Rousseau's ideas were, then, put into practice by Pestalozzi, Herbert, Froebel and several other educators. This emphasis in education generated a lot of new ideas and approaches in the field of education. Research in child psychology gained momentum. Educational psychology assumed greater importance. Methods of teaching and curriculum construction began to be considered from psychological point of view. McDougall made valuable contributions to child psychology. Psychology of individual differences came into prominence. It was considered desirable to make education flexible in view of specific differences in the nature of children. Psychoanalysis assumed still greater importance by bringing unconscious nature of the child into the picture.

3. Playway Method of Teaching. Naturalism made a very great contribution to teaching method at the early stages of education. Playway method was exclusively the contribution of naturalism. Even this method is considered important by educationists. The psychology of playway method was made explicit by Rousseau and several other naturalists. It was emphasized that all learning should take place in the spirit and by the method of play. Play reveals the child's nature most clearly. It is considered nature's mode of education. To James S. Ross "Playway in its manifold forms in the outstanding general method of creative education and it is essentially naturalistic." It is a method of teaching which includes all methods of learning which foster the spirit of joyous spontaneous creative activity. At Neill's Summerhill school children play all the day if they want to as childhood is playhood. Playway method has become the ideal of all infant schools. Montessori, Froebel and A.S. Neill developed methods of educating children which prominently use playway method of teaching-learning. In fact invention of playway method was a great contribution of naturalists to education.

4. Principle of Self-Education. This was another contribution to education made by naturalism. Rousseau's negative education was another name for child's self-education. He emphasized that it is child's natural development which should form the basis of child's education. For natural development self-education was the only means. The naturalistic educator should leave the child to himself. He should be there to only observe the child, not to give him knowledge or information. He should only provide an environment in which the child undergoes certain experiences and learns through them on his own.

5. Principle of Direct Experience of Things. Learning by doing or learning one's own experience is considered important even today. This was first emphasized by the naturalist philosophers. Rousseau said, "Give your scholar no varbal lesson; he should be taught by experience alone." Direct observation of things around and direct contact with the persons of object were considered important for this reason. It was stressed that science, instead of being taught through lectures, should be taught through experimentation in the laboratory; Geometry by actual measurement of the places around and geography by taking the pupils to various parts of the country. Similarly, the child should be taught concepts of responsibilities, duties and obligations by direct experience of social life. For this reason it was insisted that the schools should have practice of self-government in which students can participate and learn through their own experience, self-discipline, self-control and self-regulation.

In this way the naturalists were responsible for most of the revolutionary ideas in the field of education that are accepted widely even today.

FEATURES OF AN EDUCATIONAL SYSTEM

Naturalism has been described to have three forms *(a)* Naturalism of physical science which has little to contribute to education, *(b)* Mechanical naturalism which regards man as a machine and has given us the behaviourist psychology and *(c)* Biological naturalism which is founded on the notion of evolution and is most important of all forms of naturalism. The materialistic explanation of the word was the ground of naturalism in education. According to naturalism the ultimate reality is nature which is material. The naturalists are empiricists and believe that all knowledge is acquired through sense organs. They believe in living according to nature. "Follow nature" is their slogan. Be natural is their motto. They hold that nature has made all persons different. The most important modern naturalist thinkers are Rousseau, Bacon, Hobbes and Herbert Spencre.

1. Naturalists View on Aims of Education. According to Rousseau education means "natural development of organs and powers of the child". He said child's first education should be negative which means avoiding teaching of virtue or truth to him. He was against imparting any education to the child in early years of life. Development of body, development and strengthening of every part of the body and making the child grow healthy and strong was considered the most important aim of education during infancy. Then, developing child's sense organs and personality were considered important during childhood and adolescence. Development of emotions and sentiments leading to development of moral and social qualities including religious sentiment was emphasized at the level of the youth between 15 to 20 years. Thus, the aim of education according to Rousseau was bodily, sensory, mental, social and moral development of the individual. Herbert Spencer (1820-1903) another modern naturalist, in his book 'Education' (1961) enumerated the following aims of education:

(a) Self-preservation which means growth and development of both the body and the mind.

(b) Earning a living.

(c) Upbringing of children which means making the students successful parents in future.

(d) Teaching the individuals how to utilize their leisure time by teaching them painting, music, sculpture, poetry, recreation.

(e) Development of citizenship through scientific study of history.

And all these subsidiary aims must ultimately aim at "preparing the child for complete living".

2. Views on Curriculum. Rousseau was against any kind of curricular teaching or learning upto twelfth year of life. He was against any kind of verbal lesson on history, geography, or even language. He was also against teaching of morality. This was his concept of negative education which suggested that child's mind should not be stuffed with information of different kinds. So he objected to the use of any text-books for education of the young child. Giving to the child a chance to learn everything through direct experience and observation is what was stressed by him by way of child's curriculum. Even morality was to be learnt by the child through natural consequences of his own action. Thus, upto the childhood stage no curriculum of any kind was needed. Formal curriculum consisting of education in natural science, language, mathematics, woodwork, music, painting, social life and some kind of professional training was suggested to be introduced at the adolescence stage. Rousseau, however, said that books do not give knowledge, they only train one to talk. So he emphasized that curriculum for adolescence should be based on active work than on books. The youth should, however, by taught history, mythological stories and religious stories with stress on moral and religious education. Spencer also, like Rousseau prescribed the formula of returning to nature as the basis of all learning. Providing an environment, to him, was enough of the curriculum. Learning by consequences was considered enough, although he said that in case of dangerous consequences the child should be fore-warned. In order to realize the aim of complete living Herbert Spencer prescribed physical education which was considered necessary for good health.

3. Views on Method of Teaching. Rousseau was against the oral and theoretical methods of teaching which was pursued in his time. Instead he recommended playway method of teaching learning. Real education to him was self-education acquired through experience and observation. Two great principles of teaching which he stressed were *(i)* learning through self-experience and *(ii)* learning by doing. Naturalism, thus, stands for a kind of teaching which is not dependent so much on schools and books, as on the "manipulation of the actual life of the educaned". Its watchword is "Back to Nature". Herbert Spencer was the naturalist who enunciated several principles of teaching such as:

(i) Proceeding from easy to difficult situations and experiences.

(ii) Proceeding from known to unknown which means the new experience to be given should follow the one which the child has already undergone.

(iii) Proceeding from indefinite (vague) to definite (clear) meaning; theredy that the teacher should make child's knowledge which is vague, clear and definite.

(iv) Proceeding from concrete to abstract which means concrete things and experiences should be presented first and abstract ones after them.

(v) Proceeding from experimental to rational knowledge. It means that the child should, first, be allowed to experiment with things around. This will prepare him to acquire and retain rational knowledge given in books.

(vi) Conforming to the stages of development which means that the method of teaching should be suitable from the point of view of the characteristics of child's development. For very young children playway is the most suitable method.

(vii) Create interest in learning by using audio-visual aids, charts, diagrams etc., in order to concretize knowledge.

Thus, playway, experience and experimentation are the most desirable characteristics of teaching method according to naturalists.

4. Views on the Place of the Child in Education. In Naturalist child is the measure of all things, the centre around which revolves every aspect of education. Naturalists' view of the child is very close to that of Wordsworth who said 'child comes from heaven trailing clouds of glory'. They are interested in the child as he is rather than as he will be. To them adult standards of behaviour are not at all important for being followed by the child. They conceive of childhood as something desirable for its own sake and expect children to be children before they become men and women. Hence, they abhor all kinds of restrictions to be imposed on children in schools. They recommend that the nature powers and inclinations of the child should be allowed to develop freely with a minimum of guidance. The naturalistic educators allow the child to follow the lines of his natural interests and to have free choice of activities with no interference or thwarting. No knowledge, no development of any kind (social, moral or religious) should be forced on the child. "These the child will forgo for himself. He knows better what he should learn, when and how he should learn it" (James S. Ross). Rousseau's negative education advised to leave the child largely to himself.

5. Views on Discipline. Discipline, according to Rousseau, is learnt by the child as a consequence of his actions. It cannot be imposed on him by the teacher. Naturalists did not support the idea of punishing the child for ensuring discipline. Rousseau said that consequence of child's action was enough and natural punishment. Oral teaching of morality through lectures and preachings was against the naturalistic philosophy. Left to himself the child will learn better discipline. This was their belief. Rousseau and Spencer both had the same views. In fact Rousseau's conception of education was it is "the process of development into an enjoyable, rational, harmoniously balanced, useful and hence natural life".

✹✹✹

6

Philosophy of Pragmatism and Humanism in Education

Pragmatism is midway between Idealism and Naturalism. It is an American philosophy typical in nature and practical in approach. The term pragmatism is derived from the Greek word 'Pragma' which means activity or the work done. Pragmatism is also known as Experimentalism because pragmatists believe experiment as the only criterion of Truth. It is noted that the fundamental start of Pragmatism is change. In this sense, no truth is permanent. It is always changing from time to time, from place to place. To them only those ideals and values are true which result in some utility to mankind in a certain set of circumstances, place or time. It is intimately connected with human life and human welfare, that is why, it is called as a humanistic philosophy of life.

Idealism is psycho-centric, Naturalism is neutro-centric and Pragmatism is anthropo-centric, according to which, man's own experiences are the centres of reality and truth. Idealist looks before and after and pines for what is not, naturalists look to present needs and problems and have no concern for future, Pragmatist looks here and now.

Idealist constructs a transcendental ideal which is beyond man's realisation. Naturalists follow the principle of struggle for existence and survival of the fittest. Pragmatists are practical people believing in finishing the book here, solving the problem now, making the social contact immediately, striking the business deal at once. Whatever they wish to do, they examine its utility and do it immediately.

Idealists live in the world of ideals. Naturalists live in the lap of nature. Pragmatists live in the world of facts. Pragmatism makes 'activity', 'engagement', 'commitment' and 'encounter' its central theme.

Different philosophers and educationists have defined pragmatism as follows :

According to Prett, "Pragmatism offers a theory of knowledge, a theory of truth and a theory of reality."

According to Ross, "Pragmatism is essentially a humanistic philosophy maintaining that man creates his own values in course of activity, that reality is still in making and awaits its part of completion from that future."

According to William James, "Pragmatism is a temper of mind, an attitude, it is also a theory of the nature of ideas and truth and finally it is a theory of reality."

According to Dr. Prem Nath, "The nature of Pragmatism is naturalistic, its duration is scientific and practicable and its aim is social and humanistic."

Pragmatism is definitely a foreign ideology. In modern times, the introduction of pragmatism to human life was first done by American philosopher G.S. Pearce in 1878 A.D. He asserted, "our beliefs are really the rules for action". Due to inhuman cruelties in England, thousands of the oppressed people migrated from their native countries in Europe to America. The new way of thinking led them to new types of activities and new ways of learning by doing and by consequences and experiences.

Forms of Pragmatism

There are different types of Pragmatism which are as follows:

1. Biological Pragmatism. According to this the capacity of a human being is valuable and important which enables him to adjust with the environment or which makes him able to change his environment according to his needs and requirements.

2. Humanistic Pragmatism. According to this 'whatever fulfils one's purpose, satisfies one's desire, develops one's life, is true.' It maintains what satisfies the human nature is only true and real.

3. Nominalistic Pragmatism. It emphasises on the concreteness of an idea. When we do an experiment we come across future solutions. Its basis is concrete. It results in some visual solutions.

4. Experimental Pragmatism. According to this whatever can be experimentally verified is true. That principle is true which can be verified as true by experiment.

5. Supporters. Perce, William James, Kil Patrick and John Dewey were the supporters of Pragmatism.

Characteristics of Pragmatism

Characteristics of Pragmatism are as follows:

1. Faith in Democracy. This philosophy believes in humanism which is in accordance with democracy. Pragmatism shows its deep faith in democracy, as democracy is a way of life and a spirit of sharing experiences.

2. It is a Revolt against Traditionalism. This philosophy is a midway between Naturalism and Idealism. It neither believes in the established beliefs nor in the objective interpretation of naturalism. It lays emphasis on the practicability of thing and activity.

3. It does not believe in eternal values. Man makes his own values. Values change according to the change of time. They are relative. There is nothing in the name of eternal values. Truth is that which works, which serves some purpose and is useful to a man. Truth is man-made and the values of life and truth always change.

4. Principle of Utility. Pragmatism believes in the priciple of utility. Utility is the measure of a view point. The thing which gives satisfaction is useful. According to this only those ideas and things are true which have a utility for man.

5. Thought in Subordinate to Action. Pragmatism sees thought as intrinsically connected with action. It gives supreme position to action.

Pragmatism and Philosophy

Metaphysics. Pragmatism regards the material world as true. It regards human being as the supreme person. He is a social being and his development is possible only in the society. To it this world is the combination of different elements. It considers truth as chaugeable. Truth is man-made. There is a change in its form and concept. Pragmatism believes in the power of God if the existence of God is helpful in the growth of human being otherwise not. It lays stress on action and its consequences. It considers reality as a process of the completion of a task.

Axiology. Pragmatism does not believe in eternal values. Man himself creates values. Values are not predetermined. Pragmatists consider consequences as the basis of selection of all types of values. If the values are useful their sellection is appropriate otherwise not. In the context of religion, Dewey has said, 'God is active relation between Ideal and Reality, They consider the use of intelligence in the solution of problems.

Epistemology. Pragmatism considers experience as the source of attaining knowledge. Human being receives knowledge through experience based activity and ideas by acting and reacting with human environment. Pragmatists consider experimental methods as the best means of attaining knowledge. To them problem, selection of problem, data collection, hypothesis and experimentation are the steps of experimental method. Truth is the outcome of expected consequences through this method.

Principles of Pragmatism

Principles of Pragmatism are as follows :

Pragmatism believes in the power of God if the existence of God is helpful in the growth of human beings otherwise not. It recognises the importance of human power. The essence of human life is humanity. The world is like a laboratory where man solves his problems. In it means are more important than ends.

1. Stress on Social Values. Pragmatists uphold social and democratic attitudes and values. Pragmatism holds that man is a social being. He is born in society and all his development takes place in and through society.

2. Principle of Utility. Pragmatism is a utilitarian ideology which holds that the reality of a principle lies in its utility. Any idea or thing which is useful to us, is proper and right. In case it is of no use, it is improper, wrong and untrue.

3. God is not Absolute. To the Pragmatists God is not infinite, absolute and immortal entity as the idealists proclaim. To them, God and Soul are not immortal and infinite. These entities as well as the religion are useful to human beings only when they serve usefully to develop human personalities, otherwise Pragmatism shows an attitude of indifference towards moral and spiritual ideals and values.

4. Emphasis on Activity. The greatest contribution of Pragmatism to education is the principle of learning by doing. It lays great emphasis on activity rather than on ideas. It holds the view that ideas are born out of activities. Man is active by nature. He learns by his activities.

5. Past is Dead. According to Pragmatism past is dead and gone. It is of no use to think and talk about what is dead and gone. To it each individual has to solve the problems of his present and future life. Hence, present and immediate future are of great value to an individual.

6. Problems are Motivating Force. According to Pragmatism, human life is like a laboratory wherein each individual undertakes various experiments to solve the problems which confront him in course of his growth and development. The success of the experiment is a search of truth. Hence, problems are the motivating force for the search of truth.

7. Importance to Human Intelligence. Pragmatism gives more importance to human intelligence and mental capacity which brings about harmonious and progressive adjustment with environment which results in human welfare and happiness. It is against old customs and traditions. It believes in realities of life.

8. Faith in Pluralism. This philosophy is pluralistic. It takes "life" from naturalism and 'Psyche' from mentalism and evaluates and explains God, nature and man. It is just in the middle of naturalism and idealism.

Pragmatism and Aims of Education

1. All Round Development. Education ensures all round development of the child. The child must develop physically, mentally, socially, morally and aesthetically. The aim of education is for development. To Dewey, "Education has no aims, only persons have aims." Therefore the aims of pragmatic education are chageable".

According to Ross, "The general educational aim of the pragmatists is just the creation of new values. So the main task of the educator is to put the educand into a position of developing values for himself."

2. Social Efficiency. Pragmatism wants to develop social efficiency in the child through education. Education wants a child to stand on his feet by providing him vocational efficiency so that he may fulfil the needs of his family and society besides his personal needs. Thus, social efficiency tries to enable him to adjust with the society.

3. Adjustment. Pragmatic education is flexible. Therefore it wants to develop a child as a dynamic and flexible intellectual so that he may adjust with the changing environment and ensure his progress by controlling it. It wants to enable a child adjust mentally for the present and future by making him as the centre of education. The aim of education is 'to direct the impulses, interests and abilities towards the satisfaction of the left needs of the child, in the environment.

4. Reconstruction of Experience. As every individual is required to solve many diverse problems in his life, the aim of education should also be the formulation and cultivation of a dynamic, adoptable, resourceful and enterprising mind. It is with such a mind that original and creative thinking is possible which will enable a person to cope successfully with the varied situations of life.

Pragmatism and Curriculum

Pragmatists want to construct such a flexible, dynamic and integrated curriculum which helps in the development of the child. According to pragmatism only those subjects, activities and experiences should be included in the curriculum which are useful to the present needs of the child and meet the future expectations of adult life as well. Knowledge, of languages, hygiene, physical training, history, geography, mathematics, science, agriculture and professional subjects is compulsory. The main purpose is to help the child more and more in his development in all the fields of human activity. Only those activities and experiences in which the child takes interest should be included in the curriculum. The curriculum should consist of such varieties of learning experiences which promote original thinking and freedom to develop social and purposeful attitudes.

According to Pragmatism knowledge is one unit. It cannot be divided into water tight compartments of separate subjects. Teaching of various units should be closely inter-linked and co-related so as to form right concept and proper understanding in the children.

Pragmatism and Methods of Teaching

Pragmatism is opposed to the traditional methods of teaching. It favours child-centred, scientific and psychological and active methods of teaching. Pragmatism has contributed significantly to the methods of teaching. Pragmatists laid stress on learning through activities and the real life situations. Their main methods are Project method and Problem-solving method. Through these methods a child attains knowledge by solving his practical problems. These methods are experimental and creative.

These methods lay emphasis on learning by doing and learning through experience. Both the teacher and taught remain active. Pragmatism does not merely insist upon practical activities but tries to provide real life experiences and real life situations so that the child gains the required insight and capacities to face and solve the problems and challenges of life successfully. To it only that method is most effective which employs correlation and integration of all subjects, activities and experiences.

Pragmatism and Discipline

To Dewey discipline is a sort of mental state in the formation of which social conditions play a major role. Pragmatism condemns enforced discipline and advocates social discipline based on child's interests, activities and a sense of social responsibility.

Pragmatism advocates the merging of play with work. This merging of play and work will develop interest and a sense of purpose in the child to do his work with joy and eagerness without interfering with the work of others. This mental condition will infuse in him seriousness, sincerity and consideration for others. He will develop self-confidence, self-reliance, co-operation, sacrifice, sympathy and fellow-feeling for others. With the development of these social qualities he will develop a sense of social discipline and moral obligation towards self and others.

Hence, according to pragmatism, the school should provide purposeful and conducive experiences to the child in a free and congenial atmosphere, which helps him becoming a true citizen in the real sense. Such activities create in children virtues like mutual respect, toleration, self-control and originality. This helps him in the training of character formation and establishment of self-discipline.

Pragmatism and Student

Pragmatism gives an important place to the child. The aim of education should be to prepare the child for the society so that he can become responsible citizen and succeed in life. This philosophy stresses child-centred education. There are three aspects of child's personality—Biological, Psychological and Social. Pragmatism lays emphasis on social aspect. This philosophy considers a child as an important part of educative process. It does not want to impose external ideas upon the child. It is in favour of giving him academic freedom. It wants to educate the child in social envionment.

Pragmatism and Teacher

According to pragmatism teacher is a friend, guide and philosopher to the child. He must educate the child in social environment so that he may attain social efficiency. There must be positive relationship between teacher and taught. His behaviour towards children must be sympathetic. His attitude should be democratic and child must have academic freedom. His function is to suggest problems to his pupils and to stimulate them to find for themselves solutions which will work. His emphasis is not on the knowledge as arranged and systematised in the textbooks. He wants the children to do one experiment or to have a particular experince. 'Doing' is more important than knowing. Like Socrates the Pragmatist teacher wants "his pupils to think and act for themselves, to do rather than to know, to originate rather than to repeat."

Pragmatism and School

John Dewey maintains that school is a 'Miniature Society'

here a child gets real experiences to act and behave according to his interests, aptitudes and capacities. Pragmatists ragard school as a social institution where the child gains real experiences of actual life which develop in him social sense and a sense of duty towards society and the nation. Group games, working in laboratories and studying in libraries with others are the various activities and experiences which inculcate in children social qualities, social attitudes together with a spirit of mutual help and cooperative activities. In this way, according to Pragmatism the school is not a centre of education alone but it is also a community centre of various activities and experiences.

Contribution of Pragmatism in Education

1. Aims. It lays more stress on social and vocational efficiency.

2. Teacher. It gives important place to teacher.

3. Student. It stresses on child-centred education.

4. Teaching Method. New teaching methods is the contribution of pragmatism.

5. Curriculum. It lays more stress on experience and learning by doing.

Evaluation of Pragmatism

1. Opposition of Pre-determined Ideas. Pragmatism opposes pre-determined ideals and values. They are man-made and change according to the changes in circumstances, time and place.

2. No Fix System of Education. Pragmatism provides academic freedom to every institution which leads them no where. Pragmatism gives no fixed ideal to education. Such an education is bound to be fruitless.

3. Opposition of Eternal Truth. Pragmatism does not have any faith in eternal truth. Pragmatists believe that if the result of an activity is satisfactory then it is true otherwise not.

4. Emphasis on Material and Negation of Spiritual Values. There is no room for spiritual values in pragmatism. It gives more weightage to material values. Without spiritual values, we can not achieve happiness, contentment and peace of mind and can go astray.

5. Laxity in Discipline. Pragmatism allows full freedom to the child which is not proper at the school stage and it leads to serious chaos and confusion.

6. Condemnation of Formal Education. Pragmatism advocates that all knowledge should be acquired through direct personal experiences. But knowledge is so vast and the span of life so short, that it is quite impossible to receive all knowledge through direct experiences. Hence, acquiring all knowledge needs personal experinces and formal education both.

7. Pragmatism is a Method Only. Pragmatism is not a philosophy of life but only a method of education, growth and development. In the words of William James. "There is absolutely nothing new in the pragmatic method. It is just empirical attitude. It has no dogmas and no doctrines save its methods."

8. Negation of the Past. Pragmatism gives undue importance to the present. It ignores both past and future. The study of past is important to understand the present. Also there is need to link the present with future.

Pragmatism believe in Pluralism which is not proper.

Merits of Pragmatism

1. Project Method. Project method is a gift of pragmatism. Through this method child attains knowledge by solving his practical problems. He performs the problematic acts in natural conditions. This method lays emphasis on learning through experiences.

2. Importance of Child. Opposing bookish knowledge and formal education, pragmatism lays great stress upon the development of child's individuality by his own efforts. This makes education child-centred.

3. Emphasis on Activity. The principle of learning by doing is the main contribution of pragmatism. Children are active by nature. It emphasises on the activity of the child. It prepares the child for future life in a very effective manner.

4. Revolutionised the Process of Education. This philosophy has infused life and zest in contribution. The concepts of 'New Education', 'Progressive Education' and Activity-centred curriculum which have changed the education outlook are the contribution of pragmatism.

5. Social and Democratic Education. Pragmatism infuses in a child a spirit of freedom, initiative, equality and also a sense of responsibility in relation to rights and duties of a citizen. This develops in the child love for democratic values and social efficiency which bring harmonious adjustment and development of personality.

6. Progressive Attitude. Pragmatism emphasizes the qualities of freedom initiative, expression, conducive experiences, congenial environment, purposeful creativity and development of human values for the welfare of whole mankind.

Pragmatism is an attitude and a way of living which, opposing the old doctrines of Idealism and Naturalism, inspires the individual to look ahead and create new values for an unknown future so that he leads a better, happier and a richer life.

HUMANISM

Humanism implies both a human and a humane approach to educational problems, human in the sense that human nature (including likes, dislikes, interests, aptitudes etc.) should not be suppressed by religion in favour of an ascetic ideal and a narrow dogmatic interpretation of the world; humane in the sense that the nature of the child and its growing mind should not be suppressed by cruel discipline, teachers and rigid methods of teaching.

Humanism is a revolt against theology, church and dogma.

In simpler words we can say that when human world and human being become the concern of philosophy the result is humanism.

It also means studies of humanities.

It also means reasonable balance of life.

It is a philosophy, the centre of whose studey is man. Man is the measure of everything.

Implications in Education

The aims of humanistic education are:

(i) **Broadly Educated Man.** To produce a broadly educated man possessing a well rounded personality who could assume leadership in church and state.

(ii) **Accomplishments.** To produce men who should have a wide range of accomplishments. They should be able to express themselves in poetry, song, dance etc. All men should be physically and mentally healthy.

Jacks says that according to Humanists human perfection must be final objective.

Curriculum

The main tenet of humanism, *i.e.,* education for all and child is the centre of all education and the broad aims of education reflect on the type of curriculum. Hans says that the humanistic curriculum had in it the 'real' studies so that those could light the minds of children since it was the pupil who came first or got priority—method and theory later.

(i) Accordingly, curriculum included the study of old classics of Greeks and Romans since early humanists considered these to possessing profundity of content,

literary style etc., and they believed that all the values such as wide leraning, all round development, life of action, qualities of artistic enjoyment could be achieved by teaching Greek and Roman literature. In comparison with literature and classics, they gave slight attention to mathematics, natural history, music etc. etc. and much less attention was given by them to the vernaculars in their curriculum. They believed that if history and ethics is to be studied—we should study those as a part of the work of the old classical writers.

(ii) Training for Good Manners such as modesty was also stressed.

(iii) Physical Education was also included in their curriculum and there was due place for it. It aimed at producing a new brave class of people.

Academician J.B. Florin and his Humanistic Curriculum. In the 18th century Florin asserted, "Philosophy and the sciences ought to be made the principal study of young persons." He classified all subjects of instruction into three groups: *(i)* Relation of man to nature, *(ii)* Relation of man to himself and *(iii)* Relation of man to other men.

He advised a ten years course for the ages seven to seventeen presuming that the boys would enter his academy with a fair knowledge of writing and reading. The subjects included all branches of mathematics, history, applied sciences for the first group; Latin, French, Italian, Grammar, Rhetoric, poetry, drawing, music and exercise for the second group; History, politics, economics and biography for the third group.

Method of Teaching

(i) It was Erasmus who had left in writing about the method. He had tried the old methods in teaching literature and he told us, "Do not give the personal account of the author—rather appreciate the work of the author." We should talk about his style, about

his vocabulary etc., rather become personal with him.

(ii) Talking about difficulties in the way of learning, humanists say that the teacher should give few simple directions to overcome difficulties. Do not hurry because learning comes easily when the proper statge is reached. Avoid difficulty which can be easily ignored. Postpone things.

(iii) For mature students, early humanists recommended lectures and debates. Independence and individuality were introduced in learning of lessons. It was a protest aganist verbalism and cram work.

(iv) Next item in the method of humanistic education was to set exercises for the matter taught. It should not be literal reproduction. The subject should be reproduced. He did not favour taking notes. He would encourage memorisation, understanding and reproduction. The substance be memorised. Let the child understand critically and then reproduce. The maxim was:—Understand—Arrange—Repeat.

Other Features

1. Discipline. Humanists believed in discipline in the schools. It was a discipline of kindness than of vindictiveness. There was an appeal to pride and ambition in the child rather than to rigors of punishment.

2. Role of Teacher. It is the teacher who is the chief agent in this enterprise of sensible integration and success or failure depends upon his outlook and methods. If he lives a unified life himself, he will help his pupils to find a unity in the multiplicity of their experience, but if he is to do all this, he will require different type of training.

✱✱✱

7

Contribution of Indian Educational Thinkers

VIVEKANANDA'S EDUCATIONAL PHILOSOPHY

Swami Vivekananda was born in 1863 in Calcutta of a famous advocate of Calcutta High Court. Narendra Dutta was his childhood name. From the beginning he was interested in religion and philosophy. But, he was totally transformed after a meeting with Rama Krishna Paramhans in 1888. Since then he had been a wandering monk. In 1893 he went to attend a World's Parliament of Religions at Chicago. His views on education are found scattered in his lectures delivered at many places in India and abroad which are, now, available in printed from titled as Collective Works of Swami Vivekananda.

Meaning and Aims of Education

To Vivekananda education was a man-making process which would mean arousing the people to an awareness of their own worth, dignity and responsibility, making them the source of all the strength and sustenance of society, creating a society which will provide a healthy milieu for the development of character and personality of all its children.

Educational Philosophy of Vivekananda and the aims of education together with the concept of education are founded on Vedanta philosophy, particularly the Advaita philosophy which says that in the lowest worm as well as in the highest human being the same divine nature is present. "The whole object of Vedanta philosophy is, by constant struggle, to become perfect, to become divine, to reach God and see God". The belief of this philosophy is that every human being is spirit (*Atma*), the soul which is immortal, evolving up or reverting back from birth to birth and death to death. Swami Vivekananda only reinterpreted the basics of Vaidik philosophy in the context of 20th century man and the society.

Swami Vivekananda had great faith in education to him, this was the basic means for achieving human excellence and solving national problems. He said there are no problems which can not be solved by that magic word "education". He defined education as the "development of faculty, not an accumulation of words". To him education was meant for the training of individuals "to will rightly and efficiently". He further said that the education that does not help the common mass of people to equip themselves for the struggle for existence, which does not bring out strength of character, a spirit of philanthropy and the courage of a lion is not worth the name. Real education, to him, means that which enables one to stand on his own leg.

Vivekananda stressed the need to educate the millions of our common people to revitalize Indian culture of the day. A nation is advanced in proportion as education and intelligence spread among the masses. National development rests upon the goodness and greatness of men; and goodness and greatness of men are determined largely by education.

Education for "total human development" was the vision of Vivekananda which, he believed, could be achieved by refining and processing of in eternal human energies through the science of man in depth (*Adhyatma Vidya*). Philosophy, the science, the art and studies of various other fields of knowledge could help nations in achieving this goal. Through education nations have to unfold the humanistic and divine possibilities lying hidden within their people and raise the levels from which their consciousness handles their external, natural and social environment. True education is that which does this.

Vivekananda was deeply spiritual and intensely human. His message is the message of humanism. But his humanism has a deeper content. He said that education which gives us intellectual energy must also give us humanistic impulse and its energy of character. If man's education combines thsese two energy sources he will become tremendously powerful, well educated, full of hope, endowed with a firm mind and will and strength of muscle and nerve. Vivekananda said "We want our education to turn out millions of such young people enjoying that unit of human bliss."

Although Swami Vivekananda was an idealist and a spiritualist emphasizing realization of divinity in man, yet he was fully aware of the need for national development to be achieved through education. He stressed education for democracy and said that strengthening of democracy was possible only through education. The strength of a democracy was seen to lie in its alert and patriotic citizens who could be produced and developed through education. All institutional education, socio-political education in a democracy, he held, should therefore be designed to produce citizens who are free, responsible and politically aware, who feel to belong to the country in which they live, who are sensitive to what happens around them. Education should produce such enlightened democratic citizens. Thus, Vivekananda, emphasized education for democracy and citizenship. He, however, was in favour of creating an ethical basis of democratic politic through education. He stressed the need for developing democratic tolerance in the people and a sense of being truly free which could be fulfilled by properly organized and rightly conducted education.

Thus, Vivekananda's educational philosophy had two major components of aims—one the individual aims and second the social aims. Under individual aims of education he emphasized total human development including physical, mental, social, cultural and spiritual development of the child. He did not leave out even the vocational development aim. In a way he stood as the embodiment of man-making education. Under the social aims of education he stressed education for citizenship and democracy, education for national integration, education for the poor and education for women, education for strengthening the whole society. In a way he stood for nation-building education.

But, these two aspects were not considered by him as separate and independent. He brought a fine systhesis between the individual and the social aims of education when he said "they alone live who live for others; the rest are more dead than alive."

Approach to Curriculum

Vivekananda held that all knowledge secular or spiritual is in the human mind. Man only discovers it within himself. It is pre-existing and is manifested in man. Knowledge is eternal. Like fire being present in the wood, it is pre-existing in the human mind. It does not come from outside. It is all inside. Man only brings it out, discovers or unveils. Soul is reservoir of all knowledge. Man takes the cover of the soul and finds that all knowledge is there. "All knowledge that the world has ever received comes from mind, the infinite library of the universe is in your mind. The external world is only the suggestion, the occasion which sets you to study your own mind. The falling of an apple gave the suggestion to Newton and he studied his own mind. He rearranged all the previous links of thought in his mind and discovered a new link among them, which we call the law of gravitation. It was not in the apple nor in anything in the centre of the earth." Thus, Vivekananda considered the curriculum just as the massive suggestion, a series of stimulations only to bring out what is there in the mind of the child. All subjects, studies and activities should be treated as a series of stimuli. These, according to him may constitute his cultural heritage found in the form of history, art, poetry, paintings, Vedas,, Upnishadas, sacred books of all religions, language, stories about India's glorious past.

He was an idealist and a spiritualist and, hence, emphasized teaching-learning of such subjects which could be the powerful source of the development of higher values and child's character. But, on the other hand, being a staunch nationalist and an aspirant for nation's economic progress and prosperity emphasized teaching of science and its all branches. He was in favour of Western technology and engineering being taught in Indian institutions as it was necessary, through them to eradicate poverty from the society. He was of the opinion that the schools should produce self-reliant individuals who can earn their living after finishing their education. Hence, it seems, he suggested that vocational courses should also form a part of curriculum crafts may be taught along with other subjects. The curriculum for girls may include "needlecraft, cookery, child-rearing and other uselful subjects.

Methods of Teaching

With regard to teaching methods Vivekananda was of the view that children should be made to learn themselves. As all knowledge is within them and learning is only a function of their mind, they should only be made active.

The teacher and the curricula should act only as stimuli. This shows that he was against child's cramming of pieces of information. The child should not be a passive recipient of knowledge.

Discussions with the teacher was considered most important a method of teaching-learning by him.

Meditation and concentration were also considered important by him as through them developed the mental powers of the child.

It was also emphasized by him that the teacher should encourage children and develop in them self-confidence for learning.

Thus, alongwith the teaching the teacher was advised to develop in children those qualities which are necessary for learning. The learner must be able to control the internal and external senses. He should control his lower nature and concentrate on learning.

Swami Vivekananda ranks among the greatest educationists of the world. Here, in the following lines, we discuss the basic principles of the philosophy of education:

1. Only study of books is not education.
2. Knowledge lies hidden in the mind of man. He uncovers and develops it by his own efforts.
3. Concentration is the key of all knowledge. For this, practice of Brahamcharya is very essential.
4. Purity of thought, speech and deed is self-discipline.
5. Education should develop the child physically, mentally and spiritually.
6. Education should develop character, mental powers, intelligence and inculcate self confidence together with self-reliance.
7. Education should foster spiritual faith, devotion and self surrender in the individual and should full development through service and sacrifice.
8. Mass education schemes should be formulated and launched.
9. Religious education should be imparted through sweet impressions and fine conduct in preference to books.
10. Boys and girls should receive the same education.
11. Specially women should be imparted religious education.
12. Provision for technical education should be made so that industrial growth leads to the economic prosperity of the nation.

13. Teacher is a friend, philosopher and guide. He should sympathetically bring out the latent knowledge in a child by inspiration and motivation.
14. There should be an intimate relationship between the teacher and the students.
15. All those subjects should be included in the curriculum which promote the material and spiritual advancement of a child.

Meaning of Education

Education is not the mass of informations which are inserted by force into the mind of a child. According to Swami Vivekananda if education meant information only, then, libraries could be the greatest saints of the world and Encyclopaedias had become seers and rishis. In his own words—"Education is the manifestation of perfection already reached in a man."

Aims of Education

According to Swami Vivekananda the following should be the main aims of education:

1. The Aim of Reaching Perfection. The prime aim of education is to achieve fullness of perfection already present in a child. According to Swamiji all material and spiritual knowledge is already present in man covered by a curtain of ignorance. Education should tear off that veil so that the knowledge shines forth as an illuminating torch to enliven all the corners by and by. This is meant by achieving fullness of the latent perfection.

2. Moral and Spiritual Development. According to Swami Vivekananda, a nation's greatness is not only measured by its parliamentary institutions and activities, but also by the greatness of its citizens. But the greatness of citizens is possible only through their moral and spiritual development which education should foster.

3. Physical and Mental Development Aim. The second aim of education is the physical and mental development of the child so that the child of today, after studying Geeta, is able to promote national growth and advancement as a fearless and physically well developed citizen of tomorrow. Stressing the mental development of the child, Swamiji, wished education to enable the child to stand on his own legs economically rather than becoming a parasite on others.

4. Character Development Aim. According to Swamiji character develoment is a very important aim of any education. For this, he emphasized the practice of Brahamcharya which fosters development of mental, moral and spiritual powers leading to purity of thoughts, words and deeds.

5. Religious Development Aim. To Swamiji religius development is an essential aim of education. To him, each individual should be able to search out and develop the religious seed embedded in him and thus, find the absolute truth or reality. Hence, he advocated the training of feelings and emotions so that the whole life is purified and sublimated. Then only, the capacities of obedience, social service and submission to the teachings and preachings of great saints and saviours will develop in the individual. Education should foster this development.

6. The Aim of Development Faith in One's Ownself, Shraddha and a Spirit of Renunciation. All through his life Swamiji exhorted the individuals to keep full confidence upon their powers. They should inculcate a spirit of self surrender, sacrifice and renunciation of material pleasures for the good of others. Education should fosts, all these qualities in the individual. He gave this call to his countrymen. "Arise, awake and stop not till the goal is achieved."

7. The Aim of Searching Unity in Diversity. The ture aim of education is to develop insight into the individuals so that they are able to search out and realize unity in diversity. Swami Vivekanandaji has further asserted that physical and spiritual worlds are one, their distinctness is an illusion (*Maya*). Education should develop this sense which finds unity in diversity.

Methods of Teaching

Swamific prescribed the same ancient spiritual methods of teaching wherein the Guru and his desciples lived in close association as in a family. The essential characteristics of those religious and spiritual methods were as under:—

1. To control fleeting mental faculties by the practice of Yoga.
2. To develop the mind by concentration and deep meditation.
3. To imitate the qualities and character of teacher intelligent and clear understanding.
4. To lead the child on the right path by means of individual guidance by the teacher.
5. To gain knowledge through lectures, discussions, self-experience and creative activities.

Curriculum

According to Swami Vivekanand, the prime aim of education is spiritual growth and development. But this does not mean that he did not advocate material prosperity and physical well-being. He feelingly advocated the inclusion of all those subjects and activities, in the curriculum, which foster material welfare with spiritual advancement. For spiritual prefection Swamiji prescribed Religious, Philosophy, Puranic lore, Upnishads, Company of saints and their preachings and for material advancement and prosperity he recommended Languages, Geography, Science, Political Science, Economics, Psychology, Art, Agriculture, Industrial and Technical subjects together with Games, sports and other Physical exercises.

Place of Child

Like Froebel, Vivekanand emphasized the education to be child centered. According to him the child is the store and repository of all learning material and spiritual. Like a plant a child grows by his own inner power naturally. Hence, advising the child to grow naturally and spontaneously, Vivekanand asserted—"Go into your own and get the Upnishads out of your own self. You are the greatest book that ever was or will be. Until the inner teacher opens, all outside teaching is in vain."

Place of Teacher

Swamiji believed in self-education. According to him each of us is his own teacher. The external teacher only guides and inspires the inner teacher (*soul*) to rise up and start working to develop the child. Hence, discussing the role of teacher Swami Vivekanand said—"Teacher is a philosopher, friend and guide helping the educand to go forward in this own way."

Education of Masses

In the times of Swami Vivekanand, education was not available to the common people. It was confined to the well to do persons only. The poor, the miserable and the lowly placed used to strave and die for hunger. Swamiji yearned to improve the condition of the masses and thus, advocated mass education as the only way to achieve any improvement in individual as well as society. Swamiji exhorted his countrymen to know—"I consider that the great national sin is the neglect of the masses and that is one of the causes of our downfall. No amount of politics would be of any avail until the masses of India are once more well educated, well fed and well cared for."

PHILOSOPHY OF AUROBINDO

Born on 15 August, 1872, in Calcutta and educated in England from the age of 7 years to 21 years Aurobindo was a top notch idealist, a unique philosopher who attempted to synthesize matter and spirit, science of the West and Vadanta of the East. To him the aim of life was to attain "Divinity" through "Integral Yoga" (development of inner self) and "Dharma" (perfection of Outer life). He said that every living being is a form, a part of the Universal Consciousness and one can come into contact with this "true" self through yoga and meditation. His assumption about life was that divinity in potential from is inherent in some amount in every individual. Realization of that is the goal of life to which education should contribute. Following are said to be the contributions of Sri Aurobindo to educational philosopher:

1. Meaning and Aims of Education. Though not much is spoken about education by Sri Aurobindo, significant ideas may be inferred about education from his philosophy. Since he was a spiritualist who saw everything in the universe rooted in the soul. They wanted education also to be rooted in the soul and "founded on the rock of the Divine", aiming at the purity and spiritualization of human life. Thus, the aim of education according to Sri Aurobindo seems to be spiritual development of the individual and the society both. The spiritual aim "regards man not as a mind, a life and a body, but as an soul seeking for divine fulfilment." Education, to him, must lead the individual to realize that "it is the some supreme force that is active in the universe. He held that physical science being necessarily in complete in the range of its inqudiy cannot help much in understanding the occult movements of the Force.

Spiritual development of the individual was emphasized by Sri Aurobindo. Education could be a tool for this development. Knowledge was unavoidable in this context. But, all these could not be the end in themselves. Education, knowledge and its related aspects were considered only the means for the ultimate fulfilment of the individual. He said emphatically that the individual should learn not to multilate or destroy his "ego", but should learn to expand it out of its limitations and lose it in something greater. Thus, to Aurobindo education is not only for the individual and his developments. Individual development was, perhaps, seen by him as a means of the development of the total mankind. He said that the individual should "learn to fulfil himself in the fulfilment of mankind". He wanted that human society, human friendship, love, affection, fellow feeling all must have spiritual basis, a pure foundation instead of being founded on the ego. This requires, according to Sri Aurobindo, a "transmutation of the very substance of human nature." Education must play an effective role in this transmutation.

"The first natural aim of the individual must be his own inner growth and fullness and its expression in his outer life; but this he can only accomplish through his relations with other individuals" and the humanity at large. This view of Sri Aurobindo emphasized the ideal of human unity. It may be inferred from this that education should aim at the development of the total humanity by developing each individual separately. The individual and the whole mankind can never be separated for achieving this objective.

Sri Aurobindo emphasize five aspects of education each relating to a specific aspect or human personality. These are physical education, education of the vital, mental education psychic and spiritual education. They are complimentary to one another and should be taken up simultaneously. This is known as the principle of integral education.

2.Contribution to Human Development. Another contribution of Sri Aurobindo was in the field of human evolution, upward movement of man from matter to spirit. To grow is the inner urge of the Divined in every one. Sri Aurobindo firmly stood for the change in man from the vital and the mental to the spiritual order of life, transference of man's centre of living to a higher consciousness, so as to enable him "to become himself", "to exceed himself", to realize that he is divine potentially. The secret of this evolution is to Sri Aurobindo, is not the intellect and will; rather it is the spirit which is higher then the reason. He calls this development a form of free-self-rule, a development from within rather. Then a repression of his dynamic and vital being from without. Through "Yoga" (Integrated Yoga) of Sri Aurobindo this upward ascent of the individual may be possible. The law for the individual, according to Sri Aurobindo, is to perfect his individuality by free development from within. Education should be made an effective tool for promoting this process of human evolution.

3. Contributing to Principles of Teaching. Sri Aurobindo once said that nothing can be taught. This principle implies that learning and knowledge are a function of child's own will and effort. Nothing can be imposed on him from outside. Hence, instead of teaching, it should be child's own self-learning.

He again, suggested that teaching should mean only to provide the most relevant experiences and most conducive environment to the child which can cater to his physical, mental, social, moral and spiritual development.

Freedom to think for himself, freedom to realize what the reality is, freedom to experiment with the Truth should essentially be allowed to the child. This is the greatest principle of teaching-learning.

4. Views About the Teacher. About the teacher's place in child's education Sri Aurobindo's position was that of a pragmatist. He had to be there very much on the scene but only as a guide, a helper. He is not there to impart knowledge, but only to help the child know how he can perfect his instruments of knowledge. He helps the child in knowing what knowledge is and how he can acquire that.

5. Contribution to Curriculum Development. Though specific suggestions about should be included in the curriculum have nowhere learn made by Sri Aurobindo inferences about this can be drawn from what is being followed at the Ashram School at Pondicherry. The curriculum includes physical and health education, teaching of academic subjects, vocational education, cultural activities, psychic and spiritual studies, education for international understanding. The emphasis, however, is on moral and spiritual development.

To sum up, the whole purpose of his teachings was "that man can achieve an extension of consciousness beyond the mental principle he will continue to be trapped by the dilemmas which beset him." Education, to him, must prepare the individual for this transformation. "Integral Yoga" was suggested by him to be the most practical and effective way of child's education for this purpose. It is only in Yoga that the psychological knowledge essential for attaining extension of consciousness and divine life exists.

PHILOSOPHY OF RABINDRA NATH TAGORE

Rabindra Nath Tagore was born on 7th May, 1861 at Calcutta. He was the fourteenth of the fifteen children of his parents.

He had unhappy schooling. He composed poems till his death on 7th August, 1941.

He own Nobel Prize in Poetry. He was a great thinker also.

His Philosophy

Tagore as an individualist, naturalist, Idealist, humanist—all these rolled into one. We shall presently examine his philosophy.

1. Tagore as Individualist. Tagore was out and out an individualist. He believed in the right and freedom of the individual to shape his life as the individual desired. Everyone knows that no two individuals are alike—so why bind all of them with the same rope? It was thus, in the development of the individual that Tagore wanted the unity of the mankind. With the development of the individual the Creator will be realised by the individual. Some of us are likely to misunderstand Tagore. The development of individual is compatible with the growth of the social units! This is not to be forgotten.

2. Tagore as Naturalist. Tagore's naturalism is based on the Indian belief in fundamental unity of creation and man's kinship with nature. The essential fact is that this world has a vital meaning for us and we have to know it, was connot ignore it, we have to establish a contact with it. This way, we shall be happy. When a man does not realise his kinship with the world, Tagore says, "he lives in a prison house whose walls are alien to him." He loved nature immensely—the moon, the stars, the hills. Nature had deeply moved him—had stirred the poet in him.

3. Tagore as Spiritualist (Spiritualism of Tagore). Tagore's naturalism as described above, paves the way for spiritualism. Music is an aid to the process. He started the Shantiniketan school to give spiritual culture to Indians. His belief was that every Indian should attain spiritual perfection.

4. Harmony with all Things. The basic principle of the philosophy of Tagore is "harmony with all things," harmony with nature, harmony with human surroundings and harmony in international relations. The highest education is that which does not merely give us information but attains our life in harmony with all existence.

5. Tagore's Humanism. According to Dr. R.L. Ahuja, the humanism of Tagore has two aspects: the actuality of individual joy and suffering and the reality of a world—culture of humanity as its background. He worked unwearingly, to relieve the distress due to flood and famine in his own villages of Bengal. Equally untiringly did he endeavour to spread to the four corners of the world the message of the coming together of the races of mankind, of universal humanity.

(i) ***Tagore's Conception of God is also Human.*** To quote him, "He is there where the tiller is tilling the hard ground and where the pathmaker is breaking stone." This is the high point in Tagore's philosophy.

(ii) ***Tagore's Conception of Universe is Purely Human.*** All values have their origin in man. Truth is realised through man. Beauty is felt as such by man. He says, "Reality is human and even Truth is human.

6. Tagore and Cultural Cosmopolitanism or Internationalism. Rabindra Nath Tagore was an internationalist.

He looked at the world as a whole. He was for unity of mankind and its brotherhood. He hated distinctions, made on caste, creed, sex. He was for the unity of soul between East and West. Thus, in conformity with his culture and philosophy, he advocated a synthesis between East and West, so that the East should give its best to the West and in return assimilate the best that Western civilization can give it. He faced the both—East and West. He was grateful to both—East and West. His University is "Vishwa Bharti". It is very much international.

7. Tagore believed in truth; beauty, peace and non-violence. He was also a lover of art, painting and music.

8. He belived in spontaneous expression and creativity of the child. This again supports the first point in the philosophy—individualism.

Educational Philosophy of Tagore

His educational philosophy sprang up from two sources:

(a) Hatred towards school.

(b) Love of nature.

To quote, "Tagore's philosophy of education is therefore, a result of the memory of his school days, when the school resembled an educational factory, lifeless, colourless, dissociated from the context of universe, within base white walls staring like the eye balls of the dead."

His contributors revolve round the two above.

Concept of Education. Education to be real must be of the whole man, of the emotions and the senses as much as of the intellect. Man in the fullness, said Tagore, is not limited by the individual but overflows in his community. And so in his school, alongwith training in individual initiative and self-reliance, equal emphasis was laid on community service.

Nor is education a plant that can be made to grow as an exotic variety in the hot house. If it does not strike roots in the soil and adapt itself to the natural environments, it has little value for the people as a whole.

In short, education according to Tagore meant development of the individual. It meant enrichment of personality and education should be Indian one and not borrowed from the West.

Aims of Education

The aims of education according to Tagore are:

1. Emancipation and Perfection of Man. About this Tagore says, "The highest education is that which does not merely give us information but makes our life in harmony with all existence." He aims at the emancipation of man from all kinds of bondages. He aims at a perfection not only of body or mind but also that of soul. It is the fullest growth and freedom of soul. In order to achieve that aim in his endeavours he makes education as broad based as possible.

2. Moral Development of the child is the second aim of education according to Tagore. Tagore attached for more significance to moral values in education than for mere results of science which produced a system and physical power.

3. Education should develop international outlook is another aim.

4. Education should be Creative. Tagore does not want education to be mere informative but desires that it should be creative also. He says, "The great use of education is not merely to collect facts, but to know man and to make oneself known to man."

5. Unity of Truth. Another object of education, according to Tagore, was that of giving man the unity of truth. He says that physical, intellectual and spiritual life are one and we must give this idea to the children. This way harmony will prevail and when we do not do this, there is a break between the intellectual, physical and spiritual life.

Of course, education is to develop one physically. It should be utilitarian too.

Curriculum

Tagore was a naturalist and also an idealist and he wants things of beauty and nice virtues to be taught in the curriculum. He lays stress on those subjects which make a child full and rich in knowledge. He also wants them to appreciate truth, beauty and goodness. This guides us towards the curriculum. Subjects recommended by him to be taught are: History, geography, nature study, language, science. Activities or finer subjects will include music, art, poetry, dancing, dramatics.

He was very particular about Music and Drama. Music is essence of life and drama releases the children's tensions and anxieties.

Methods of Teaching

Methodology. Rabindra Nath Tagore does not believe in routine methods of teaching. He broke new ground in the methodology of teaching. His belief is not in routine methods of teaching. Even at the outset, to quote Dr. R.S. Maini, when he opened his new school, he declared that the ordinary routine methods of teaching were not to be expected in his institution. To quote Tagore, "Those who still require an artificial method of feeding in their lessons, who need constant watching and goading from their teachers will find themselves out of place in Vishwa Bharti." He rejected mechanical methods of teaching. These methods were uninspiring. Tagore wanted the boys to progress at their own rate without being goaded by others. Tagore points out, "When I was young I gave up learning and ran away from my lessons. That saved me and I owe all that I possess today to that courageous step taken when I was young. I fled the classes which gave the instructions, but which did not inspire. One thing I have gained, a sensitivity to the touch of life and of nature who speak to me."

What then is his method?

It is clear that his method of teaching is method of freedom in teaching as well as learning and, therefore, does not like the lessons being forced upon the children.

Secondly, it is activity method. He wants teaching-learning to be a joyous adventure, full of thrills, wonders, surprises. It could be Heuristic approach. Let the child find out through activity. It is also sense training through and through. It is also naturalness in teaching. School is not to be a factory and learning has got to be enjoyable.

His approach is Gestalt approach. He believes that children learn their lessons with the aid of their whole body and mind, with all the senses fully active and eager. He thus, believes whole methods of teaching rather than in part methods.

He also believers that child's mind is quite sensitive and it will pick up things of its own.

Discipline

Tagore does not want that we should be harsh to children. They should be treated with all symapthy and consideration. Discipline was never, in fact, a serious problem for Tagore.

Tagore says that if the atmosphere is good, discipline problems will not arise. It is only control that breeds in scandals and indiscipline. So where there is freedom—no question of indiscipline. He also believes in self-discipline. He wants children to experiment but not in indisciplined manner.

Tagore recognizes that the boys are full of enthusiasm and when they find opportunities for self-expression, they may be little uncontrollable. He could rather enjoy the children expressing themselves freely in their outbursts of playful spirit which may seem uncontrollable, but not tolerate the repression of the child with no freedom to expand. Therefore, after analysing the psychological cause of indiscipline, he gave the children unrestricted freedom to do whatever they liked. This way, many psychological complexes are eliminated and "naughtiness" seldom occurs.

Further, man should be disciplined through art. Tagore discovered that the secret of maintaining discipline lies in the development of integrated personality. It is basically discipline of freedom.

Role of Teacher

Role of teacher is important. He is the Guru. He is to guide the students. He is to keep them on the track. He is also to keep in contact with them. Teacher is also to remain learner throughout his life. He who fails as a learner, fails as a teacher.

Vishwa Bharti University at Shantiniketan

To give his ideas and ideals a practical shape, Tagore founded what is now known as Vishwa Bharti University at Shantiniketan (Railway Station Bolpar in West Bengal). It is an international university for Tagore believed in internationalism very much. Vishwa Bharti means a place where universal knowledge is given or gathered. In fact, Vishwa Bharti University has grown out of an ashram founded by father (Maharishi Debendra Nath Tagore of the Brahmo Samaj Fame) of Rabindra Nath Tagore in 1863. Since 1921, it is recognised as a university. It is said that India needs more such type of universities.

Why of Shantiniketan? The Vishwa-Bharti University at Shantiniketan was opened with the following aims:

(i) To bring learned people from East and West together.

(ii) To promote internationalism.

(iii) To help Indians create.

Tagore said that our knowledge was second-hand knowledge. There was nothing original in it. At Shantiniketan, all freedom will be given to create.

(iv) Lastly, to provide for the fullest development of man.

The Main Faculties of Vishwa-Bharti University

1. **Vidya Bhawan :** It is school of research. Here research is carried on in all languages and in Indian Philosophy.

2. Teacher's College.
3. Patha Bhawan (Just ordinary school).
4. Industrial Training School.
5. Music and Drawing School (Kala Bhawan).
6. Hindi Bhawan.

Other Features of Vishwa-Bharti

1. It is located in natural surroundings.
2. More stess is laid on teaching and learning of music, art, drama, poetry.
3. Classes are held in the open under the trees.
4. Students themselves make rules and run the university.
5. Individual attention is paid to each and every student.
6. Unlike Gandhiji, Tagore did not lay much stress on manual work. He stressed on something fine and delicate. He did not reject manual work altogether.
7. Atmosphere is homely, prayers are sung and due stress and place is given to extra curricular activities.

In fact, what Tagore said is fully practised here. Students work hard here.

EDUCATIONAL PHILOSOPHY OF GANDHIJI

Gandhiji, the Father of the Indian Nation, the apostle of Truth and Non-violence, was born on the 2nd of October, 1869 at Porbandar in Kathiawar. Gandhiji's mother was a saintly woman. She had a strong influence on his life. After studying Law in England, he started practice in Bombay, but he could not earn sufficient to live on. He went to South Africa. His experiences in England, India and South Africa made him bitter against the British Rule. What he did for the liberation of the country is known to all of us. At present we are concerned with his Educational Philosophy.

Background of His Educational Philosophy

There are three important elements in the background of his educational philosophy:

1. His philosophy of life.
2. His dissatisfaction with the British System of Education.
3. His educational experiments at Tolstoy Farm, Sabarmati and Sewagram Ashrams.

1. His Philosophy of Life. He had Faith in God. All things move due to God. To him God is every thing—"Life Truth, Light and Love". Other important principles of his life were Faith in Truth, Ahimsa—Creed of Non-violence and Dignity of Labour.

2. His Dissatisfaction with the British System of Education. British System of Education did not suit to the Indian Socio-Economic conditions. Teeming millions of Indian were wrought in ignorance, superstition, intertia and illiteracy. This education is not related to life. It makes the Indians foreigners in their own homes.

3. His Educational Experiments at Tolstoy Farm, Sabarmati and Sewagram Ashrams. In these Ashrams, the inmates, living and working together, adopted certain codes. All the inmates were to work with their hands. There was no servant. Every job was performed by the inmates. Gandhiji found that manual work has great virtues in its trail. One can learn and can also be self-sufficient. These experiments encouraged him to put forward important principle of the education philosophy *i.e.,* earn while you learn.

His Educational Philosophy

There is a general tendency among educationists and laymen to identify Gandhi's educational philosophy with Basic Education or Wardha Scheme of Education. Basic Education is, no doubt, an integral part of Gandhi's educational philosophy but it is a scheme or programme of education not synonymous with Gandhi's philosophy of education, which aims at bringing about a revolution in the hearts and minds of men all over the world. Basic Scheme is primarily meant for children between 7 and 14 years of age.

Concept of Education

According to Gandhiji, "By education, I mean an all-round drawing out of the best in child and man—body, mind and spirit." The aim of education is not literacy. Gandhiji laid emphasis on the development of the whole personality. Education which draws out the best or Truth consists in the development of the mind and body with a corresponding awakening of the soul. "True Education", says Gandhiji, "is that which draws out and stimulates the spiritual, intellectual and physical faculties of the children."

Aims of Education

Aims of education are implied in the very meanings of education. He has given two sets of aims—*viz.,* immediate and ultimate aims of education.

1. Immediate Aims. Immediate aims, include 'bread and butter aim', the cultural aim, the harmonious development of all powers, the moral or character development aim and sociological aim.

2. Ultimate Aim. Ultimate aim of education is identical with the goal of life, which is 'Self-realisation'. Self-realisation is the realisation of the self-proper. True education should result not in the material gains but in spiritual uplift.

Gandhiji laid great stress on religious education which teaches fundamental virtues of truth, love, justice and non-violence. According to Gandhiji, "Like without religion is life without principles." Gandhiji is also of the opinion that God could be achieved not by returning into jungles but by living in a society and serving it. He preferred to call a student "Brahmachari", a searcher after God.

Self-realisation can take place through self-control, character and abstinence.

1. Cultural Aim. Cultural aim refers to the refinement of the personality. Mere knowledge is not enough. Education should lead to that quality of mind which may be reflected in daily conduct. Speech, behaviour and manner must be refined. Culture brings in humility and frankness. Education should not take Indian children away from its own culture. There is a need of synthesising cultures so that one could inherit world cultures. This aim enables the students to assimiliate and appreciate other cultures.

2. Bread and Butter Aims. This is also called utilitarian aim. It is due to this aim that he gave the principle of 'self-supporting education'. The educand should not only be made capable of earning his own livelihood in later life after school but also during the schooling. The child must be an earning unit who must be self-sufficient right from the beginning of the education of the child. This aim is really an important aim of even modern education.

3. The Moral or Character Building Aim. It is the chief aim of education. The central purpose of education is to build character. If choice is to be made between character and other things in life, then every thing else can be sub-ordinated to the former.

Man must be a man of word. He must be ready to do something for the humanity at the first call to this conscience.

4. Sociological Aim or Training for Citizenship. Gandhiji reconciled the individual and social aims of education. In democracy the first slogan is 'Educate your Masters'. Thus, Gandhiji advocated 'Universal education'. Every member of this Samaj should be educated so that he could uplift it. He must have qualities of a good citizen. Essential qualities are—spirit of courage, self-sacrifice and industry.

5. Harmonious Development Aim. Harmonious development or perfection of nature is another aim that

Gandhiji advocates. Harmoniously developed person is that who adjusts to his life and environment. He laid greater emphasis on the development of 3 H's *i.e.,* Head, Heart and Hand than on 3 R's *i.e.,* reading, writing and arithmetic. Present system of education leads to unbalanced development.

Curriculum. Gandhian curriculum includes following subjects:

1. Basic craft which may be agriculture or spinning and weaving or cardboardboard work and mental work.
2. Mother tongue both as a language and as medium of instructions.
3. Domestic science for girls at higher stages. At lower stages same for boys and girls.
4. Arithmetic/Mathematics: More emphasis is to be laid on numerical and geometrical problems connected with craft and community life.
5. Drawing, Painting and Music.
6. Social Studies.
7. General Science.

Methods. Gandhiji framed teaching through physical and mental activities. Activity is the starting point of his teaching. Gandhiji advocated teaching through a method.

Craft. Correlated knowledge should be given through a craft.

Discipline. The spirit of non-violence should prevail in the school. Love and truth should be the basis between the teacher and the taught. Self-discipline is the only discipline worth the name.

Basic Education. Gandhiji's philosophy is reflected in Basic education. The four features are:

1. Education should be free and compulsory for all children between the age group 7-14 years.

2. Mother tongue should be the medium of instruction.
3. Education should be craft-centered.
4. Education should be self-sufficient.

CHARACTERISTICS OF THE EDUCATIONAL PHILOSOPHY

Education, to Gandhiji, was a means to achieve perfection of individuality on the one hand and an instrument of service to the nation on the other. Thus, individual and social both the aims of education were considered by him equally important. "By education I mean an all-round drawing out of the best in child and man—body, mind and spirit", he said. This in other words meant development of the whole child, the whole personality of the child. Harmonious development of all the aspects of human personality such as physical, intellectual and spiritual was emphasized by him as an individual aim of education. Emphasizing the social aim of education he said that the individual has a responsibility to work for the welfare of the whole society. "Willing submission to social control and restrain for the sake of the well-being of the whole society" were considered by him important attitudes to be developed in the people through education. Good of the individual and good of the society were inter-dependent. So education should be both for the child as well as for the state.

Education, to Gandhi, was something more than literacy. Though he did not belittle the improtance of vocational aim of education, self-realization and knowledge of the Ultimate, God were considered the ultimate aims of education. Emphasis on vocational aspect led him to say that education has to be self-supporting, a theory which culminated into his system of basic education.

Cultural refinement of human personality through education was also considered important by Gandhiji. But, it was Indian culture that was emphasized by him. Culture, according to him was in quality of the soul which was reflected in all aspects of human behaviour. For achieving this kind of cultural refinement he emphasized the study of the Geeta and the sacred books of all other religions.

Gandhi attached much importance to character education and moral development of the child through education. This would mean to him development of such qualities in the individual as purity of personal life, self-restraint, service of humanity, courage, strength of conviction, righteousness and sense of responsibility. The attitude of "Ahimsa", non-violence was the supreme value to be developed in the people through education.

The ulitimate aim of education according to Gandhiji is the Self-Realization. All other aims are important as they lead to self-realization. Self-realization, to him, means realizing that the ultimate reality, the Truth is the universal soul, some unknown supreme power and that the man is only a spark of that which fuses with that supreme ultimately.

Curriculum

Gandhiji considered elementary education the most important phase of the educational system. He, therefore, expressed his views only about the curriculum of primary stage curriculum. About this stage he said that intellectual development alone should not be emphasized. The curriculum should be so designed that it caters to the development of all the aspects of child personality. Physical, social, moral and spiritual development, too, are important. Hence, there should be provision in the curriculum for activities, experiences and subjects of knowledge that can help achieve these developments also. He, then, suggested to make the curriculum activity centred by introducing teaching of some craft like spinning, weaving, handicraft, book craft, art, agriculture, pottery etc., whichever is close to the child's life in his environment. Besides, he recommended that mother tongue should be the medium of instruction at this stage. It was also suggested by him that mathematics, social studies, drawing and music should necessarily included in the curriculum. General science including biology, chemistry, physical science, hygiene, nature study, physical education and general knowledge of astronomy were also recommended to form the basis of the curriculum. He also suggested that upto class V boys and girls should be subjected to the same curriculum. But, after that girls should be taught home science instead of general science.

Method of Teaching

Gandhiji once wrote in Young India (1921) that "schools and colleges should become almost, if not wholly, self-supporting". He, then emphasized that teaching should be done through arts and crafts, work and play, voluntary activity and self-choosen activity.

Gandhiji said that the method of teaching should be such as it provides to the child freedom, a chance to come into closer contact with the teacher, a chance to be an active investigator, observer and experimenter.

Craft-centred teaching and correlation method may be said to be the most important ingredients of the educational method Gandhiji suggested. Correlation method would mean relating the knowledge, of each subject being taught to the craft on the one hand and to the child's life on the other. Gandhi, emphatically, demanded that craft should be made the center of all education, centre of the school life. The idea, afterwards, found an expression to the Basic Education System which was introduced in all the states of the country.

❋❋❋

8

Contribution of Western Educational Thinkers

FROEBEL'S EDUCATIONAL PHILOSOPHY

Froebel (1783—1852) was a great educator of Germany. He also had a neglected childhood and boyhood and so he had to roam about from place-to-place, learning, studying and trying various professions. He also started his own schools in Switzerland and Germany but these could be flourish for want of proper finances and because of official restrictions. He, however, brought out his world famous books on education during this period which include "The Education of Man", "Pedagogies of Kindergarten", "Mother Plays and Nursery Songs" and "Education by Development". These books mainly deal with the education of children, below the age of seven years.

1. His Philosophy. Froebel's philosophy is of absolute idealism. He mainly pressed two great things, namely, his 'idea of unity in diversity' and his 'theory of development'.

With regard to the former, he viewed this whole universe as a unity from God—the Absolute. In his book, "The Education of Man", he remarked, "The whole world—the All, the Universe—is a single great organism in which an eternal uniformity manifests itself. This principle of uniformity expresses itself as much in external nature as in spirit. Life is the union of the spiritual with the material. Without mind of spirit, matter is lifeless, it remains formless, it is mere chaos. Only through the entrance of the spiritual into the material, does the cosmos originate....Every creature, object is matter, informed by spirit....God is the presupposition, the condition of their existence. Without God, they would not exist. God is the only ground of all things. God is the all-comprehending, the all-sustaining. God is the essential nature, the meaning of the world. He further says, "All things have come from the Divine Unity (God) and have their origin in the Divine Unity. The Divine affluence that lives in each thing is the essence of each thing."

With this belief Froebel formulated the principle that there is unity of man, nature and God. Men must be aware of this Absolute Unity of Universe. The real purpose of education was "to expand or develop the life of an individual until it comprehends this existence through participation in all-pervading spiritual activity."

Regarding his theory of development, he said that there is an absolute goal towards which all things are growing. This absolute goal is realized through the presentation of symbols, representing the various aspects of the Absolute. These symbols are called "gifts" which we shall discuss later.

Development can be produced only by the exercise or use of faculty; physical, mental or spiritual. If mind is to be developed, it should be exercised and so is with the development of the body. Effective development is possible only if the exercise arises from the thing's own activity. "Each individual must develop from within, self-active and free, in accordance with the eternal law, because full development comes only by spontaneous self-activity". Froebel advocates balanced and unified development of body, mind and soul.

2. His Concept and Aims of Education. To Froebel, education is growth from within. It is a development by which an individual realizes that he is one unit of the all-encompassing unity. "It is development by which man's life broadens until it has related itself to nature; until it enters sympathetically into all activities of society, until it, participates in the achievements of the race and aspirations of humanity." Education is to unfold the child's innate powers and awaken his spiritual nature so that he may have a spiritual union with God.

Regarding the functions of education, Froebel remarks, "Education should lead and guide man to clearness, concerning himself and in himself, to peace with nature and to unity with God. It should life him to a knowledge of himself and of mankind, to a knowledge of God and a nature and to the pure and holy life."

As regards the aims of education, Froebel wants all-round development of the individual, so that he may be able to express the spiritual, the Divine, that slumbers in him. Like Rousseau, Froebel education should lead to moral improvement, religious uplift and spiritual insight. Then the child will be able to realise that he is component of all-pervading spirit, which is Absolute Unity.

Finally, education should enable the child to enter sympathetically into all activities of society and participate freely in its achievements and aspirations.

3. Froebel's Kindergarten. Froebel, however, attached great importance to education in the child's early life. He thought that if the education of pre-school years was not properly reformed, no tangible improvement could be made in school education. This led him to establish a school for small children between the ages of three and seven. This school was named "kindergarten" or the *garden of children.* The chief characteristics of the kindergarten are:

(i) Self-Activity. Self-activity is spontaneous in which the child carries out his own impulses and movites. Such activity directs the growth of the child along the lines of racial development. So it merges the individual spirit with the spirit of humanity. Self-

activity, in fact, is self-realization through which the child comes to know of his own nature as well as the life around him. Thus, self-activity not only fills the gap between knowledge and action but also gives joy, freedom, contentment and peace of mind. Self-activity is promoted through song, movements and construction.

(ii) ***Social Participation.*** Froebel believes that man is essentially a social animal by nature. It is the primary instinct of man to live in the company of other persons. So unlike Rousseau, he emphasised the social aspect of education and advocated that home, school, church, vocation and the state, should all provide opportunities to children for social participation. By participating in co-operative activities, the child not only receives physical traning but also intellectual, social and moral education.

(iii) ***Creativeness.*** Child is creative by nature. If he is given some material, he will at once try to create new forms and combinations with that material. "Since God created man in his own image, man should also create and bring forth like God," Froebel also believes that every man's mind, soul and hand are inseparable, although they are independent parts of him. Mind and soul express themselves through physical activity and expression. It is, therefore, that thinking must express itself in doing, otherwise education will reman unproductive.

4. Methods of Teaching in the Kindergarten. Froebel's Kindergarten is a miniature state for children in which they move freely and joyfully, of course, with due consideration for each other. There are no books prescribed. The entire school programme gives training in self-expression through song, movement and construction. Out of these three, the child automatically learns the proper use of language. But these three modes of expression are not generally separated from one another, but they often go together, so that the entire process may become one organic whole. For instance, when a story is told or read, it is expressed in a song, dramatised in movements and gestures and finally illustrated by construction work from blocks, paper, clay, drawing or other material. Through such a procedure, "thoughts are stimulated, imagination vivifies, hands and eyes trained, muscles coordinated and moral nature strengthened."

5. Teaching through Gifts and Occupations. Gifts and occupations of Froebel are the most conspicuous contribution to the methodology of nursery education. Gifts are simple educational toys which are presented to the child in a definite order, without charging their forms. The child is given the freedom to handle them in any way, he likes.—While gifts signify the material, occupations represent activities which are suggested by that material and which can be continued with its help. Gifts are in the shape of wooden balls of different colours, wooden spheres, cubes and cylinders of different types and sizes. Additional gifts are in the form of wooden squares, triangles, tables, sticks and rings. Occupations include activities like construction with paper, clay, wood and materials.

It may, however, be noted that gifts and occupations have a definite purpose behind them. They train the senses of sight and touch. They give the idea of size, form and surface. They also develop the number sense and artistic consciousness. In this way they facilitate further instruction in Algebra, Geometry, Trigonometry and Drawing. And as Rusk says, "By his methodological arrangement of the gifts and occupations, Froebel nevertheless founded a new type of educational institution and although his system too readily lent itself to formalism by later generations of teachers who had not the spirit of the natter, it ameliorated the lot of countless children."

6. Teaching Through Songs. In the Kindergarten, education is generally imparted through songs. It is, therefore, that songs are included in the daily school programme. All the songs, selected and included by Froebel, are about the common objects of life. They relate to nursery games and satisfy some physical, intellectual or moral needs of children. These are arranged no accordance with the development of the child. Each such song has three parts *(i)* a motto for the mother's guidance *(ii)* a verse for singing to the child and *(iii)* a picture illustrating the verse. There are in all fifty play songs of this type. Besides these play-songs, Froebel also devised such nursery rhymes, as "Jack and Jill", "Humpty Dumpty" and "Cyndrella". The main aim is to enable the child to use his senses, limbs and muscles and to make him familiar with the objects, around him.

7. Teaching Through Play. About play, Froebel remarks, "Play is the characteristic activity of childhood. It is the highest phase of child-development—of human development to this period, for it is self-active representation or the inner-representation of the inner form, inner necessity and impulse. Play is the purest, most spiritual activity of man at this stage and at the same time, typical of human life as a whole—of the inner, natural life in man and all things. It gives, therefore, joy, freedom, contentment, inner and outer rest and peace with the world. It holds the source of all that is good."

It is through play that the child discloses his real self and clearly indicates his interests. So Froebel gives a prominent place to play activities in his Kindergarten system. He has rather based the educational process in early years on play. He utilizes play for cultivating in child the habits of action, feeling and thinking. Courage, instinct and motivation are also developed through play. But Froebel's play activities are all very well-directed and guided by the teacher.

8. Other Subjects of the Curriculum. Besides spontaneous self-activity and play activities, Froebel has also recommended manual work, nature study, natural sciences, languages, art and religious instruction. About the inclusion of manual work, Froebel says, "Scholastic education of our times leads children to indolence and laziness and a vast amount of man-power remains undeveloped and is lost. Manual work is necessary condition of the realisation of pupil's personality; through it, he comes to himself." Nature study creates a sense of wonder and admiration in the minds of children for the work of God and, therefore, he believed that it would result in religious uplift and spiritual insight. Natural sciences including Mathematics, which gives an insight into the laws that govern human life. Languages establish the inner living connection among the diversities of things. Art activities like singing, drawing, painting, clay-modelling, wood-work and leather-work provide the soul with opportunities for expression in those outward forms.

9. Role of the Teacher. Teacher in the Kindergarten acts as a gardener, whose function is to see that young plants (small children) under her care, grow according to their own natural course of development. Froebel compares young growing children with plants and, therefore, he asks the teachers to let the children grow and develop in accordance with their natural endowments. He says, "The tree germ bears within itself the nature of the whole tree. So the development and formation of the whole future life of each is contained in the beginning of its existence."

So the teacher is instructed not to distort the natural endowments, powers and tendencies of children by undue and wilful interference in their activities. The teacher is simply to redirect the child's growth to natural direction when she feels that the child is going astray. According to Froebel, education is controlled development so it is the duty of the teacher to control this process.

10. Discipline. Discipline, according to Froebel, is not a set of rules and regulations, imposed upon children. It is a way of living and doing which gives children a strong will. In the Kindergarten, discipline is of protective and co-operative type. Spontaneous and play activities, games and strories, art and crafts, gifts and occupations, all provide sound physical and mental training to children and teach them discipline.

11. Contribution of Froebel to Educational Theory and Practice. Froebel's Kindergarten system attracted the attention of the educational world to the proper education and training of pre-school-going-age children. Although this stage is the most important stage of child development, yet its education was so far neglected altogether. The Kindergarten system soon became very popular throughout Europe and now it has firmly established itself in the shape of reformed nursery schools throughout the civilized world. Froebel has really shown the right road to further advance. His main contribution to educational theory and practice is as follows:

(i) ***Emphasis on Nursery Education.*** As we have stated above, it was Froebel who greatly emphasised the importance of pre-school education. He often said, "All school education was yet without a proper initial foundation and until the education of the nursery was reformed, nothing solid and worthy could be attained." He was a great lover of young growing children. So he made a minute study of their nature, aptitudes, interests and endowments and then gave to the world a theory and practice of education for the pre-school period, which had very largely been neglected so far.

(ii) ***Respect for the Child's Individuality.*** All the modern educators have a great respect for the child's individuality. They consider the school as a "temple where they are to pay homage to the individuality of the child". But it was Froebel who first realised the value of "discovering and developing individuality by means of initiative, execution and co-operation in the educational process." It is in the wake of Froebel that modern educators recognise the child's individuality and work it out by means of the child's own initiative and effort.

(iii) ***Self-Activity in Education.*** Although the concept of education as a process of learning through self-

activity is not original, yet Froebel by making spontaneous inner activity of the child as the very basis of all learning, attached a new value to the native capacities of children in scheme of studies. He said that children were not only receptive of knowledge, they were also very active in the expression. So at the pre-school stage they should be allowed to see, handle, arrange, rearrange, make and unmake things themselves.

(*iv*) ***Learning through Arts and Crafts.*** Modern progressive schools fully recognise that creativeness is a great insentive to work and to learn. So the child is made to create and construct things with his own labour and effort. In Basic education also a great stress is paid on learning through arts and crafts. It was Froebel, who was an early advocate of the inclusion of manual work in the school curriculum. In "The Education of Man," he says, "Manual work is a necessary condition of the realisation of the child's personality. Through it he come to himself." So he included various arts and crafts like drawing, painting, wood-work, leather-work, clay-modelling, paper-cutting, cardboard work and embroidery etc., in pre-school education.

(*v*) ***Emphasis on Sense-Training.*** For sharpening the intelligence of pupils, Froebel emphasised sense-training, against merely verbal instruction. Since senses are the gateways of learning, their training must form the first step in the child's education. Froebel's gifts and occupations are especially devised for training the senses of children.

(*vi*) ***Sociological Aspect of Education.*** By laying stress upon activity and social participation and by transforming school into a miniature society where children develop the power of doing things in a social atmosphere, Froebel brought sociological aspect of education into limelight. It is this aspect which is greatly emphasised in modern education. Froebel wanted education to fit the individual for full life within the group, so that he may adjust himself properly to his physical and social environment. For this purpose, he recommends that primary virtues like co-operation, sympathy, fellow-feeling and responsibility be developed in children in the school community. So Froebel is looked upon as the father of sociological trend in education.

(vii) ***Play-Way in Education.*** Modern educators stress that children should be taught through play-way. It was Froebel who based all the early education of the child on play by identifying play and work as one. This doctrine of play forms the centre of mordern education and has had the greatest influence on educational theory and practice. In modern progressive schools, the project and other new methods as well as all types of experimental and creative activities are based on play-way.

(viii) ***Inclusion of Nature Study in Curriculum.*** Froebel gave new stimulus to the aims and methods of teaching Nature Study. He regarded the study of nature as a means of realising the presence of the all-pervading Diving Spirit, in the Natural phenomena. It is, therefore, that he recommends the study of nature page to page, as a living expression of Divine life. He main aim of including this subject in the school curriculum was moral and religious uplift of the child, by coming into contact with nature.

Thus, we can conclude by saying that Froebel's Kindergarten system aims at the complete development of the individual child. "It is by far the most original, attractive and philosophical form of infant development, the world has yet seen." This is the only reason why this system has now spread in all the progressive countries of the world.

Some critics of Froebel say that tiny rots of three or four years cannot undertand his philosophic principle of "Organic Unity". Then symbolism involved in gifts is also too difficult to be understood by immature brains. Furthermore, there is no correlation in the subjects and activities in the Kindergarten system. Everything is taught in isolation. Another defect pointed out by them is that Froebel stresses the sociological aspect to the neglect of the child's individuality.

PHILOSOPHY OF ROUSSEAU

In modern times, we make use of a number of progessive methods of teaching and a variety of audio-visual aids, to make classroom teaching effective and attractive. But upto the seventeenth century, there was no systematic organization or arrangement for imparting education to children. Schools in those days were very few and those that existed, were the terror of pupils and the slaughter-houses of mind. They followed no methods and used no aids. Every teacher had his own methods to follow. Severe punishments were given to pupils and all types of rods, canes and sticks were used for this purpose. The early educators, if any, "had confined their education to the training of the governing classes of the community and until the time of Comenius, it was only idealistic. There were many who could hazard the suggestion that all in their childhood be instructed in learning, in their own native tongue." During the seventeenth, eighteenth and the nineteenth centuries a number of educationists were born who, in fact, revolutionised education, Rousseau, Froebel, Montessori and Dewey are the most prominent among these.

Rousseau (1712-1778), was the great educator of the 18th century and one who belonged to the new school of education. Rousseau's life was greatly influenced by the prevailing atmosphere of society in France, his native country. In the beginning of the 18th century, the privileged classes in France, flourished at the cost of the poor and the helpless. Hypocrisy, artificiality, cruelty and despotism of the privileged classes, led to discontentment among the common people.

However, in the later half of the 18th century a new era of 'Equality, Liberty and Fraternity,' began in France which revolutionised the entire French society. Rousseau and Voltaire were the pioneers of this new era. It was a result of these new ideas that in the sphere of education also many new changes found their way. Children began to be treated well, properly understood and humanly educated.

1. Rousseau's Philosophy and Concept of Education. Rousseau's Philosophy goes by the name of "Naturalism". The keynote of his philosophy was to have a "Natural State, a Natural Man and a Natural Civilisation". He felt that all ills and miseries in the Modern world were due to a departure from the previous "State of Nature". He declared, "Everything is good as it comes from the hands of the Author of Nature (the Creator), but everything degenerates in the hands of man." He believed that child was essentially good but was made bad when he came in contact with society and its environment. He contended that "man in society is born, lives and dies in a state of slavery. He is fettered by our institution, which drags him away from his good nature." So Rousseau pleaded, "Leave the child alone. Let him be a natural man rather than a civilized man. Let him have a state of nature rather than artificial surroundings that stunt his proper growth and arrest his natural development." Thus, Rousseau preached for a life according to nature—which was simple and real and free from all customs, traditions and conventions. He, in fact, wanted to educate the child for manhood and not for citizenship.

It should, however, be clearly understood that by Natural State and Natural Man, Rousseau did not mean the primitive social order and the savage man. He believed that human institutions were one mass of folly and contradictions. To regain the old vitality and happiness, human society should give up the present artificial modes of life and revert to the natural state. He favoured natural civilization, free from all artificial and rigid barriers that pollute the goodness of our nature. The Natural man of Rousseau's conception was a fully developed Man enjoying social life, without being carried away by the passions and prejudices of society. Reason was the only guiding force in producing natural Civilization and Natural man by Natural State also he meant 'a simple farming community or state, without the evils of large cities, corrupt rulers, social classes and luxury. His Natural Man is a true man, who is 'governed and directed by the laws of his own nature rather than those of social institutions. Natural powers, emotions and reactions are most trustworthy as basis for action, rather than reflections or experiences that come from association with society.' The catch-words of Rousseau's 'Naturalism' were freedom, growth, interest and activity. And all these words are the life and soul of modern progressive education.

2. Three-fold Meaning of Nature. Rousseau made use of the word 'Nature' in a very wide sense. He gave three-fold meaning to it, namely:

- ***(a) Isolation from Society.*** Rousseau advocated that children should be saved from the evil influence of society. They should be isolated from society and brought up in contact with the beauties and wonders of nature. This, however, does not mean no-education. It simply signifies a non-social education *i.e.,* an education which is not based on meaningless traditions and formalities of society. For Rousseau, society was not natural, but an artificial product, the outcome of a contract and evil. Nature and society, thus, become opposed to each other. Nature is accordingly, defined 'negatively to society'. It is a preventive education saving the child from the evil influences of society.
- ***(b) Contact with Natural Phenomena.*** Education according to child's nature, must be provided in natural environment. Rousseau himself was a great lover of nature, mountains, streams, sun-rise, sun-

set, solitude and country life. He, therefore, recommends contact with hills, streams, plants, trees, animals, birds and physical forces of all kinds. One who is brought up and taught in natural environments automatically becomes a 'natural man' He follows nature and obeys, the voice of his own conscience.

(c) ***Instinctive Make-up of the Child.*** Instinctive make-up means the native instincts, tendencies and capacities of the child. Rousseau believed that learning takes place when the child is free to develop and grow according to his natural impulses. So education must start from the child's instinctive tendencies and should be based on the same because these tendencies are more reliable bases of education than experiences, gained from society. According to Rousseau, "Education is no longer a procedure, artificial, harsh, dull, unsympathetic and repressive of all natural inclinations. It is, on the other hand, an organic growth. It is a development from withim."

3. Three Source of Education. At the outset of his book "Emile" Rousseau states that education comes from nature, from men and from things. In other words, the problem of education is the relationship of man to his physical and social environment. Explaining these sources of education, he says, "The internal development of our organs and faculties is the education of nature; the use we are taught to make of that development, is the education given by men; and the acquisition made by our own experience on the objects that surround us, is our education from things." In other words, by education from nature, he meant development according to the child's natural endowments and capacities. By education from men, he emphasised the importance of social environment, teaching how to make use of that development. By education from things, he understood physical environment, helping to gain experience by ourselves. He says that the harmonious development of these three factors constituted an ideal scheme of education.

Such harmony in education is possible by subordinating the education of men and things to that of nature because we have no control over nature. We must, therefore, direct the other two, to ensure co-operation of these three factors for imparting ideal education.

4. Rousseau's Theory of Negative Education. As we have already stated, Rousseau believed that everything is good as it comes from the Author of Nature. Everything degenerates in the hands of man. By saying so, he meant that child is good; but it is society that makes him bad. So he advocated that first education should be purely negative. The child should not be taught the principles of truth and virtue but guarded against vice and error. In his own words, "I call a positive education one that tends to form the mind prematurely and to instruct the child in the duties that belong to man. I call a negative education on that tends to perfect the organs that are the instruments of knowledge and endeavours to protect the way for reason, by the proper exercise of the senses."

5. Rousseau's Aims of Education. Before Rousseau's time, the aim of education was either spiritual or social or vocational, Efforts were made to mould the child into the artificial forms of conduct, satisfactory to the judgment of adults in society. The child was trained to speak, think, act as a miniature adult without any consideration of his natural instincts and interests. Rousseau revolted against this wrong concept of education. He believed that education was a life-long process, which began from birth and ended only with the end of life. It was development from within and not an imposition from without.

So Rousseau's aim of education was the attainment of fullest natural growth of the individual leading to balanced, harmonious, useful and natural life. The real aim of education is to help the child to live his life. He says, "To live is not merely to breathe. It is to act, to make us of our organs, senses, our faculties and of all those parts of ourselves, which give us the feeling of our existence."

This general aim of education was split up by Rousseau, according to the nature, at different stages of human development.

(i) In infancy *i.e.,* from birth to the age of five years, the aim of education is to develop a well-regulated freedom. For realization of this aim, he recommends purely physical education in an atmosphere of perfect liberty.

(ii) In childhood *i.e.,* between the age of five and twelve, the main aim of education is to provide the child with the strength which he needs for the attainment of well-regualated freedom. So at this stage also no formal education is recommended, but the continuance of the same physical care and natural education, Rousseau's advice for this period is, "Exercise the body, the organs, the senses and powers and keep the soul lying fallow, as long as you can."

(iii) In boyhood or pre-adolescent period *i.e.,* from twelve years to fifteen years, the aim of education is "to acquire such knowledge which may satisfy the wants of the child and must be functionally useful". This is the period for intellectual education—the period of instruction, labour and study.

(iv) In adolescent period *i.e.,* from 15 to 20 years, the aim of education is the training of heart, to make the child loving and tender-hearted so that he may live peacefully in social relationship. In this period religious, moral and social education is recommended. In the previous periods, the child has already developed physically and intellectually. He must now grow emotionally, aesthetically, socially and morally. The sex instinct, which is

suficiently developed by this time, is to be sublimated by re-directing it to the love of some noble idea and by keeping the young person occupied in work and activity.

6. Role of the Teacher. Rousseau assigns a very minor place to the teacher in the educative process. He is not called an instructor but only a guide. His main responsibility is to motivate the child to learn. This he can achieve by exploiting the innate tendencies of the child. He must possess a profound understanding of the child's nature and be able to control his emotional reactions. He is not to impose any rules of control upon the child. He is to allow him perfect feedom and guide him properly.

The following are the chief characteristics of his theory of Negative Education:

(a) ***No Time Saving.*** According to Rousseau, in childhood no time should be saved. It should rather be lost. Let the child run, jump and play all day long. In all these activities he will have a continuous reconstruction of experience which is nothing but education, pure and simple. Time lost on play and recreational activities in childhood, is not lost but profitably gained. Childhood is not the time for intellectual pursuits.

(b) ***No Social Education.*** In Rousseau's time, society was corrupt to the core. So he wanted children to be isolated from such a society and to educate them in the midst of nature till their power of reasoning and judgement is perfected, with which they are in a position to protect themselves from the evils of society.

(c) ***No Habit Formation.*** In his own words, "The only habit which the child should be allowed to form is to contract no habit at all." Young children should not be made slaves of rigid habits. They should be

left free in all their activities. If any habits are to be formed in childhood, let them form natural habits.

(d) ***No Book Learning.*** Rousseau says, "I hate books because they are a curse to children. They teach us to talk only that which we do not know. Instead of making the child stick to his books, I keep him busy in the workshop; his hands will work to the profit of his mind." Rousseau felt that readymade material found in books, was of little advantage. Let children gain knowledge by their own efforts and through different types of experience.

(e) ***No Formal Discipline.*** Rousseau is in favour of free and positive discipline for children. Let the children suffer natural consequences of their own actions without the intervention of humam beings to protect or punish and in this way they will set themselves right. If a child breaks a window pane, let him sit in the cold wind that gushes in, as a result of his folly. If he climbs a tree, let him fall down and learn not to do so again.

(f) ***No Direct Moral Education.*** Rousseau is not in favour of direct teaching of morals. Let the child be left free to act and learn what is right and wrong, by the consequences of his own actions. He says, "Much more harm than good is done by your ceaseless preaching and moralising." He further says, "Inflict on the child no sort of punishment and never make him ask your pardon. As there is no moral quality in his actions, he can do nothing wrong.

(g) ***No Sticking to Traditional Precedure of Education.*** Rousseau was greatly disgusted with the prevailing social, political, economic, religious and educational conditions in his country. So he said, "Follow the reverse of the current practice and you will almost do right." He challenged the traditional procedure

> of education saying, "Give me a child of twelve who knows nothing at all. At fifteen I will restore him to you, knowing as much as those who have been under instruction from infancy, with the difference that your scholar only knows things by hearts, while mine knows how to use his knowledge.

It will, thus, be clear from his theory of Negative Education that many of its principles have been accepted by the modern educators. No doubt, at times, Rousseau went to the extreme. But it was natural and he had to eradicate wrong social practices like a reformer by focusing public attention to those practices. His play-and-activity principles in a child's education, his free and positive discipline, his advice against formal book-learning and his principle of no direct moral instructions of children, have all been incorporated in modern educational theory and practice. However, it is his theory of natural consequences which is not acceptable and dependable at all times.

CONTRIBUTION OF MADAM MONTESSORI

Madam Maria Montessori (1870—1952) was an Italian lady-doctor, who later became a world famous educationist. She entered the field of education through her interest in mentally deficient children. She studied those childen very intensively and reached the conclusion that mental deficiency was due to dullness of senses and that if their senses could be properly trained, those children could acquire some knowledge. Ans she actually succeeded when she tried the experiment. This lead her to employ that very method on educating normal children and she achieved far better results. Thus, her approach to education is scientific and rational as against that of Froebel's metaphysical. She is the originator of the 'Montessori Method'.

1. Concept and Aims of Education. According to Madam Montessori, "Education is the active help given to the normal expansion of the life of the child." She said that every child is different from others, physically as well as mentally. Each has peculiar powers and endowments. So the child's individuality must not be crushed or suppressed through collective teaching. Each child should be paid individual attention and allowed to progress at his own pace. Education should enable each child to adjust himself to his immediate environment. She wanted that each child should develop from within and not from without. Education should guide the process of unfolding the hidden powers of the child in a way that he becomes what he is destined to become.

2. Practical Working of Montessori Method. Froebel called his school "Kindergarten" or "The Children's Garden". Montessori called it "the Children's House". It is the place where children are taught in homely atmosphere, which is very congenial to the development of pupils individuality.

"The children house" is a many-roomed school with a nicely laid-out garden. It has separate rooms for study, lunch, manual work, games, amusement and rest etc. All these rooms are properly equipped and furnished. These are looked after by the children themselves, who not only clean and dust them but also lay the tables and set the chairs. The Montessori school has no fixed time-table because class is only a unit of organization and not a unit of teaching. There are no punishments and rewards. The child's sense of achievement is the only rewards and self-development is the greatest pleasure. Each child is free to choose his own activities, interest and inclinations.

For children below the age of six, three types of exercises are given in a Montessori School:

(a) ***Exercise for Practical Life.*** In Children's House, pupils are given exercises for practical life. They are taught how to wash their hands and clothes, how to sweep the rooms, dust the furniture, set the tables, clean their nails, brush their teeth, polish their shoes and comb their hair. Exercises are also given to train children in movements, necessary for dressing and

under sing themselves. It is, in fact, a training in liberty, for freedom. According to Montessori, does not consist in having others at one's command to perform the ordinary services, but in being able to do these oneself and in being independent of others.

Montessori has also devised certain formal gymnastic exercises, which develop co-ordinated movements in the child. For these exercises she has also devised special apparatus. Muscular education and training is given through walking, holding objects and hand-work, Rhythmic exercises are also provided. These exercises not only make children healthy but also give them training for practical life.

(b) ***Exercises for Sense-Training.*** Montessori attached more importance to sensory training than learning, thinking or reasoning. She, therefore, devised apparatus for providing exercises in sense-training. The Didactic Apparatus sharpens the pupils' senses and accelerates learning. The varied material includes blocks, cylinders, paper, cabinets; coins, tables, pencils and wools of different colours, boxes, balls, cubes, rods and water of different temperatures. This material is meant to give perception of size, form, weight, touch, hearing and colour etc. The sense of touch is developed by presenting water at different temperatures to the child. Sand-papers of graded roughness are also used for this purpose. Perception of size is developed through handling a series of wooden cylinders of varying heights and diameters. Series of blocks and rods of graded diameters are also used for this purpose. Sense of hearing is developed through boxes, containing pebbles and other sound-producing material. Sense of weight is cultivated through blocks and tables of wood of varying weights. Colour sense is trained through samples of wood of different colours, arranged and graded according to the depth of colour, as we have already stated under the 'Principle of self-education'.

(c) *Didactic Exercises for Teaching 3R's.* After sensory training, children are taught reading, writing and arithmetic. In her system writing starts before reading. For this purpose, she depends upon the psychological principle of "Transfer of Training". In her own words, "Preparatory movements could be converted and reduced to a mechanism by means of repeated exercises, not in the work itself, but in that which prepares for it."

(i) **Teaching of Writing.** The procedure of teaching consists these steps:

(a) *Recognition of the forms of Letters.* For this purpose, letters of the alphabet are cut in sand paper and pasted on cardboard. The children are asked to pass their finger over these letters. In this way they gradually learn to manipulate a pencil. The same exercise is then practises with closed eyes.

(b) *Control of Pen.* Then the pupils are asked to place the metal frame on a piece of paper and draw a line round it with a coloured chalk. The same thing is repeated by placing the metal inset. In their way, two figures are produced on the paper. The intervening figure is then filled up with another piece of chalk. While making upward and downward strokes, the pupils are not allowed to move their pencils or pieces of chalk, outside the outline. Thus, they learn the necessary control of pen.

(c) *Learning of Phonetic Sounds.* While the pupils are tracing out letters, the teacher tells them their sounds, which they are asked to reproduce. This prepares them for reading.

(ii) **Teaching of Reading.** About reading, Montessori says, "Reading is the interpretation of an idea from the written signs and not merely breaking at print. Until the child receives a transmissions and of ideas from the written word, he does not read." Her material for reading consists of slips of paper or cards, on which words and phrases are written in bold scripts. The child is given a card, containing the name of a familiar object. He tries to utter the sounds and then repeat them faster and faster. When the child is able to pronounce the word correctly, he is asked to place the card under the object, whose name is written on it. Similarly sentences, describing actions or expressing commands are written on paper or card-board. The child selects a card, reads it mentally and does the action contained in it.

(iii) **Teaching of Arithmetic.** After sufficient writing and reading, Montessori wished that children should be introduced to the four fundamental rules of arithmetic. But there is no originality in the methods of teaching arithmetic as advocated by her. It is the same old procedure of teaching by means of coloured beads, numerical rods, wooden spindles, sand-paper numbers, simple boxes, printed shells and such other attractive material as could be made available. Thus, addition, substraction, multiplication and division were taught. The device, generally used, was the 'Long Stair'. Consisting of a set of ten rods, varying in length, from one to ten decimetres. Each rod was divided into a number of parts, painted red and blue respectively.

3. Principle of Montessori System of Education. The important principles of the Montessori System are:

(a) The Principle of Individuality. As we have stated above, Montessori believed that each child has got his own peculiar interest, aptitude, capacities and endowments. He can, therefore, develop them in his own peculiar way and at his own rate and speed. Thus, individual differences must be recognised both physically and mentally. She says, "The child is a

body which grows and a soul which develops. Such a mysterious thing should neither be marred nor stifled. Educational activities should be so planned that a child's individuality must be unfolded to the full." So she recommends observation of each child, proving him the environment, suited to his individual normal growth and thus, educating him individually.

(b) ***The Principle of Sense-Training.*** Like Rousseau and Froebel, Montessori also stresses that senses play a very important part in a child's education because these are the gateways of knowledge. She believed that mental deficiency was due to the dullness of senses and therefore, proper training of senses was necessary for acquiring knowledge. From a study of children she realised that senses of children were particularly very active between the ages of three and seven and a such, a lot of learning could take place during this period. She, therefore, devised graded apparatus for providing sensations of weight, colours, sound, touch and temperature etc. and this enabled children to discriminate between different stimuli.

(c) ***The Principle of Self-Education.*** Montessori believed that self-education was the best method by which a child can learn in his own way and of his own speed, without any interference from outside. Knowledge gets a new meaning altogether when it is self-sought and self-caught. She, therefore, stressed that we should never goad on the dull child and check the bright one. In case of error, she recommended the use of Didactic Apparatus, which controls every eorror and helps the child to correct himself automatically. This apparatus enables even dull and defective children to receive education. In fact, it is a substitute for the teacher.

(d) The Principle of Liberty. For self-education, children should have an atmosphere of freedom and liberty. This principle of liberty has come out of her concept of education as development. It means that as education is concerned with the unfolding of the child's nature, his innate faculties and latent potentialities. The child must be allowed maximum freedom to unfold himself without any check or hindrance. Thus, freedom is the most suitable medium for the development of human personality. So she says, "The school must permit the free, natural manifestation of the child if he is to be studied in a scientific manner. The method of observation is established upon one fundamental basis—the liberty of the pupils in their own spontaneous manifestations which necessitates independence of action on the part of the child.

4. Place of the Teacher. Montessori recommends "consciously controlled and systematically directed" education for young children. This control and direction is to be provided by the teacher, who should be an expert guide and excellent organizer. The teacher in Montessori system is called a "directress", who should be well-versed in child psychology. Montessori says, "The broader the teacher's scientific culture and practice in experimental psychology, the sooner will come for her the marvel of unfolding life and her interest in it. The teacher must allow full freedom to the child and not to interfere with his activity. She is simply to observe and intervene only when absolutely necessary. She is to act as a stage director in this self-educative process. Virtues and not words are the main qualifications of the teacher. She should be partly a scientist, partly a doctor completely religious."

5. Montessori's Contribution. Dr. Maria Montessori's work has considerably influenced modern educational theory and practice, especially in case of children at nursery school stage. Her gospel of love, respect and sympathy for the child has been accepted all over the world. Her system of child education has become so popular that the word "Montessori" became synonymous with "child". All values her system have been absorbed and put into practice by the modern nursery school. Her main contribution is as follows:

(a) ***Scientific Concept of Education.*** Dr. Montessori started life as a doctor and, as such formulated her method of teaching young children in the light of her experience and experiment.

She gave us observation, experimentation and other scientific methods in education. She never insisted on material and method as the last words in the field of child education. She rather gave a scientific approach to education by breaking away from old traditions.

(b) ***Emphasis on Individual Teaching.*** As against collective and class reading, Montessory stresses individual treatment of each child. Because of individual differences in physical and mental make-up, each pupil should be observed, studied and handed in a different manner. Thus, like the modern educators, she made child as the "unit of teaching" in place of class.

(c) ***Psychological Approach to Education.*** Like Froebel, she has also given emphasis on sense training, which is based on psychological principles. By introducing exercises for practical life, she has enabled children to meet everyday situations themselves. She has advocated auto-education in an atmosphere of freedom and in the spirit of play. She has also emphasised child's development from within through his own efforts. All these principles have made *learning* more important than *teaching,* which is universally accepted today.

(d) ***Love and Respect for Small Children.*** Montessori often said that child-education was the most important problem of humanity. It is, therefore, that it should receive the best attention of the Government and the public. In her own words, "The child's soul which is pure and very sensitive, requires our most delicate care". For her "child was God, her school was the temple and deity of the temple was the essence of childhood." The profound love for children, that she had compelled her to travel from one corner of the world to another to start institutions for them, based on her system. She also stayed in India from 1939 to 1951 and conducted a number of training courses for teachers in her system of child education.

(e) ***Learning Through Exercises.*** The most conspicuous contribution of Montessori is the Didactic Apparatus, which she devised for imparting sense training, muscular co-ordination and instruction in 3 R's. It was really a new experiment to teach writing before reading, but the experiment was successful in actual practice.

6. Special Role of the Teacher. In her system of education there are no *teachers* because they do not teach. They are simply *directors* because they direct and guide the movements of children. They only provide the proper environment and material at the right moment and then observe auto-development of children. Thus, in Montessori system, the child is more active than the teacher. He learns by participating fully in the reading-learning processes. Thus, the teacher has to play a different role altogether. "Instead of facility of speech, she has to acquire the power of silence, instead of teaching, she has to observe and instead of the proud dignity of one who claims to be infallible, she assumes the venture of humanity."

7. Limitations of her Method. In spite of such a unique contribution to the field of child education, the Montessori Method also suffers from certain limitations. *Firstly,* she has neglected play activities of children, which are most valuable in a child's education. *Secondly* she gives too much stress on Didactic Apparatus. In fact, her entire method rests upon this apparatus. Exercises with this apparatus, as recommended by Montessori, are so limited that a child cannot express himself fully. *Thirdly,* she has neglected social factor in the education of children. She looks only to individual development. This is the reason that in Montessori method there is a little of music songs, dramas, dances and group activities, which are all so essential for social training. *Lastly,* her method is very costly. Teachers of the concept of Montessori are not available to majority of our schools, especially in villages. So this method is not suited to Indian conditions.

Montessori Versus Froebel

Both Montessori and Froebel have oganised schemes of educating pre-school age children. Both of them consider education as the process of unfolding. Both lay stress on self-expression and self-activity in an atmosphere of freedom. Both advocate play-way methods of imparting education. Both respect the child's individuality and have profound love for the child. Both are in favour of sense-training for sharpening the intellect of children. Both recommend self-education on the part of the child, with his own efforts, while teacher should be in the background, to play the part of an observer and a guide. Both are idealist thinkers. To Montessori, child was God, while Froebel wished education to lead and guide a man to unity with God.

However, there are also certain points of difference between these two educators. While Froebel's theory is based on metaphysical, assumptions, Montessori's method has a scientific background and therefore, her approach is based on practical considerations. *Secondly* in the kindergarten, the children are taught in groups while in the Montessori, individual work and individualism is emphasised. *Thirdly,* kindergarten, social training is one of the basic principles. It is imparted through movement, plays, action songs, group activities and co-operative occupations. *Fourthly,* Froebel advocates a good use of stories, fairy-tales, fables, songs, dramas and poetry for stimulating the imagination of pupils. Montessori neglects altogether the training of imagination in her system. *Fifthly,* in Montessori system, writing, reading and arithmetic are provided, while there is nothing, of the sort in kindergarten. *Sixthly,* in Montessori, sense training is provided through Didactic Apparatus while in kindergarten, it is given through gifts. *Seventhly,* while in Montessori, daily life activities are given prominence, in kindergarten, manual activities like clay-modelling gardening, wood work, paper-cutting, etc., emphasized, *Eighthly,* teacher in a kindergarten school is like a gardener, looking after tender plants. She is to guide children's activities and may interfere when they go a stray. In a Montessori school, the teacher is simply to observe children, handling didactic apparatus. *Lastly,* kindergarten system can be introduced in any infant school without much difficulty as gifts can be got prepared locally according to needs. It can therefore be medium of mass education. On the other hand, the Montessori Method cannot be applied in that Didactic Apparatus. Moreover, teachers with knowledge of experimental psychology and laboratory procedure are not available.

CONTRIBUTION OF JOHN DEWEY

John Dewey (1819-1952) was a famous American philosopher, psychologist and educator. Being brought up in rural environments, he realized from the very beginning that traditional methods of instruction were not at all effective and that social contacts of everyday life provided effective, dynamic and unlimited learning situations. These very ideas formed the foundation of the educational theory, formulated later by him. His outlook on education reflected the Industrial Revolution and the Development of Democracy. He believed in the dynamic nature of things and values. So he changed with the change in ideas, as a result of experience and experimentation and finally emerged out as a Pragmatist.

Today, he stands in the front rank of the world educators. His works on education are a great source of inspiration and hope and help in developing our experimental and scientific attitude of mind. Perhaps no other educator has written so much on educational problems as John Dewey.

1. Dewey's Philosophy—Pragmatism. Dewey's Philosophy represents a happy blend of naturalism and idealism because it is based on the evolutionary concept soft Darwin and Pragmatism of William James. Like Darwin he believes that world is still in the process of making and that life in this world is an every-changing and self-renewing process. Like William James, he believes that whatever useful is good and whatever good, is useful. Truth is also that which works, which fulfils our purposes and satisfies our desires.

For John Dewey there are no eternal and absolute values. All values change with time and space. Man is the creator of his own values. What is true today may cease to be true tommorrow. Man's life is a series of experiments and purposeful action. "Everything is provisional, nothing ultimate. Knowledge is always a means, never an end iteslf." It is purely instrumental. Hence, the title of Dewey's philosophy is "Instrumentalism".

Then Dewey believes that knowledge and thinking are closely associated with action. They are tentative plans of action. They have to be tested by action and by knowing the result of their being acted upon. He affirms, "The essence of pragmatic instrumentalism is to conceive of both knowledge and practice as means of making good. It does not imply that action is higher and better than knowledge and practice inherently superior to thought. Constant and effective interaction of knowledge and practice is something quite different from an exaltation of activity, for its own sake. Action, when directed by knowledge, is method and means, not an end. The aim and end is the securer, freerer end more widely shared embodiment of values in experience, by means of that active control of objects which knowledge alone makes possible."

Further-more, he is convinced of the organic relationship between the individual and the society, to which he belongs. He is conscious of both the physical and the social environment. Self can neither grow in solitude nor in natural surroundings. For his proper growth an individual must live both in natural (or physical) environment and (human or social) environment. Man is not a solitary self but an individual, who lives with the rest of mankind. "He is a citizen, growing and thinking in a vast complex of inter-actions and relationships."

Lastly, Dewey holds that barriers of creed, religion, language, nationality and colour have divided humanity and separated man from man. These barriers must be broken to establish harmony between individuals and groups and ensure the process of human growth. To him, growth stands for the "being process" and not for the "done product". Not perfection as a final goal, but the ever enduring process of perfecting, maturing and refining, is the aim of living. He further declares, "The bad man is one, who is beginning to deteriorate, to grow less good. And the good man is one, who is moving to become better." This is the function of education to break the barriers of separation and bring men and nations together for establishing a happier and nobler world.

2. Dewey's Educational Theory and Aims. About the importance of education, John Dewey writes, "What nutrition and reproduction are to physiological life, education is to social life. Education is a social necessity. It is a means of social continuity of life. It is a means by which a person is helped to have useful and helpful experience." All this he said in the light of the rapid changes in social and economic life of his own time.

Defining education, Dewey says, "Education is development of all those capacities in the individual which will enable him to control his environment and fulfil his responsibilities." It means that education extends the limits of human possibilities. It is progressive both for the individual and the society. Thus, education, to John Dewey, is a bipolar process. It has two sides, the psychological and the sociological; neither of the two can be subordinated or neglected. The psychological side is the study of the child, with all his inclinations, instincts, endowments and interests. It forms the very basis of education. The sociological side is the social environment in which the child is born, lives and grows for society. On a further analysis of his educational theory, we find the following four fundamentals:

(i) ***Education as Growth.*** Growth is the real function of education. It, therefore, must lead to growth. But growth is not directed towards any pre-determined goal or end. The end of growth is more growth and so the end of education, more education. An individual is a changing and growing personality and education is to facilitate that growth. It is, therefore, the duty of the teacher to provide opportunities for proper growth by arousing the instincts and capacities of children and by providing to them the solution of those problems which make the children think.

(ii) ***Education as Social Efficiency.*** Man is a social animal who continuously draws energy, strength, knowledge, experience and attitudes in a social medium. As a social being, he is a citizen, growing and thinking in a vast complex of interactions and relations." He owns character and mind, habits and manners, language and vocabulary, good taste and aesthetic appreciation, to his interaction with the social consciousness of his community. When as an individual he shares such rich resources of a good society, he should also be ready to give back to that society and thus, help other members to develop. It is the function of education to teach him this give-

and-take process and make him aware of his social obligations. Education must transform the immature child into a social human being. It is in this sense that education becomes a social process and social efficiency becomes the aim of all education.

(iii) ***Education as Reconstruction of Experiences.*** According to John Dewey, experience is the only source of true knowledge. One experience leads to further experiences and each new experience calls for the revision, modification or rejection of the previous experiences. In this way the old pattern yields palce to a new pattem. Dewey says, "We should so regulate the learning and experiencing activities of the young, that a newer and better society will arise in the end." Therefore, there is a need of continuity of experiences, helping man to grow physically, mentally, socially and morally. Education must create environments for the promotion of continuity of experiences. Dewey, therefore, conceived of education as a process, involving continuous reconstruction and reorganization of experience. He says that education is by experience, for experience and of experience.

(iv) ***No Fixed Aims of Education.*** However, being a pragmatic education, John Dewey has no fixed aims of education. He believes that since physical and social environments are always changing, aims of education must also change. They cannot be fixed for all times to come. Thus, he revolted against the traditional aims of education—namely: the moral aim, the disciplinary aim and the knowledge aim etc., of the nineteenth century. He rejected the very idea of education as preparation for future life and said that education must cater to the present needs of the child rather than the future because the child is not interested in the unknown future. He

therefore, said that educational aims must be restated and re-formulated in the light of the rapid social and economic changes in present day life.

(*v*) ***Education as Life.*** Dewey believes that education is not a preparation for life. It is life itself. "Life is a by-product of activities and education is born out of these activities." School is now taken as a miniature society which faces problems, similar to those faced in life outside. For education, pupils should be made active participants in the social and community life of the school and thus, trained in co-operative and mutually helpful living. They should be encouraged to face actual life problems in the school and gain varied experiences. As our children are required to live in a democratic society when adults, they must experience same life in the school.

3. His Concept of an Ideal School. Dewey considered ideal school as an enlarged ideal home. In this home, the child learns to subordinate his interests to the general interest of the household. Here, he learns the habits of obedience, regularity, hardwork, cooperation, sacrifice, fellow-feeling, patience and discipline. In the ideal school, teachers play the same part as parents at home. Being better equipped than home, the school must provide ideals, high and noble and worthy of being pursued and lived upon. These ideals are quite in conformity with the ideals of society which the school is required to serve.

Then the ideal school of Dewey's concept, is a society in miniature in which real life experiences of the community are provided on smaller scale. It is an activity school, wherein ample opportunities are provided to the child to construct his experiences, under the scientific guidance of teachers. In this ideal school, the child learns by doing and by actual participation in purposeful and intelligent activities. These activities include cooking, sewing, wood-work, weaving as well as other occupations and violations. Thus, the schools provide various types of social, economic and moral experiences of practical utility.

4. Dewey's Ideal School. Dewey was dissatisfied with the existing system of education. In his opinion, the Industrial Revolution, the development means of communication and transport, various discoveries and inventions of science and ideals of democracy, had brought about extra-ordinary changes in social life. As such, an ordinary school had not been able to keep pace with these changes. It could not give the present day child an exact idea of the social, political and economic life of the community around him. It is, therefore, that social education is not connected with his daily life. John Dewey wanted to bridge this gulf between school life and home or social life, outside the school.

5. Scheme of Education. Dewey outlined a definite scheme of education, according to the stages of mental development of the child. These stages were:

(a) Play period from 4 to 8 years of age

(b) Period of spontaneous attention from 8 to 12

(c) Period of reflective attention from 12 onwards.

In the Play Period, the child studies the life and occupations of the home. Then he studies larger social and community activities on which his home-life depends. Finally, he learns about the development and significance of other occupations and inventions. In the last year of this period, he also learns reading, writing and geography.

In the period of spontaneous attention, the child understands the difference between means and ends. He is able to act for the solution of practical problems of life. At this stage he is also taught social studies with a view to make him understand how man achieved his purposes under various conditions in different periods of history.

In the period of reflective attention, the child is grown-up enough to raise new problems and find out their solutions.

At this stage he acquires definite skills and arts so that after leaving the school, he should adjust himself as a useful and efficient member of society.

6. Curriculum. Dewey's curriculum is not a mere scheme of studies. Nor is it a list of subjects. It is an entire range of activities and experiences, because to him subjects are only summaries and recapitulation of human activities. Dewey does not recommend any readymade curriculum. He rather wants the curriculum to grow out of the pupils own impulses, interest and experiences. It consists of activities and projects, leading to reconstruction and re-organization of experience. Thus, he makes occupational activities or crafts, the core of school curriculum. He also includes moral, aesthetic and religious education in the curriculum. But this education is also imparted through parctical experiences and not through "chalk and talk lessons," in the classroom. In his opinion, "Purposeful activity and a curriculum comprising standard factors of social life, would give the children more interest and insight, through the functioning of intelligence and will, in the achievement of self-control and the appreciation of social values."

7. Dewey's Contributions and Influence. John Dewey is, by far the most original thinker in the field of educational philosophy. He stands in the front rank of the educators of the world. It is under his influence that today we find freedom, happiness and friendliness in American schools. Dewey is a philosopher of the present dynamic age, which is dominated by the forces of science, technology, industrialism and democracy. He has made an original approach to the problems, confronting man to-day and has offered sound solutions for them. To educators, he has given a new progressive outlook and called it life itself. He has also given new aim of education, new curricula, new methods of teaching, new role of the teacher and new concept of discipline. In fact, he glorified every aspect of education that he touched. His watch-word,

"Progress more and more progress; growth, unlimited and illimitable," has given a new impetus of education.

Rousseau glorified the individual at the cost of society. This was not a balanced approach. Dewey fused both the psychological and the psychological aspects of education. He said that education is impossible without social medium. Education must proceed by the participation of the individual in social relationship, with other persons. Children should, therefore, be acquainted with social institutions and industrial processes by creating the same environment in the school and by actual living and working.

Another great contribution of John Dewey is democracy in education. Democracy stands for providing equal educational opportunities to all. It thus, stands for free universal education. It emphasises education through cooperative and shared efforts, in a social medium, to secure the best for the individual and the society. It also emphasises the breaking down of social, national, religious and economic barriers between man and man, group and group and nation and nation. So John Dewey says that it is the school which can contribute a lot in this direction by training young children in experimental thinking and democratic co-operation.

Then, his Project Method is the practical outcome of his philosophy. It is based on "learning by doing and experiencing". This method encourages pupils to learn through self-effort and creative activity in real life situations. It is based on the fact that different branches of knowledge are not separate. They are studied separately for the sake of convenience alone. It incorporates integration and correlation of activities and subjects. It upholds the dignity of labour, favours social discipline and stresses problem solving, in place of cramming and memorisation.

❋❋❋

9

Socialisation and Social Change

Socialisation is a social process and it has been variously defined. Some of these definitions are the following:

According to E.A. Ross, "The development of we feeling in association and the growth in their capacity and will to act together."

According to E.S. Bogardus, Socialisation is, "The process whereby persons learn to behave dependably together on behalf of human welfare and in so doing experience social self-control, social responsibility and balanced personality.

According to V.V. Akolkar, "The process of adoption by the individual of the conventional patterns of behaviour is described as his socialisation, because it occurs on account of his integration with others and his expression of the culture which operates through them."

Socialisation then, is process by means of which the individual learns to behave according to the social traditions and conventions. The human child has a remarkable capacity to imitate others and hence, he develops according to the environment into which he is born. Man, being a social animal, tries to win the appreciation of the group in which he lives and hence, he naturally tries to imitate the culture of that group. It is through socialisation that he is transformed from the animal into the human and it is socialisation which gives—him a balanced personality. The social aspects of the personality is no less inportant than the individual aspect.

Socialisation teaches him to retain control over himself in the interest of others. It evolves a we feeling or community feeling in him and there by invests him with a sense of responsibility.

The Process of Socialisation

Individuals influence each other by imitation, suggestion and sympathy, besides which the process of socialisation is furthered by many social institutions. Man is the product of many social processes such as praise and blame, cooperation and conflict, submission and ascendancy and these forces create the individual's personality. Education is the most potent agency of socialisation available to society.

Factors of Socialisation

1. Socialisation in the Family. The family plays a very significant part in the individual's socialisation because the child spends his early formative years in the home. He learns much by observing the people around him, by imitating them, by indulging in activities which win their approval and avoiding those which bring their disapproval and immediate punishment. It is the family environment which can create good habits in him, because the child's moral code is conditioned by the system of reward and punishment which prevails in the family. And, it is also in the family that criminal tendencies are first generated. In the book *New Light on Delinquency and its Treatment,* Healey and Bronner have pointed out that juvenile delinquents are frequently found in those families in which the fulfilment of social relationships has been hindered at one time or the other. Freud and other psychoanalysts have demonstrated that the child remains throughout life whatever he is made out to be in the family. In his *"Psychological Factors in Marital Happiness"*, Termann has theorised that only those individuals can enjoy marital bliss whose own parents had been happy and contended. In the preface to *'Women of the Street'*, a depth study of the prostitutes of London, it has been commented that the problem of prostitution is, in reality, a problem of the relationship between the children and parents.

The family plays a very significant, perhaps the most significant role in the individual's development. Freud and other psychoanalysts believe that the impressions made upon the child's mind at home determine the child's personality as an adult, for in childhood, the child's mind is very flexible and susceptible to any influence. The parents' love for the child makes a deep impression on him. And, although it is true that exclusive love and affection have detrimental effects, the complete absence of affection creates complexes in the child's mind, which later disbalance his personality. His personality is also influenced greatly by the behaviour of his brothers and sisters towards him. Adler, the famous psychologist, has stressed the fact that the order of the birth of children in the family distinctly and separately influences the personality of each child. The eldest child's mental make up differs from that of the last. Besides, all great thinkers and philosophers have admitted the importance of their mother's love as far as their personality development is concerned. In India, people often gauge the personality of a young marriageable girl by observing her mother. And, as far as marriages are concerned, more attention is paid to the prospective bridegroom's parentage than to his own personality, for the family makes a lot of difference.

The family's influence does not end with the individual's entrance into adolescence, for even then the influence continues. Complete absence of control often results in moral degeneration among the young people, while excessive control manifests itself in repressed personalities and narrow minds. Only reasonable restraint and freedom can help the individual to develop a balanced personality. After marriage, the individual's personality is also exposed to the influence of his partner's personality, his or her health, mental attitudes, family background, physical beauty, attainments, etc. The ability to beget children or not is another factor which plays a significant role in the individual's personality development. In fact, considerable literature has been devoted to the subject of family's influence upon the personality by sociologists, psychologists and anthropologists.

2. Socialisation in the School. After the home, the child is exposed to the school which also influences him, for the school is nothing less than a miniature society to him. It socialises him, gives him an opportunity to manifest his qualities, instincts, drives and motives and helps to develop his personality. For the child, the educator's personality and character provide a model which he strives to copy, thereby consciously or unconsciously moulding his personality. This is ture only of those teachers who succeed in arousing in the child's mind an attachment and love for themselves. Every little action, every movement, speech, etc., impresses itself on the child's mind. On the other hand, he is often repelled by some teachers and he wants to contradict them through every act. This repulsion may be conscious or unconscious, but it drives the child away from such a teacher. The child is attracted by the other teacher who wins his sympathy and it is from this teacher that the child wants to win praise and appreciation. He fears the frown of his teacher, he imitates him persistently. Apart from the teacher the child is also influenced by his colleagues and his status and role in his school groups plays a large part in determining the status and role he is to occupy in society in later life. During the process of education, the child's personality develops under the impact of the other personalities with whom he comes into contact. In the school the child is disciplined. He is aware that disobedience brings immediate punishment, but too strict a system of discipline restricts the child's mental growth and may even drive him to criminal activity. On the other hand, complete absence of control may either make him liberal, free and independent or impulsive and impish.

INDIVIDUAL AND SOCIAL AIMS OF EDUCATION

Apparently it seems that individual and social aims of education are two rival camps, two rival claims of the individual and of the society. All educational aims tend to lay stress on either the one or the other. But the difference is merely one of emphasis and a synthesis of the two is possible if the extreme view of these is avoided.

The extreme view of social aims of education originates in the totalitarian philosophy of the state which says that the state is an entity over and above the individual citizen, superior to him in every way and transcending all his desires and aspirations. Hence, it follows, the aim of education should be the GOOD OF THE STATE. In the interest of the good of the state, it is argued that the state has a right to determine and dictate what shall be taught and how it will be taught. Similarly, who will be taught what is determined by the consideration that how best he will serve the state. From the primary stage to the University the children should be taught that the state or the society is absolute.

The extreme view of individual aims emerges from the philosophy of individualism which emphasises the individual rather than the society. Expressed in T. Percy Nunn's words it says that "nothing good enters into the human world except in and through the free activities of individual men and women and that educational practice must be shaped to accord with that truth." This is an attempt on asserting the importance of the individual and safeguarding his indefeasible rights. Hence, it stresses that the aim of education should be to secure for everyone the conditions under which individuality is most completely developed. Except this ideal of developed personality, according to this extreme view, there is no other aim of education. Nunn claimed that laws of nature would support this aim. In a slightly different way it means "self-realisation". Thus, development of "individuality" and the "Self" is the only aim of education according to the extreme view of individual aims of education.

These two extreme views as such have no possibility of any compromise or synthesis. But, in their moderate form a synthesis is possible. If both these aims are interpreted and understood slightly in different ways, they may appear to be the one and the same thing. And this way of understanding them alone is more, positive and realistic more so in a democratic country like India.

Synthesis. If instead of "education for the state" we say, "education for social service" or "education for citizenship" emphasising the good of the community only on the one hand and "spiritual individuality" instead of only "individuality" or "self-emphasising the importance of the development of the responsible man" the compromise between the two becomes possible. If we believe that the greatness of a society or the state is an outcome of its democratic institutions and responsible citizen the two aims appear just one as one cannot take rise without the other. It is the virtues of the individuals that make a society or the state great and glorious. The interests of the state are enhanced by the development of virtue and wisdom in the individual and individuals find their best chance of self-development in the service of the state or the society. It is a fact that only in a social medium man's individuality can be fostered and personality exalted. The individuality of a person or his so called personality can be expressed and understood only in social terms. The very concept of individuality will be meaningless without a reference to what he is expected to be in relation to his society. A charming personality, *for example,* means what the society means by being charming how the society defines and describes it. As Nunn puts it "man's nature is social as truly as it is self-regarding". Thus, as Ross has expressed it "the individuality is of no value and personality is a meaningless term apart from the social environment in which they are developed and made manifest." Self-realisation can be achieved only through social service and social ideals. At the same time social ideals of real value can come into being only through free individuals who have developed valuable individuality.

Professor Bagley of America tried to synthesise these two aims into one by saying that education should aim at developing "social efficiency" in the pupils. It was defined by him as consisting of three components: *(i)* economic efficiency, *(ii)* negative morality and *(iii)* positive morality. This point of view stresses that all the activities of the individual are to be valued with reference to his social obligations. On the other hand social institutions exist only to make the individual life better, fuller, richer, happier, more secure and more fruitful.

Thus, , there should not be any conflict between the social and individual aims of education. They are the two sides of the same coin, self-realisation and social service are complimentary to each other. They can not be separated and pulled apart. If one single heading, theme or title has to be found for both of them, it may be "Welfare Aim of Education", meaning, thereby, seeking welfare of the individual as well as of the society, the state through education.

SOCIAL CHANGE

Social means concerning society and change means deviation from existing pattern. In this sense, social change means change in the structure and functions of human society. In fact human life is not static. It is under a constant change in the ideas, attitudes and values of an individual. This changing process brings changes in the social structure and in other social attributes also. In fact, styles of living are changing so fast today that it is difficult to keep pace with the changing ideas, beliefs, life-styles and material pursuits for more and more human welfare. This change in social structure is known as social change.

To understand the meaning of social change, it is essential to know the meaning of 'change' and 'society'. 'Change' means alteration of an item under consideration either in part or whole. It is a variation from previous state or difference through time. Therefore going by these two definitions we can say that social change is the change in social relations.

According to Davis, "By social change is meant only such alterations as occur in social organisaton *i.e.,* in the structure and functions of a society."

According to Dawson and Gettys, "Cultural change is social change, since all culture is social in its origin, meaning and usage."

According to Ginsberg, "By social change I understand a change in social structure, *e.g.,* size of a society, the composition or balance of its parts or the type of its organization."

According to Jenson, "Social change may be defined as modification in the ways of doing and thinking of people."

According to MacIver and Page, "Social change is the change in society. Society is a network of social relationship. Social relationships include social processes, social patterns and social interactions. Social change can be defined as change in social relations itself."

Some scholars depict the process of social change in the following manner:

Change in the experience of individuals

↓

Change in the attitude of individuals

↓

Change in the social interactions

↓

Change in social relations

↓

Change in social structure

Social change

On the basis of above definitions, we can say that any change in the social structure or its functions is a social change.

Social change is accepted as such only when the majority of individuals in a society accept it in their life, behaviours and beliefs.

In short, social change means replacing the old with the new in the society. It can be a modification of the old also if not total replacement. It can be a new mode of thought, a new attitude towards work, worship and wealth, a new behaviour pattern and so on. It can take various forms.

Different Aspects of Social Change. Social change is related with all types of changes related to society. It includes all aspects of society.

Economic Aspect. Change relating to industry, business, agriculture, productive process etc. comes in this aspect.

Political Aspect. It is related with change in administration and political power.

Moral Aspect. It is related with change in values and thoughts.

Scientific and Technological Aspect. It is related with change due to scientific and technological development.

Religious Aspect. It is related with change in religion and religious institutions as—Church, Temple and Gurudwara.

Factors Affecting Social Change

Social change is the product of the interaction of many factors which are as follows:

1. Geographical Factors. Change in the Geographical environment has great effect on human society. Climate is the only reason of rise and downfall of civilisations and cultures.

Geographical factors comprise all the inorganic (Non-living) phenomena which exert an influence on human life. Theoretically, such a definition would include even the physical state of other planets in our solar system. Practically, however, the geographic factors may be limited to the climate and its influences including temperature, sunshine, rainfall, relative humidity, prevailing winds and other climatic possibilities. Every man lives in particular geographical conditions which do affect the social life, *e.g.,* social life of people living in plains is different from those living in hilly areas.

The inhabitants of West Bengal and other regions near sea depend more on fish for their food as fish are available in these areas in large number and at ease.

When natural calamities such as flood, drought, famine etc. uproot innumerable families, the individuals involved from new social relations which as a result bring about social change. Natural catastrophe encourages geographical mobility and people moving to a different place and culture adapt themselves to it.

2. Psychological Factors. The psychology of human being may itself become the cause for social change. Man by nature loves change, desires to invent new things in every sphere and is always anxious for novel experiences.

As a conequence of this, attitude changes and rituals, customs, traditions etc., also go on changing in the society in a continuous manner. This does not imply that whatever is new is considered superior to the old. On one side man wants to preserve the good elements of what is old and simultaneously attends to what is new. In this process of interaction between the two tendencies change in social relationships takes place which leads to social change.

3. Biological Factors. The important biological factors affecting social changes are: The plants and animals in the area and the human beings themselves. Man uses the available plants and animals according to his culture and traditions. He destroys the enemies like insects, poisonous plants, bacteria and dangerous animals with the best available means. The biological environment is dynamic and we find change in the climate, change in soil composition, drying up of lakes or streams etc., which spell the doom of some organisms and encourage new opportunity for others.

4. Technological Factors. Social change is brought about mainly due to the following technological factors:

(a) Development of new methods and processes of agriculture.

(b) Development of means of transport.

(c) Development of means of communication.

(d) Use of machines in industries.

Technology is nothing but applied science, which helps in bringing social change with the changing needs of the society. The development of technology has led to the establishment of factories, urbanisation and industrialisation. Therefore, new classes emerged. People of different regions started migrating to industrial areas for want of work and stayed there which led to the mixing of different cultures. The increase in the number of educational institutions, facilities of bank, opening of new business centres and expansion of trade and commerce are also its products. As a result of industrialisation joint family system has broken and is fast being replaced by single family system.

Technological development has resulted into many material and non-material changes in our society such as:

(a) Abolition of untouchability and weakening of caste relationships.

(b) The manner of preparing our food, standard of living, decrease in the death rate, development of scientific attitude and emergence of new values such as equality, liberty, justice, secularism, brotherhood, co-operation and fellow feelings etc.

5. Cultural Factors. Culture encompasses values, styles, ideals, beliefs, traditions, emotional attachment etc. These affect the society to a great extent.

Main Factors in Bringing Social Change in India

The main factors of social change in India are as follows:

1. Science and Technology. Scientific and technological discoveries and inventions have caused several far-reaching social changes in the lives of people in developing as well as developed countries. Television, Films, Video and other scientific inventions have completely changed our mode and style of living, modes of thinking and consequently social relations.

2. Sanskritisation. It is the process by which a low Hindu caste, or tribe or other group changes its customs, rituals, ideology and way of life in the direction of high caste. Generally such changes are followed by a claim to a higher position in the caste hierarchy than that traditionally conceded to the claimant caste by the local community.

3. Social Mobility. Social mobility means position in social sphere. This mobility occurs in 'vertical' or 'horizontal' directions. It can be 'individual' or 'group mobility'.

Vertical mobility implies movements up the social or occupational ladder, accompanied by rise in status, position, income and economic condition etc.

Horizontal mobility means change in place without accom-panying rise in social or economic status.

4. Modernisation. Modernisation means the change in the values, attitudes, relationships, associations, social institutions etc., on the pattern of the so called modern culture of U.K., U.S.A., Japan, France etc. A country can evolve its own model of modernity as well by developing its own ideas on style of living and technology.

5. Indianisation. A glimpse of Indianisation is noticed in dress, meditation, religious songs, prayers, celebration of Indian festivals and customs. Integration with Indian culture and civilisation is known as Indianisation.

6. Secularisation. Secularisation implies rationality, differentiation, religious toleration, naturality, broad outlook and unorthodoxy. It implies that various issues in personal and social life are evaluated not from religious point of view but from utilitarian point of view.

7. Westernisation. This is the process of social change in India by which the culture, traditions style of living and values are changing as the western culture considerably affected the Indian culture and society. Under the British rule the Indians have not only adopted the western technology and educational system but also they have accepted the western manners and habits in the matter of food, dress, social relations, mode of living, recreation and system of marriage etc.

8. Urbanisation. A significant feature of this change is the continuous migration from rural areas to the urban areas. This social change leads to the same problems as that of industrialisation. Urbanisation leads to growth of towns, cities and urban centres, industrial towns, business projects, educational, commercial and trade centres and religious cities etc.

9. Politicisation. There was politicisation due to leaders' political outlook, manifestos of political parties and awareness about the rights and duties of citizens, regional, national and international relations. The advancement of democracy, the spread of education and the mass media greatly promoted politicisation throughout the country resulting in vast social changes.

10. Hinduisation. The tendency and efforts of several tribal communities in India to enter the broadfold of the Hindu social structure are implied by this process. *For example* a section of the Bhil tribals has now become Bhil caste in Hindu social structure. By doing so they think that they have gained social status.

11. Industrialisation. The spread of industrialisation gives rise to crimes, strikes, prostitution, drinking, trade unionism and agitations. Other changes which take place due to industrialisation are: Growth of educational institutions, banks and business centres, extension of roads and other civic amenities.

12. Planning and Law. Law also helps in bringing social change in the society. People have the tendency to oppose new changes in the society but they are forced to accept these changes if enacted as law. And then these changes become the part of their life, *for example* Zamindari system, privy purse, slavery, exploitation and untouchability etc., have been abolished by law.

Role/Importance/Functions of Education in Social Changes

Education is an important instrument to bring social revolution. Among all the instruments education is considered as the most powerful. Education for all, at all levels and at all ages of children is the only remedy to bring about the desired social change in Indian society.

The relationship between education and social change takes a dual form—education as an instrument and education as a product. This implies that education as an instrument is used as a means for bringing about desired changes in the society and in the later case changes in the educational structure follows as a consequence of changes which have already taken place in the society.

There are three types of relationship between education and social change which are as follows:

1. Education as a Necessary Condition of Social Change. Historical experience of advanced countries has shown that for any social revolution education is the pre-condition. Illiterates remain satisfied with their existing conditions and feel that they are destined to be what they are. They never bother to exert to bring change in their present social and economic conditions. They are guided by orthodoxy, traditions and fate rather than by rationality in their actions. Education helps people to make them rational in their thinking and approach.

2. Education as an Outcome of Social Change. There is interdependent relationship between education and social change. On the one hand it brings change in social conditions. On the other hand it is influenced by social change, which means social change helps spreading education. Education follows social change. It has its place before and after social change. First come social changes and then teaching process is changed according to those social changes. Education system changes according to the needs of society.

3. Education as an Instrument of Social Change. Education as an instrument of social change means how education helps people to bring social change. Education changes the outlook and the tradition approach towards social and economic problems. It sharpens the skills and knowledge of the children. Technical education helps in the process of industrialisation which results in vast changes in society. Education not only preserves the cultural traditions *i.e.,* customs, traditions and values etc., of the society but also transmits them to the next generation. It also motivates the children to adopt new pattern in order to remain dynamic and forward looking. Education fulfils the needs of the society and propagates such ideas which promote social changes in all fields of life.

Functions of Education as an Instrument of Social Change

Education fulfils the needs of society and propagates such ideas which promote social change in all fields of life. In this way, education becomes a social process by means of which society moulds children according to its needs and approved patterns of behaviour. Functions of education as an instrument of social change are as follows:

1. Stabilizing Eternal Values. Education protects eternal values, saves them from pernicious effects of social changes and promotes their knowledge and acceptance in such a manner that inspite of social changes, people in general keep faith in these values. In our society such eternal values are of moral and spiritual nature. Education should protect, preserve and promote these values.

2. Increasing the Areas of Knowledge. Education promotes in the individuals the capacity to increase the scope of knowledge more and more for their benefit. It opens new areas for investigations and researches, which bring about desirable changes in material as well as non-material aspects of culture. Thus, education prepares ground for the advent of social change.

3. Leadership Role in Social Change. Education provides leadership in social change. Education makes people capable to initiate and guide for needed social changes by fighting succesfully against social evils, customs and blind traditions. Thus, people become capable for realising their own true personality to the full and promote social welfare to greater and greater extent.

4. Evaluation of Social Change. Education lays down the required standards and criteria of values with reference to which this process of evaluation takes place effectively and only after that, desirable social changes are propagated wheres the undesirable ones discarded.

5. Education Accelerates Social Change. Education tries to banish social evils, blind customs and traditions through various social reformation projects, political movements, social service schemes and also tries to bring in 'needed social changes and reforms'. *For example,* in India public movements and agitations against child marriage, forced widowhood, untouchability and social injustice resulted in desirable social changes.

6. Education Prepares People Mentally for Social Change. It prepares the mentality of people to welcome and adopt desirable social changes easily. It may be noted that people will welcome and adopt any technique or pattern only when they become convinced of its utility and desirability. Education, thus, structures a wholesome and conducive environment for these social changes to become acceptable to all.

It tries to remove the mental reservations and complexes in the minds of people which obstruct the progress of change.

Education provides necessary training in skills and occupations and thus, produces the needed competent personnel for manning the different specialised jobs in modern industry, business, educational and research establishments and other secondary associations.

Education is expected to change the values and attitudes of the people and to create in them the urge of the necessary motivation to achieve social class ascendency, social mobility and/or their sanskritisation.

Modern education can mould people into enlightened, emphatic, risk-taking, thick-skinned, industrious and mobile personalities.

Education can be of immense help in bringing about democratisation, secularism, national integration as well as economic prosperity and proper political socialisation.

Education can cut down the thick roots of traditions, superstitions, ignorance and backwardness etc.

Education prepares the society for the initial cultural stock inherent in determined plans of modernisation. Elvin Toffer's thrilling book '*Future Shock*' tells us about it.

Education can prepare the society for the cultural imbalances that inevitably characterise the social transitional situation and should endeavour to prevent, as far as possible, shocking conditions and during the long transitional phase, it can discipline the people to withhold immediate gratification in the interest of future inputs for the furtherance of the long-range plans of modernisation.

❋❋❋

10

Social System and Family

It is a well known fact that family is found everywhere and it is concomitant with group life. Society and State derive from a circle of intermarrying families banded together to satisfy their basic needs. Sociologically and historically, the family may be viewed as a group consisting of two or more parents and their children. Such a view suggests itself because there have been great variations in the number of parties entering into the marriage union. Although the family is universal, no particular form of it is primary or inevitable. Like all other institutions, it is a social product subject to change and modification. In. response to varying conditions, different forms of the family have appeared from time to time. But in the present day world Patriachial family organised under the system of monogamy is most prevalent isntitution. In such a kill-group that it is both an association and institution and very essential to the life of society.

Main Functions of Family

It is an open secret that family plays an important role in the life of society. There is no other human group that dominates the life of the individuals, more than family. It is in the light of this hard fact that, Maciver says, "Of all the organizations, large or small, which society unfolds, none transcends the family in the intensity of its sociological significance. It influences the whole life of society in innumerable ways and its changes, reverberate through the whole social structure. It is capable of endless variation and yet reveals a remarkable continuity und persistence through change." The family occupies a vital place in the working of social order and it is so because it performs certain characteristically significant functions. Davis has characterized the main social functions of the family in four divisions. These are reproduction, maintenance, placement and socialization of the young. It also performs individual functions but these are the corollary of its social functions. However, Davis has said, "From a sociological point of view we are mainly concerned with the social functions and consequently we stress the four functions mentioned here as being the core functions with which the family is always and everywhere concerned. There may be great variation from one society to another in the precise manner and degree of fulfilment of theee functions, but the four mentioned above seem to be the ones which universally require a family organization."

Lundberg has also mentioned a number of basic functions of the family. In them he has included the regulation of sexual behaviour and reproduction, care and training of children, co-operation and division of labour and primary group satisfactions. Besides, there are many auxiliary functions as well. Maciver divides the functions of the family into two categories. They are the essential and non-essential functions of the family. Under the essential he includes three functions *(i)* Stable satisfaction of sex need. *(ii)* Production and rearing of children and *(iii)* Provision of a home. Under the non-essential functions he mentions religious, educational, economic, health and recreation, which he says have now been transferred to specialized agencies in society. In short, the various functions of the family can be mentioned in the following way:

Essential Functions of Family

The essential functions of the family are those functions, which it has to perform exclusively. They can neither be shared with any other group nor they can be delegated to any other association. They are the functions, which in every age and in any form the family must perform and there can be no deviation from them. Some of them are *(i)* Satisfaction of Sex need. *(ii)* Production and rearing of children and *(iii)* Provision of a home. They are in a way the primary functions of the family, for the doing of which some sort of family group has ever to remain in existence. This fact is aptly testified by Reuben Hill in these words, "Family life is probably more than a social habit. The family may be viewed as a device for solving certain fundamental problem, which must be faced by any group of people who live and work together in a society. As a problem-solving device it has simplified the social life of many of its members. Through it sex partners are sorted out and their sex drives are harnessed and linked with the love sentiments to weld together conjugal units into which children can be born, cared for and reared to adulthood. Within it all the basic elemental needs are met and kept from becoming individual problems, which if left unsolved might demand collective action. It simplifies life to live in a family and that is true for adults as well as for children. Certain basic needs of affection, intimate response, recognition, personality, expression, growth and security are met through the family which are not met satisfactorily elsewhere." In view of these facts the important essential functions of the family can be explained in some detail in the following manner:

1. Satisfaction of Sex Need. This is the first essential function, which the family performs. Satisfaction of sex instinct brings the desire for life-long partnership among male and female. The satisfaction of sex instinct makes for normal personality. If sex instinct is suppressed, it may produce personality maladjustments and disrupt social relations. The modern family can satisfy this instinct in greater degree and in a better way than the traditional family. In the old family the sexual act was combined with reproduction and the fear of pregnancy as a result of inter-course prevented the couple to satisfy their sex urge. But in modern family the task of sexual satisfaction has been eased by the invention of contraceptives and other methods of birth-control. It has now become a primary function of the modern family. According to Reed, "The fundamental function of the family is to regulate and gratify sexual needs. Manu accepts sexual satisfaction besides production as the aim of family. Vatsyayan also regards sexual satisfaction as the primary objective of the family. This function is so important that Havelock Eills remarks, "With failure of sexual harmony the marriage structure rests on shifting sands.

2. Production and Rearing of Children. The inevitable result of sexual satisfaction is procreation. The task on race perpetuation has always been an important function of the family. It is an institution par excellence for the production and rearing of children. The function of child-rearing is better performed today than in the past because now more skill and knowledge are devoted to the care of the unborn and new-born children. The infant death rate has shown a market declare. In the achievement of this result specialized agencies like nursing child welfare centres have come to the aid of the family. A close study of the available statistical data reveals that the number of illegitimate children is falling down, the practice of prostitution is vanishing away and the number of marriages is increasing rapidly. It is a pointer to the fact that the function of procreation of race is only performed through family.

3. Provision of Psychological Satisfaction and Security. Another fundamental and universal function of the family is to meet the psychological needs of its members. Ogburn has included affectional functions in the necessary or vital functions of the family. According to Groves it is the functions of the family to provide opportunities for the establishment of intimate relations. Burgess and Lock have written, "Mutual affection is becoming the essential basis of marriage and family:" The individual receives affection, sympathy, love and psychological security in the family. The relations between man and woman in the family are not exclusively physical. Profound conjugal affection for each other is generated in husband and wife by working together in the family and by sharing each other's joys and sorrows. An all around development of individual is not possible in the absence of family love. The family has an important part to play especially in the development of the child's personality. Ralph Linton has written that merely the satisfaction of bodily needs is not sufficient for the proper development of the infant.

4. Provision of Home. The desire for a home is a powerful incentive for men as well as women after marriage. Man after the hard toil of the day returns home where in the midst of his wife and children he sheds off his fatigue. Though. In modern times there are hotels and clubs which also provide recreation to the man but the joy that a man feels within the congenial circle of women, parents and children stands far above the momentary pleasure. Which is provided by club and hotel. In spite of these re-creative agencies the home is still the heaven and sanctuary where its members find comfort and affection.

5. Protection and Care of the Young. It is another essential function of the family and it may be said to be a corrollary of its sexual and procreative functions. According to Groves the protection and care of children is one necessary function of the family. The human child is the most helpless and weak being. A family is needed in order to maintain its existence and to ensure its coordinated and balanced development. Its balanced development is achieved with difficulty and that too with the care of the parents and other family members. It is right that in the modern age this function of the family is losing much of its past significance and it is being handed over to the subsidiary agencies. But all the same it still continues to be one of the essential functions of the family and the Indian families are particularly known for this function.

Non-Essential Functions of the Family

The non-essential functions of the family are those functions which it performed in the traditional society but which it is giving up one by one in the modern times. These functions are being either delegated to the subsidiary agencies or they can be shared with other groups. They are no longer the exclusive function of the family but still in some societies the family is associated with them in some form or the other. The Indian society is one such example where the family despite so many modifications and being placed under limits has been laying its claims on the so-called non-essential functions along with the essential functions. Some of the non-essential functions of the family can be enumerated in the following order:

1. An Economic Unit. A very important non-essential function of the family is that it serves as an economic unit. In the traditional family most of the goods for consumption were made at home. The members of the family were all engaged in the family occupation. The ancient Hindu joint family served as a sort of mutual insurance society. It was a unit of production and the centre of economic activities. However, in the present time the importance of family as an economic unit has been lessened because most of its economic activities have been taken over by some outside agencies. The members of the modern family do not work together as they did in the old family. They are engaged in different activities outside the come. Moreover the family has not even remained the unit of production as most the goods for consumption including even the food are purchased ready-made from the market. But with all these shifts in the family as an economic unit, it has not been reduced to a passive body. This is to say that the old pattern has not been destroyed, it has been merely changed. In the family one or the other profession is still carried on though of a different sort and in a different atmosphere.

2. Centre of Education. One more function performed in the family is the education of children. The family is an important education agency. The child learns the first letters under the guidance of parents though today he learns them in a nursery-schoo1. The traditional family was the centre of vocational education because the children from the early childhood were associated with the family task. The modern family has delegated the task of vocational education to technical institutes and colleges. But despite all this the role of the family as a center of education has not vanished completely and in a somewhat modified form it still continues to perform some of the educational functions. For instance, it is even now in and through family that the people learn their social habits and moral virtues. It is in no way an in significant function for which the Indian families are conspicuously known and popular.

3. Centre of Religious Activities. Another non-essential function, which the family performs is of a religious character. It is a centre for the religious training of the children who learn from their parents various religious virtues. In the old family, different religious practices like idol worship, yagya, religious discourses and sermons by pandits were carried on which made the outlook of the children religious. The modern family, however, does not observe religious practices and has become secular in outlook.

4. Centre of Recreation. The old family provided recreation to its members. They used to sing and dance together and visit the family relations. In modern times family relationship is individual rather than collective. The present forms of recreation such as bridge tennis carrom and movies, provide for only individual or couple participation. Moreover, recreation is now had in club or hotel rather than in home. In this way, there has also occurred a shift in the recreational functions of the family. However, it needs be said that in countries like India having close ties of ancient culture the family is still acting as a centre of recreation at least in the rural areas.

5. Guardian of Culture. The family keeps the culture of society, alive. It moulds its members according to the social culture. The children are educated in the various aspects of culture from their infancy. The family creates such an environment for them that they learn to live and behave in acccordance with their culture. The elderly members of the family impart training in matters of conduct, thinking religion and ethics etc. to the children. The family is aptly described as the maker and guardian of Culture.

It is clear from the foregoing facts that there has come about a great change in the functions of the family whereas about a hundred years back the family was more of a community, it has become today more of an association. The very importance of the family has been loosened. It is no longer a home for recreation of its members, a school of education for children or a centre for their religious training. Many family duties, which were performed formerly by the parents have now been transferred to external agencies. The functions of a modern family are very much limited both in their number and extent. Even the task of procreation has suffered a setback. Of course the task of satisfaction of sex need is better performed, by modern family. In short, the family has lost some of its former: functions. It is to be, however, remembered that though there is a loss of functions the family is not going to perish. There are certain functions for this performance of which no human society can do without family. Thus, it may be said in the end that despite its structural and functional changes, the family still plays a significant role in social strength and social solidarity.

FAMILY AS A SOCIAL SYSTEM

It is customary to regard family as a social system. In fact there are many kinds of social systems and these are composed of variety of elements. So far as family is concerned, it fulfills many of the conditions, which go to make it a social system. It is for this reason that family is characterised as being a perfect social system and this notion fully holds good at least in the case of joint family. Defining social system Talcott Parsons writes, "The social system is composed of the patterned interaction of members. It consists of interaction of a plurality of individual actors, whose relations to each other are mutually oriented through the definition and mediation of a pattern of structured and shared symbols and expectations." Similarly C.P. Loomis is also of the opinion, "Socialogists frame of reference is inter action, characterised by patterned social relation that display in their uniformities social elements articulated by social processes, the dynamics of which account for the emergence, maintenance and change of social system."

When these observations are applied on family, it becomes clear that the family is contained in a number of elements, which are found in every social system. These are some of those elements of which most family groups consist and on the basis of which family is entitiled to be called a social system.

1. Status. Every family consists of a number of persons and all of them have a certain status. This status of the members of a family is normally determined on the basis of age and sex. But sometimes learning and occupation also have some effect in this matter. The status of parents is always higher than that of the children. Similarly in a family sons enjoy better status than daughters. Status helps in making gradation in the position of the different members of their family and their social relations are determined in accordance with their position. Since father's status in the family is the highest of all, he is authorised to perform all the family responsibilities. The eldest son being next in importance to his father automatically obtains the same position after his father's death.

2. Privilege. In a social system every unit is gifted with a certain kind of privileges. These privileges also go with the roles that they perform and the status that they hold in a social structure. It is through the enjoyment of privileges that a unit is enabled to do its responsibilities nicely under all circumstance. It is this element that gives stability and continuity to a social system. The Same thing can be said in the case of family as well. The members of the family are always in the enjoyment of certain privileges according to their status. It is by the exercise of these privileges enjoyed by the members that structure and functioning of the family remain intact.

3. Sanctions. The sanctions determined by the social values and Ideals play in important part in the field of human conduct. The social sanctions make a distinction between what is right and what is wrong in the activities and behaviour of the individuals. Society permits its members to do certain things and forbids them to do others and thereby lays down a standard for the general conduct of its members. The members are allowed to do only those things, which are beneficial for the life and stability of the social order. In this way sanctions also help a lot in the strengthening of a social system. They maintain discipline and orderly conditions in it. This element is found in abundance in the working of the family as well. There are some set rules and codes of behaviour which are binding on the members and which they cannot ignore easily. Thus, the family as a social system depends largely for its life and sound working on a set of rules, which operate in the form of social sanctions. The more active and forceful are these social sanctions, the more solid and the longer lasting will be the structure of the family. This is why in the past families were more integrated and well disciplined because there was more force behind the social sanctions.

4. Role. All the members of the family perform a certain role and it is by this means that the working of the family is made possible. The roles that the different persons perform are determined and conditioned by the status that they hold in the family. In fact every status has a correspondent role attached to it. Role is the outward manifestation of the status and, thus, both of them go together. Every member of the family while performing his role keeps in view his status in the family and does the things accordingly. The role maintains the balance of status system and thereby keeps intact the structure of the family. Since, there are a variety of status differing from person to person, so there are a number of roles varying from person to person according to his status. For Instance, the role of parents in the family is quite different from that of the children but it needs be said that the functioning of the family can go well only if all of its members perform their respective roles properly.

5. Necessities and Aims. Every social system consists of the needs, aims and ends of the people. They are related to the level of cultural and economic progress of the society. Sometimes they are also concerned with the social development of the people. Men have some basic needs and the fulfillment of them is the chief aim of a social system. For realization of these aims a social system has to set before it its certain ideals and ends. In this way needs and alms play a vital role in the efficient working of any social system. Family as a social system is concerned with fulfilling some-physical and social needs of the people. There are some basic needs like sex impulse, procreation of race and the provision of home, which cannot be met elsewhere except in the family. These needs aim at ensuring good life to the people. It is right that in the modern times many of the functions of the family have been taken over by some other associations, but all the same there are some primary functions which must be performed in the family in all civilized societies.

6. Sentiments. Sentiments occupy an important place in a social system. The sentiments especially influence collective life. It is under their influence that an individual gives preference to collective interest over his own individual gain. They develop general working patterns of different groups, which afford stability and uniformity to a social system. Family as a social system gives expression to a number of sentiments. The chief among these are a sentiment of love, the sentiment of co-operation, sentiment of sympathy and the sentiment of respect. These sentiments form the be all and end all of family life.

7. Power. In every social system there exists a supreme power which acts as a controlling figure in it. It, on the one hand, resolves the conflicts of different units and on the other, keeps intact the unity of that social system. The family as a social system vests its supreme power in the father or husband who supervises and controls the activities of other members. There can be no challenge or disobedience to the command of the head of the family. Only such families last long in which there is unity of command and a well-knit controlling power.

8. Ideal Principles. The family, as a social system, derives its life out of the inter-relations and inter-actions of its members. Every member of the family has a special function to do and a particular role to play for its well-being. There is great need of making. It certain that all the members of the family do their part well. For this purpose there exists some ideal principles. These principles maintain solidarity and balance in the family. These principles are in the form on unwritten maxim and are based on common consent. They are so vital to the social life that they cannot be set aside easily and in their absence a good family life cannot be made possible.

Thus, it is clear from the above facts that family is truly a social system because it contains most of the basic elements of a social system. It is right that in the modern times family is undergoing great changes. As a result of this fact it is feared that family may not lose in course of time, its character of being a social system. But such doubts appear to be unfounded because there are so many elements of social system, which cannot vanish from family. Thus, in the end it can be said that family is definitely a social system with this much exception that it has been more apparent in a joint family.

Difference between Family and Society

There is a general agreement on this point that both family and society are not only natural but also necessary for mankind. They are very old organizations which have been working since the time immemorial and which are bound to exist till the unknown future. It is neither possible nor desirable to challenge this assumption. But despite all this they cannot be viewed as identical terms. There exists a broad and clearly visible line of distinction between them.

To begin with, the first mark of distinction between them is the flame as is between the whole and a part of a thing. Society is the collection of different communities, associations and institutions while family is one of them. It is an association and also an institution serving some of the basic needs of the individuals. In this way society is the whole of organizational pattern of human relationship of which family is a component part.

Secondly, from the structural point of view society is much bigger than family. The family is a small kin-group, which consists of father, mother and their children and in some cases it may contain some other close relatives. But on the other hand, society is a large organization, which is composed of several families and clans. Thus, family may be said to exist within society and not society within family.

Thirdly, from the standpoint of their origin also a distinction is drawn between them. Many sociologists are of the opinion that the first and the primary unit of human organization in this universe is family and not society. The family later on developed and assumed the form of society. In this way, society is the developed form of family and family in the matter of origin is regarded as prior to society.

Fourthly, the membership in a family is always limited and definite but this is not the case with society. The members of a family always live in that very family and they cannot change their family affiliations at their own sweet will. But there is no such limit on the members of a society. People can change their membership of society at their own pleasure. They may leave one society and join another and they are under no check in such changes. Thus, while the membership of a family is natural and inborn, the membership of society can be in some cases the work of human wishes and efforts.

Lastly, from the view-point of their functions and nature, the structure of the family is becoming more and more simple day by day while the structure of society is becoming increasingly complex. There used to be in the past huge joint families, which have now become small simple single families. On the other hand, with the passage of time the society is constantly growing in bigness of size and complexity of structure. However, despite all these differences the two organizations must always work simultaneously and live together.

DIFFERENCE BETWEEN MODERN FAMILY AND TRADITIONAL FAMILY

Family is a very old social group. It has been in existence since long times. It is older than society and as old as human life itself. But despite all this, it is not a static institution. It is always changing with the march of time. It is for this reason that the structure of the modern family is not the same as it was about a century ago. In order to emphasise this fact, J. Rumney and Joseph Maier observe, "Although the family is universal, no particular form of it is primary or inevitable. Like all other institutions, it is a social product subject to change and modification." Similarly Nimkoff and Ogburn also write, "The family has changed a good deal in the past and has assumed many different forms and functions. The family has proved to be a very resilient and flexible institution. Despite radical changes in form and functions, the family has continued to exist in every society known to us. It should be clear from these facts that family is undergoing constant changes. As a result of this the modern family has become much different from the ancient family. In short, some of the main points of difference between them can be shown in the following way.

1. Replacement of Joint Family by Single Family. To begin with a fundamental difference between the modern family and the ancient family pertains to its size. In the ancient societies joint family system was the order of the day. There used to be families of very big size consisting of the members of many generations. Not only parents and their children but also the families of their brothers, grand parents and the widow daughters of the same family used to live in one house. Such family group was like a social unit and many a time the number of its members exceeded even a hundred, but in the modern times single-family system has become the order of the day. Now joint families have broken up and their place has been taken over by single families. The modern families are quite small in size consisting of parents and their small children. Even the grown up children after their marriage separate themselves from their parents and establish their own families. At present the number of membership in a family hardly exceeds ten persons or so.

2. Change in the Position of Women. *Secondly,* an important point of difference between the traditional and modern families relates to the position of women. Formerly, the women occupied a very low position in the family. They were just slaves to men possessing none of their own individuality. They had no rights nor any freedom. They had to carry out the dictates of the male members of the family. But now her position has changed altogether. In modern famdy the woman if not the devotee of man but an equal partner in life with equal rights. The husband now does not dictate but only requests the wife to do tasks for him. She is now emancipated of man's slavery. She can divorce her husband as the husband can divorce her. She can sue the husband for her rights and likewise be sued in turn. Thus, the position of the women has changed in the family with the changing times.

3. Modern Family no Longer a Social Unit. *Thirdly,* the traditional family was regarded as a social unit, whereas the modern families have become individualistic in outlook. In the ancient times all the members of a family lived at one and the same place and they were bound together by a thread of the commonness of residential and social conditions. All the physical and social needs were fulfilled in the family and there was no necessity of any outside agency to interfere in the human life. But such is not the case in the modern families wit the disintegration of joint family system. The family in the modern time has lost. Its character as a social unit. The people have become more Individualistic In outlook than they think of common interests. Now even the members of the same family live scattered at different places and do separate occupations.

4. Economic Independence of Women. *Fourthly,* a very important feature of modern family is the economic independence of women, while such a thing was not found in the traditional family. Previously, women were dependent on men for the fulfillment of all their needs and wants. They had no independent economic resources of their own to support them. They were confined within the four walls of the home and all their basic needs of food, clothing and shelter had to be met in the family by men. Women could own neither property nor could they hold any occupation. Marriage was a compulsory bond for them, which they had to undertake for the fulfillment of economic, needs. But now the position has changed altogether. Women in modern family have attained an increasing degree of economic dependence. It is not only the husband who leaves the home for work but it is also the wife who goes out of doors, for work. The percentage of women employed outside the home is continually on the increase. They are now property-owners as well as wage earners and do not want to lag behind men in any way. This economic dependence has largely affected the attitude of modern woman. Formerly, she had no choice but to find a male partner who could marry her and support her economically. She now does not feel helpless before man, settles matters with him in terms of her own right. She is not a slave of the man who provides her with food, clothing and shelter but she can now earn her own living. Such a feature did not mark the traditional family.

5. Decline of Religious Control. *Fiftly,* while the traditional family was religious in outlook, the modern family is secular in attitude. The religious rites of the traditional family such as early prayer, yagya etc., are no longer performed in modern family. Marriage also has become a civil contract rather than a religious sacrament. It can be broken at an hour. The authority of religion over the conditions of marriage and divorce has markedly declined. Divorce is a frequent occurrence in modern family. In traditional family it was a rare phenomenon.

6. Decreased Control of the Marriage Contract. Marriage is the basis of family. In a traditional family the parents contracted the marriage. The marriage ceremony was based on the principle of male dominance and female obedience. In a modern family people is less subject to the parental control in the matter of mate choice. The partners themselves do not settle the marriage and it can be undone at their own will.

7. Modern Family no longer an Economic Unit. *Seventhly,* the traditional family was an economic unit, which the modern family has, ceases to be now. The traditional family was all at once a production and consumption unit. It was self-sufficient in economic needs. All the active members of the family were employed in the family occupation. All the articles of consumption could be prepared at home. There was no cause of depending on outside agencies for the sake of economic gratification. But the modern family does not possess such a character. It is no longer a self-sufficient unit. The members of the family have to seek outside help for finding a suitable occupation. It has also ceased to be a unit of production because most of the articles of daily need are now obtained from the market. In this connection Gisbert has aptly remarked, "The modern family is no longer the Economic unit that it was in the Middle Ages where production, distribution and consumption developed in the home as a self-sufficient unit in an agricultural and handicraft economy. It would be misleading to say that the family is losing its economic functions, but it is certainly transforming them considerably."

8. Abandonment of non-essential Functions. *Lastly,* the sphere of activities of traditional family had been much larger than that of modern family. The modern family has given up a great many functions, which were performed by the traditional family. These functions have now been taken over by specialized agencies. According to Jay Rumney and Joseph Maier, "Compared with the family of medieval times the functions of the modern family are few. All but gone are its economic, educational, religious and protective functions. They have been transferred to the State, the Church, the school and industry." Not only this much but many of the traditional tasks of the household such as cooking and baking, cleaning and washing are also performed outside the household by specialized agencies. In this way while the traditional family performed both essential and non-essential functions, the modern family is concerned with the doing of essential functions.

It is clear from the foregoing facts that the family has been subjected to profound modification of an economic, social and biological nature. The modern family is no longer the economic and self-sufficient unit. But despite all this it may be said, that the family still remains a strategic social institution. The loss of its functions and the change in its structure has not destroyed its basic position. Thus, it may be said in the end that the modern family has considerably changed from the traditional family, but this process of change has been all at once the result of changing needs and current circumstances.

CHANGES IN THE MODERN FAMILY

It is a well know fact that change is the law of Nature. There is no human organization on social institution which has remained uniform and static at all times and under all circumstances. It has to move and change with the changing conditions, or it is apt to become obsolete and go out of existence. This rule is fully applicable on the age-old institution of family as well. The family as it is now is much different from what it was a few generations ago. Several changes have taken place in its nature and structure with the result that it has undergone an overall transformation. Whereas about a century back the family was more of a community, it has become today more of an association. According to Ogburn and Nimcoff, "The family has changed a good deal in the past and has assumed many different forms and functions. The family has proved to be a very resilient and flexible institution. Despite radical changes in form and function, the family has continued to exist in every society known to us."

It points to the fact that in the recent times many changes have occurred in the family and some of them may briefly be mentioned here.

Referring to some of the changes occurred in the modern family and the forces bringing about them Davis writes, "Modern civilization characterized by an elaborate industrial technology, a high degree of urbanization and a great amount of geographical and social ability, has sheered away the extended kingship bonds.. The role effective kinship group is now the immediate family and even this unit has lost in size and function. True, the immediate family has gamed in importance by being freed from the control of extended kindred, but it has declined in importance in other ways."

It is clear from this statement that in the modern time a large number of changes have occurred in the organization and working have the family and several factors has been operating to bring about these changes. Some of the more important changes in family life need be mentioned here in order to reveal its present position.

(i) To begin with, the joint family system is declining and in its place single-family system is coming into prominence. Unlike the large family of traditional society the modern families are small in size. They

consist of the husband, wife and their minor children. This is of course the first and the fundamental change that has occurred in the structure of family.

(ii) There has taken place a change in the mutual relation of husband and wife in the family. Unlike old times women have become independent and self-reliant in many ways. Now that the women have gamed equal fights with men, their mutual relationship has undergone much change. Mowrer has correctly written of modern woman that 'she is no longer the drudge and slave of other days.'

(iii) The modern family is no longer a permanent association. It is precarious and can be rendered void at any time. Marriage has been reduced to a mere social contract, which it is not difficult to break in the event of even the slightest friction. According to Maciver, "The Modern family in comparison with the ancient and medieval families is very weak and unstable."

(iv) In the modern time there has occurred a change in the mutual relation of parents and children. The control of parents over their children has lessened a great deal and now the family discipline is not as tight as it was in the ancient families. The children have become less obedient to their parents and they are very particular about their freedoms and rights.

(v) There has come about a good deal of change in the extent of family functions. Many of the functions which family performed previously are no longer under its care. They have been transferred to several external agencies. The family has ceased to be an economic as well as social unit. When compared with the family of medieval times, the functions of the modern family are few. All but gone are its economic educational, religious and protective

functions. They have been transferred to the State, the church, the school and industry.

(vi) The modern family is under less religious control. It has been replaced by legal control. With the decline of the Influence of religion the family morals have also become comparatively loose. The modern family has become secular in outlook and it has given up many of its religious activities.

(vii) The rigidity traditionally associated with marital and sexual relationships no longer characterizes the modern family. The use of contraceptive and means of birth control has rendered the size of the family very small. There is not much affinity among the blood relations of the family. In this way the relations in the family have become more formal and mechanical in Nature.

Lastly, the family seems to be coming on the verge of disorganization. The number of divorces is on the increase. The control, which the family exercises over the individual is being lessened rapidly. Thus, the family has undergone a good deal of transformation in the present century.

Factors Responsible for Changes in the Family

It is clear from the foregoing facts that a large number of changes have occurred in the structure of family. This process has not completed yet and is liable to continue till indefinitely even in the unknown future. There is not one but many factors which are working at the root of all these changes.

Referring to some of these factors Jay Rumney and Joseph Maier write, "The modern family which is still essentially patriarchal in character has been shorn of much of its power. The State is tending to become a super-parent, having arrogated to itself much of the patriarch's authority. Profound economic changes since the Industrial Revolution have deprived the family of its economic functions as a unit of production. It is now mainly a unit of consumption. The new economy, requiring the use of womanpower opened up new occupations to women, they became economically in dependent of their husbands. The political and economic emancipation of woman as well as periods of prolonged unemployment undermined the authority of the father, especially if his earnings were surpassed by those of his wife and children. A new morality emerged in conflict with the traditional moral standards. Large families became rare. Urbanization led to a wide dissemination of contraceptive knowledge. The small independent if nit, consisting of parents and one or two offspring became the rule. Thus, lit short, some of the causes and factors of family changes may be explained in the following order.

1. Impact of Industrialization. The first important factor bringing about changes in the structure of family has been the force of industrialization. The Industrial Revolution substituted the power machine for the manual tool. As new techniques of production advanced they shelved the old family of its economic functions. New factories with heavy machines have been set-up which have taken both the work and the workers out of the family. Now cloth is produced not on the family handloom but in the textile mill. Thousands of workers who are drawn out of home are required to work in the factory. Not only males but females also have begun to go to the factory for work. The work of women has become specialized like that of men. They instead of being busy with the multifarious tasks of the family have started going to workshops and factories for work. As a result of it women have become as good the earning members of the family as men. This earning power of the women has made them free from dependence on men.

2. Effect of Urbanism. An inevitable result of industrialization has been the, growth of urbanism. Urbanism has materially affected not merely the size of the home but also the essentials of the family life. It has substituted legal controls for informal controls and has brought the family into competition with specialized agencies. The result is that many of the family functions have been taken over by the external agencies. *For example,* the educational, health and recreational functions of the family are now performed by schools, hospitals and recreational centres respectively. Under the joint force of industrialization and urbanization the family has ceased to be a social as well as economic unit. The joint family system is vanishing and in its place the single-family system is becoming the order of the day. It has even affected the mutual relations of the different members of the family. To quote Davis," It has forced individuals to co-operate with countless person who are not kinsmen. It has also encouraged them to join special interest groups thus, drawing them out of the unspecialized and heterogeneous family with its wide sex and age differences." In this way urbanism and industrialization have caused considerable modifications in the structure of family.

3. Decline of Religious Control. The modern family has become secular in its outlook because of the decline of the force of religions. Marriage has become a civil contract rather than a religious sacrament. It can be broken at any time. The authority of religion over the conditions of marriage and divorce has suffered a great decline. Divorce is a frequent occurrence in modern family while in traditional family it was a rare phenomenon. Religion has been a great uniting and solidifying factor in the, family. And with the loss of its force the family is bound to undergo disintegration.

4. Effect of Changing Mores. The mores concerning family life are constantly changing and this factor has. Also greatly affected the organization of family. Now the mutual relations of different members of the family have undergone remarkable change and it is all the result of changing mores. According to Maciver and Page "The basis of husband wife relationship in the family is no longer domination but co-operation". Previously everywhere, the wife was dominated by the husband and so the family stability survived because of the unity of command. But with the removal of this dominance the family organization has been exposed to powerful perils. Thus, as a result of all these factors the family organization is not stable and it is undergoing quick modifications. But notwithstanding all these facts the family still continues to be a strategic social Institution.

5. Social Mobility. The critics are of the opinion that social mobility has cut still deeper into the family organization. In so far as individuals improve their class status by virtue of their own achievement rather than by birth, an intrinsic function of the family is lost to it. In this connection Davis writes, "In a completely open society where all vertical positions were filled purely by individual accomplishment, there could scarcely be a family organization; each family member would tend to find himself in a different. Social stratum, from the others and the invidious sentiments thus, brought into the family circle would prove incompatible with family sentiment." The organizations of the family can remain intact only if its members feel dependent on it for their personal advance in life. If this requirement is fulfilled by some external factors, it adversely affects the family organization. This is exactly what is happening in the present society. People do not feel themselves so much? Attached to family because so many external factors are on their disposal to help them in their individual development.

SOCIOLOGICAL SIGNIFICANCE OF THE FAMILY

The family is by far the most important primary group in society. Historically it has been transformed from a more or less self-contained unity into a definite and limited organization of minimum size, consisting primarily of the original contracting parties. On the other hand it continues to serve as. a total community for the lives born within it, gradually relinquishing this character as they grow toward adulthood. The family more profoundly than any other organization, exists only as a process. Referring to the sociological of the family Maciver and Page opine, "Of all the organizations, large or small, which society unfolds, none transcends the family in the intensity of its sociological significance. It influences the whole life of society in innumerable ways and its changes reverberate through the whole social structure. It is capable of endless variation and yet reveals a remarkable continuity and persistence through change. Thus, in short, family is the first and foremost organ of society and this fact can be proved by the following arguments:

1. Universal in Character. The family is the most nearly universal of all social forms. It is found in all societies, at all stages of social development and exists far below the human level, among a myriad species of animals. Almost every human being is or has been a member of some family. There is no other social group that can equal family in this matter.

2. Nuclear Position in the Social Structure. Family is the nucleus of all the social organizations. Frequently in the simpler societies, as well as in the more advanced types of patriarchal society the whole social structure is built of family units. Only in the higher complex civilizations does the family cease to fulfill this function, but even in them the local community, as well as its divisions of social classes tends to remain unions of families. One of the first definitions ever given of a community made it "a union of families" and for the local community the definition, with some qualification, still holds today.

3. Formative Influence. Family is also significant because it exerts the profoundest formative influence on the life of the individuals. It is the earliest social environment of man's life and plays a vital role in moulding it. No other organization can compete with family in this respect. According to Maciver, "In particular it moulds the character of the individual by the impression both of organic and of mental habits". Its influence in infancy determines the personality structure of the individual. It is largely from his parents that the child receives his physical inheritance and mental training, on the basis of which he leads the whole of his life. It is well-said by a critic, "To be well-born is to possess the greatest of all gifts. To be ill-born there is nothing which this world can offord that will be adequate compensation for the lack of good heredity." Thus, family has come to surpass all other socia1 organizations in the matter of formative influence on human personality.

4. Performance of Basic Functions. The significance of the family as a social institution may be measured by the number of basic functions it performs. Compared with the family of medieval times, the functions of the modern family are few. All but gone are its economic, educational, religious and protective functions. They have been transferred to the State, the church, the school and industry. Notwithstanding the loss of functions, the family remains a strategic social institution. It is our parents that first cure us of our natural wildness and break in us the spirit of independency we are all born with. It is to them that we owe the first rudiments of our submission and to the honour and deference which children pay to parents all societies are obliged for the principle of human obedience", writes Mandeville. In addition to performing this all-important function of socializing the individual, the family regulates sexual relationships, provides for the affectional needs of its members, makes possible the prolonged care, which children require and transmits the values of the culture. It remains a powerful agent of social and political control and economic differentiation. Children generally stay in the social class to which their parents belonged. They inherit both the property and the cultural advantages, which its possession offers.

5. An Important Agency of Social Control. Family is an important agency of social control. Family controls sex passions in society. A strict control over sex relationships is necessary for maintaining the order otherwise society will disintegrate. In all cultures, family exercises some degree of control over the unmarried members from falling into bad habits. No parents would like their children to adopt the career of crime. The children under the influence of their parents drop bad habits and learn good habits. In the making of great men families have always played a major role. In this way the making of a good citizen in society depends upon the parents.

6. Proper Organization of Society Dependent upon Family. Proper social organization largely depends upon sound organization of families. If in a particular society families disintegrate, that society can never be safe and sooner or later it is found to meet its doom. This is why at all times one major cause of social disorganization has been family disorganization. Families develop the characters of the members of the society. In the opinion of ADLER, a man's role in the family determines his role in society. There is no exaggeration in calling family a cornerstone of society.

7. Family is Vital to the Process of Socialization. Another point of significance of family is that it plays a vital role in the process of socialization of the individuals. Merrill is of the opinion that family is an enduring association of parent and offspring whose primary functions are the socialization of the child and the satisfaction of the members. It is in the family that child learns all good and human qualities like sincerity, sympathy, self-submission, consciousness of responsibility and so forth. It is the character developed in the family, which helps the child in becoming an important and responsible member of society. F. J. Wrightwas quite correct in saying that in every family, the child gets an opportunity for free expression of thoughts and developing his entire personality. It has been conclusively proved that the proper development of the child is impossible without a good environment in the family. The tendencies and habits, which he acquires in the family remain with him for the whole of his life. It is in view of this fact that Freud says, "The view-point of a child towards the senior in the family determines his attitude and viewpoint towards the elders in society."

8. Family is the Conveyer of Culture. The family not only moulds character and personality of the individuals, but it also imparts its culture to them. It is while living in the family that the child acquires knowledge about the culture of society. It is an efficient vehicle for the transmission of culture from one generation to another. It is a very good socializing agency that makes the people social and cultured beings According to Deway and Tufts, "The family is a social agency for the education and protection of the race." It is through family that the individuals come to know the customs, traditions, social values and cultural background of their community. Family provides them knowledge and understanding of the past and thereby prepares them to live well in the future. Thus, in all these ways family plays a vital role in the field of preservation and transmission of social culture.

It is clear from the above account that family is the most important social institution. No other human organization can overshadow it in the matter of sociological significance. This fact is true not only from the structural view-point, but also from the functional stand-point. There are some functions of the family, which no other group can undertake successfully. There are some clear uses of the family, which no one can derive from any other group. Without family the process of socialization would remain incomplete, the task of preserving and transmitting culture to posterity would be half done and there would be no organization to safeguard their social and cultural values. Its significance also lies in the fact of its being the oldest and universal human organization. It is even the parent of society whose structure is raised on the foundations of family. If family were to vanish, it would expose the whole human race to the horrors of complete decay. The present changes in the family need not be taken to mean the signal of its possible downfall in the future; it is rather a process of its adjustment to the current needs and the changing times. Family in the past has remained an indispensable social system and it is sure to continue as such in the future as well. Thus, on account of its strategic position the family more than any other group exerts persistent, intimate and far reaching influence on the habits, attitudes and social experiences of the people. It plays the foremost role in the formation of personality. It occupies a key place in social organization.

✱✱✱

11

Social and Culture

The human infant is an organism with fundamental physiological processes: The assimilation of food, the respiratory and circulatory functions, the elimination of bodily waste, the neuro-muscular functions which co-ordinate these operations and so on. On the basis of these physiological processes rest certain fundamental drives like hunger, bodily protection and sex. These drives or motives originate from the organic needs of the body and are important for the survival of the individual and the survival of the species. Hence, they are called biogenic drives or biogenic motives. Further these are unlearned. As Sherif writes, "No matter what the social setting or 'culture pattern' may be—imperial or colonial, western or oriental, highly industrial or primitive, leisure class or poverty stricken, Christian or heathen, man eats, drinks, breathes, sleeps and tries to keep warm in order to carry forward the most essential complex of his pre-occupations, living—that is, just keeping alive as a biological organism". These are basic needs not only among human beings of all the various nationalities and cultures, but they are also common to the human beings and animals. As the individual grows he acquires various means of satisfying these basic wants. There is another important aspect of the individual, his flexibility, his ability to modify his actions. The ability to learn is thus, the other fundamental feature of the organism. This ability also, the human being shares with animals. Adaptability to new situations is something common to all living creatures; only with the increase in the complexity of the nervous system there is an increase in intelligence, the ability to learn, from species to species in the biological evolution. And thus, we find, that the human being inherits biologically certain constant drives as well as certain flexibility or learning ability. The upper limit to one's ability to learn is something biologically given. Of course, both the actual operation of the basic needs as well asthe effectiveness of the ability to learn are conditioned by the social as well as cultural processes. These two sets of the biologically given do not operate in vacuum as the individual is exposed to the environmental influences which modify or affect both of them. Further there are individual differences, variability, not only in intelligence, learning ability, but also in the strength of drives. This fact is liable to be ignored since we are impressed by differences in ability among individuals and by resemblances in basic drives among human beings. Also, the success in measurement of differences in ability has been considerable in comparison with the measurement of differences in drives among human beings. Personality measurement programmes are largely preoccupied with measuring differences among individuals regarding traits and temperaments and not regarding the basic drives themselves. This is a fertile field for animal psychologists. The experimental work in this field is today confined to the measurement of the strength of drives among animals in the sense of differences between the various drives and not in the sense of differences in the strength of drives between individual animals of one species.

Thus, we find that the newborn infant enters the family equipped with an organic constitution on which are based the basic drives as well as intelligence and ability to learn. The growing child makes demands upon his society for his survival and the society makes demands upon him. In the process of making his demands and in meeting the demands made on him, he is socialized. He gradually develops his personality. His survival depends on the physical care as well as the affection bestowed on him by his mother and others in the family. By the second year he learns language and learning this means of communication increases his inter-relationship and interaction with other people. Gradually he is given a place (status) in the family and he takes on certain functions (role). On the basis of his role and status he develops specific habits, attitudes and values. In short, he becomes a personality. The helpless bundle of protoplasm becomes a human being. As Kimball Young writes "It is from this configuration of family members and others closely associated with them that the social self-emerges. The child is not born human or social. He is at the outset an organism belonging to an animal species.

With the growth in experience and the growth in the acquisition of language there is a growth in internalization. We may disagree with Watson regarding his view that thinking is subvocal talking. But there is no doubt that he drew our attention to a very important aspect in the development of the individual. It is now well recognized that the process of internalization both with respect to thinking and with respect to assimilation of attitudes goes on as this time in the life of the child. By the second year he starts learning to speak. The child often speaks what he does. Gradually he gives up talking aloud. As Freud has shown, around the age of four and five the process of identification with parents goes on. He adopts the external commands of parents and other adults as his internal laws of command and develops his superego. Both these internalized processes of thinking and conduct are very important elements in the socialization of the child as we shall see later on. Thus, in his development the child is affected not only by what the other persons in the family do to control his behaviour, he is also affected by his own thoughts and attitudes, some of which are conscious and some inaccessible to consciousness.

There is yet another aspect of the growth of the individual which must be taken into account. The individual is not only socialized, he also influences others and socializes them. He participates in the society both by being influenced by others and by influencing them. The individual is not only the product of culture he is also the transmitter of culture; he may even alter it.

Society

As we have just now seen the individual becomes a personality because of his contact with other human beings within the family and outside. The social act is an interaction of individuals. The mother-child relationship is the basic social act with which each human being starts. This parent-child relationship, as we shall see below, is something which goes back to animals, birds and even insects. All the various patterns of social interaction start from this basic mother-child social relationship.

The sociologist classifies social interaction into two types: Primary and secondary. The family, the play-group, the village neighbourhood are all primary groups. They are characterized by intimate face-to-face contact. "The simplest, the first, the most universal of all forms of association is that in which a small number of persons meet 'face-to-face' for companionship, mutual aid, the discussion of some question that concerns them all, or the discovery and execution of some common policy". The primary group may be free-functioning and informal as in the play group and friendship or it may be formal as in an interview, in the classroom or in the office and factory. In contrast in secondary relations there is formality, specialized group roles as between teachers and students, buyers and sellers, officials and citizens. There is no intimacy. The social interaction is not between persons but between representatives of positions in a formal order. As the complexity of .society increases the social relationships become more Impersonal. In the village every person knows every other person. But in a large city one may not even know one's neighbour or a person living in the next 'flat' in the same building. The religious organization, the political party, the state itself are examples of secondary associations. With industrialization and consequent urbanization there is the formation of 'mass society'. Large numbers of people live together as in our modern cities and social relations become impersonal in their relationship to each other and there is the feeling of loneliness. When you go to a theatre by yourself, you feel lonely, though there may be hundreds of people around you. There is no relationship of intimacy. There is a curious combination of rationality and irrationality in mass society. Advance of industrialization is based on advance in science, technology and organization. But urbanization leads to impersonal relationships and hence, the increase in the influence of suggestion and propaganda. Crowd behaviour becomes an important aspect of mass society. " The impress of mass society upon men and their culture constitutes one of our most crucial problems of personality balance, sense of emotional security and moral use of power".

Similarly the other classification into 'in-group' and 'out-group' is also of great value; Sumner used the term , 'in-group'. We learn to divide people into the 'we' and the 'they'. The groups with which we identify ourselves constitute the in-group. The individual develops attitudes of identification with the persons of the family, caste, neighbourhood etc. The persons-forming the 'other' groups are looked upon with fear, suspicion or dislike as groups which are antagonistic to the progress and welfare of our group.

Differentiation of functions is another basic interaction. Varying combinations of these elemental processes of interaction are at the basis of class and caste differences in society. On the basis of differentiation of functions and the development of specific functions or roles in the group, the various modes of social interaction arise. There are the basic differentiations of function in the home which have given rise to the roles of husband and wife, social roles of the sexes, ages etc. Even within the home an individual is assigned a more or less limited and well-defined social role. This is particularly conspicuous in the Indian joint family. The individual learns the behaviour appropriate to that role, as otherwise he will not be socially acceptable. These roles whether within the house or outside in the society at large keep changing and necessitate further learning. With age and circumstance the role changes; from being a son, a man changes to being a father, from pupil to teacher, from a subordinate to the position of headship and from the labourer to the manager.

But we have to bear in mind that the interaction arising out of the social differentiation imperceptibly involves cultural factors also. It is neither possible nor necessary to draw here a hard and fast distinction between the social and cultural aspects. On the other hand this should not lead us to ignore the distinction between the social and cultural aspects.

Social and Cultural Aspects

It will be of great advantage for clarity of thinking if we recognize the distinction as well as the relation between the two aspects. Probably the use of specific terms may help to attain this end. We may use the terms inter-personal relationship and socia-cultural relationship to differentiate between these two kinds of interactions, the former indicating interaction between individuals involving either little or no cultural and institutional factors and the latter involving them to a high degree. As Lapiere and Farnsworth write: "In the more stable social systems at least, the most important human needs are satisfied through institutional mechanisms ... these mechanisms subordinate momentary considerations to long run aims. Individual needs of an immediate character are, therefore, generally satisfied in interactional situations of other than the institutional type—in what may be termed 'interpersonal' situations. The individual needs from which inter-personal situations arise and through which they are organized are often incidental outcomes of institutional membership and are seldom in antagonism to institutional membership. But the pattern of situational interaction is primarily a function of the particular personalities involved in the situation". Thus, we find that it is necessary for us to bear in mind the distinction between social behaviour which does not involve, or involves very little cultural aspect and that which involves the cultural to a high degree. This distinction is rather hard to appreciate when we are dealing with social behaviour among human beings since no human being can survive if he is not brought up in a family, in a group with its own cultural heritage, simple or complex. But this should not make us overlook the fact that social behaviour is prehuman, precultural. There is a social factor even at the level of unicellular organisms. "The interaction between organisms is one of the most fundamental of biological. If chasing and pursuing among human being is a social fact, why is it not when it occurs in the amoebla?... The social is literally an aspect of the biological. There are, so far as we know, no organisms without social contacts". We shall see the various aspects of social behaviour in animals in the next chapter.

Even among human beings we find instances of purely social, interpersonal, relationshhips among infants and children. It is only with growth that the child becomes conscious of his affiliation to a family, religion, profession of father ete. Similarly we find in congenial situations the least intrusion of cultural factor. Children, adolescents as well as adults at play will be hardly conscious of their institutional affiliations. When we react in a familiar way to strangers on the road, at the market or office, in a bus or train, we are making more or less purely social, interpersonal contacts. Similarly in friendship there is much that is not cultural. Friendship may be based not so much on demands and expectations involving the particularcultural setting of the individuals, but on the more basic sentiment formation, on the continuous or frequent satisfactions regarding personal needs of affection and security. Attention may be drawn to the very illuminating analysis made by La Piere and Farnsworth of the hypothetical situation of two men meeting on a very narrow path. Since the path is narrow and since each has to go past the other to reach his goal there is an interactional situation. There are so many possible ways of resolving this problem. One may step aside or both may argue or even come to blows. "Our problem is not what they do, but how they come to do whatever it is that is done. In this respect we may distinguish three basic and in a sense mutually exclusive types of adjustment: first, if they have never faced such a problem before, they may be forced to the trial-and-error devising of an adequate pattern of interaction; second, if they have met on this or another path before, they may now utilize the adjustment technique that they have previously devised: Finally they may employ a conventional method of adjustment that has been handed down to them as a part of social heritage". Obviously the first two methods of solving interactional situations are more 'interpersonal' or 'personal-social' and the third way is definitely 'socio-cultural'. It was conventional in old India for the untouchable to step aside or even to turn back and run away if he met a peasant or a Brahmin in a narrow path. Similarly the peasant has to react stepping aside when he met a Brahmin. Social inequality gave rise to certain conventional ways of reacting in a social situation. Similarly sex or age or wealth may determine who is to step aside. Even today the Government publishes the order of precedence for introduction to political dignitaries. Not infrequently conflicts may arise about such status considerations, involving a resistance to accepting the conventional as well as when there is a desire to change the conventions to suit one's notion about the dignity of one's office. Thus, when two people meet the social interaction may be just interpersonal or socio-cultural.

It is a familiar fact that in India the person with the highest level of human development is the Sannyasin who has no cultural affiliations and hence, is capable of meeting other human beings as human beings. He sheds in-group, out-group attitudes and looks upon all human beings as in-group. Of course it cannot be denied that this essentially human attitude is the result of great cultural effort. It is similar to rule of law or justice. Justice is not pre-judiced by colour, caste, creed, sex and other considerations. It must be acknowledged that a country as well as an individual can rise above cultural affiliations which limit social contacts only through a realization of the abiding values, which is itself conditioned by cultural development.

Culture

As we have seen above the anthropologists use the term Culture to refer to the social heritage of a group of people. It is the more or less organized and persistent patterns of habits, attitudes and values which are transmitted from generation to generation. Every human infant is not only exposed to a culture, but assimilates it and in its turn transmits it. "The Culture consists of the shared behaviour, beliefs and material objects belonging to a society or part of a society". Often the terms "Social" and "Cultural" are used as interchangeable. *For example,* culture is looked upon as the social heritage. There is no doubt that cultural patterns are transmitted through social interactions. But as we have seen above we cannot say that all social interactions are cultural.

Culture implies heritage, transmission of modes of acting, feeling and thinking from generation to generation. There are the material as well as the non-material aspects of culture. There are the physical objects like the houses tools, machines and so on which form part of culture. There are also the attitudes, beliefs, knowledge and skills which form part of culture. But a division of culture on this basis is hardly satisfactory since objects have no meaning apart from the thought and action patterns. Consequently it may be asserted that the essence of culture is the attitudes and beliefs transmitted from generation to generation rather than the mere physical objects. The use of electrical equipment designed by Americans does not make Indians Americanized, nor the use of American cars and armaments. Similarly by learning Vedanta the American does not become Indianized. Neither the adoption of objects nor the adoption of ideas of one culture by another makes the synthesis of culture. It is the upbringing that is really significant. People of different cultures become Americanized by living there for a couple of generations. Similarly in the ages gone by, people of foreign cultures became Indianized by living in India and assimilating Indian ways of life.

The individual is exposed to and moulded by the culture of the group into which he is born. Culture is the framework within which the individual grows and develops. A distinction is made between universals and alternatives. The cultural universals are the more or less generally accepted and expected patterns of behaviour. The individuals in a culture earn to behave in certain detinite patterns towards others. This is at the basis of social conformitv, typical behaviour of individuals, *e.g.*, in the dress of individuals belonging to a particular language group in India. There is conformity not only in learning the given language but also in innumerable other aspects of behaviour, thought and belief. This does not however, mean that there is absolute uniformity. There will be minor variations. This is what Linton called the 'alternatives'. There are variations in details though there is uniformity in general. Experience further shows that in any group though there is general conformity, there are also considerable variations, some individuals departing a great deal from the 'universals' of the culture. No individual is completely culturally determined. Every individual is unique in any culture. Though we must recognise the common and general features we should not overlook the unique and autonomous aspects of an individual. The uniqueness may be based on individual differences in ability, aptitude and learning. The impact of the culture on the individual is not identical in every case. Further every individual sooner or later is exposed to influences which are not completely pre-determined by culture. He meets other people outside the culture. Travel on the one hand and books, radio, cinema, theatre, newspapers on the other, expose an individual to many influences outside the culture.

A few examples will bring home the fact that social behaviour is culture determined. What is 'correct' behaviour in one group may be just the opposite in another group. Touching vessels with right hand wheh one is taking food with the right hand is taboo in one group but quite correct in another group. Similarly while drinking coffee out of the cup is approved behaviour in one, drinking it from the saucer may be the approved behaviour in another group. Thus, the approved behaviour of one group might shock another group. An Indian will be shocked at the behaviour of the western people where men and women walk holding their hands or arm-in-arm. Similarly while the South Indian greets the intimate friend or relative with a bare namaskar or at the most with a hand-shake, the North Indian embraces him. A South Indian may feel very uncomfortable when a close friend of his from the north expresses his joy and affection in the manner approved in the north. Examples can be multiplied by daily observation of similarities and differences in social behaviour. Those ways of behaving and thinking accepted in a group become part of the culture.

Unlike birds and animals man is born physically immature. The infant cannot move about or protect himself from the natural hazards. For years he has to be looked after if he has to survive. Further the world of the human being is far more complex than that of the bird or animal. By mere trial and error learning he cannot sunive. "Thus, the Society that makes possible the survival of the individual through infancy and childhood also makes necessary the acquisition by him of social adjustments which are so complex that they can be learned only under social guidance. As the infant grows into the child and from thence, on until death, society more or less effectively and always in exceedingly complex ways, trains him into rhe social patterns of behaviour necessary for survival under the particular conditions of social life". Thus, we find that just as biological heritage determines man's organic potentialities, the social heritage determines a good part of his behaviour, attitudes, belief and skills. The difference between the two heritages is that while the biological heritage is a product of natural forces, the social or cultural heritage is a product of human experience. During certain ages in certain cultures, due to comparative social stability the people may believe that the accepted social practices are divinely ordained. But historical researches on the one hand and anthropological field studies on the other have conclusively shown that there is nothing 'natural' or inevitable in social practices. Social system in any group is man-made. Further it is continually changing in every group. Only in some groups the change is gradual while in others it may be more rapid. The differences in culture are due to the differences in social heritage based on varied experiences of different groups in their adjustment to physical nature and to the presence of other human beings.

This implies that with the change in experience, with the change in situations, there will be changes in culture. A further implication is that such changes may be facilitated by acceptance or resisted by the individuals in the group. These changes may be due to one or a few of the individuals. Thus, on the one hand social heritage determines the behaviour of the individuals in a group and on the other hand some individuals may affect the social heritage. There is thus, a continuous action and reaction between social heritage and social change. In some societies in some ages social heritage may be more strong while in some others social change may be more strong. The change itself may be progressive or degenerative; or the lack of change or resistance to change may also lead to stagnation and may even affect the survival of the group. Thus, we should not commit the fallacy of looking upon society as a sort of mechanism which automatically shapes human beings into pre-determined patterns. Nor should we commit the opposite fallacy that every individual is free to grow up in any way he likes. It is necessary for every individual to learn the social adjustments acceptable to the group. We may even say that there is no choice here at all since during the long and important period of infancy and childhood it is the parents and others in the family and neighbourhood that make the individual to adopt the social adjustments peculiar to the group. But later on when the individual grows and obtains insight into the social situations and needs he may bring about social change. Thus, the individual starts with social conformity with more or less resistance and later may bring about social change with more or less success. It may even be .asserted that social change is not always a dramatic phenomenon produced in a striking way by a leader.

As we have seen above, the publication of Patterns ot Culture in 1934 by Ruth Benedict and Sex and Temperament in Three Primitive Societies in 1935 by Margaret Mead marks a significant step forward in the growth of social psychology. In the two books there are six short and vivid sketches of different cultures. They showed that the social unit encourages the development of certain qualities and prevents the growth of some others by penalizing them. The amiable Arapesh and the suspicious Dobuans were shown clearly as the product of their different cultures. These studies showed that we can look upon each group as the product of one among several possible culture patterns.

***

12

Social and Mobility

It is customary to stratify society on several basis. A very important basis is that of wealth, power and prestige. The social divisions formed on these bases are known as social classes. Thus, in general terms a social class is a category or group of persons having a definite status in society, which permanently determines their relation to other groups. The relative position of the class in the social scale arises from the degree of prestige attached to the status. *For example,* the prestige enjoyed by the ruling classes in every society is superior to that of the domestic servants or public sweepers. The term social class has been defined in a number of ways by the critics. Therefore in order to understand this term fully the viewpoints of some eminent writers may be quoted here.

Lapiere writes, "It is a portion of community or collection of in1ividuals, standing to each other in the relation of equality and marked off from other portions by accepted or sanctioned standards of inferiority and superiority."

According to Max Weber, "Classes are aggregates of individuals who have the some opportunities of acquiring good, the same exhibited standard of living".

In the opinion of Ginsberg, "A social class is one of two or more broad groups of individuals who are ranked by the members of the community in socially superior and inferior positions."

In the words of Maciver, "A social class is a portion of community marked off from the rest by social status."

According to Ogburn and Nimkoff, "A social class is the aggregate of persons having essentially the same social status in a given society. "

In view of these observations it can be said that each particular class has its own particular social behaviour, its standards and occupations. It is a culturally defined group that is accorded a particular position or status within the population as a whole. The relative position of the social class in the society arises from the degree of prestige attached to the status. Wherever the considerations of status, lower and higher, limit inter-course, there social class exists. Such is the basic criterion of social class.

In a social class there is *firstly,* a feeling of equality in relation to members of one's own class, a consciousness that one's mode of behaviour will harmonise with the behaviour of similar standards of life. Individuals belonging to the same social class are expected to maintain similar standard of life and to chose their occupations within a limited range. There is realisation of a similarity of attitude and behaviour with members of one class. *Secondly,* there is a feeling of inferiority in relation to those who stand above in the social scale. *Thirdly,* there is the feeling of superiority to those below in the social heirarchy.

Main Attributes of Class-System

Like caste-system class-system is also having its distinctive attributes. This is a why it holds a position of its own in social organization much distinct from caste system. To begin with the fundamental attributes of a social class is its social position of relative inferiority or superiority to other classes. It is the social position, which determines for its possessor the degree of respect, prestige and influence. The arrangement is much like the army with its officers, commissioned and noncommissioned. In Rome, for instance, there were the slaves, plebeian and" five superior classes. According to Maciver. "It is the sense of status, sustained by the economic, political or eccestiastical power and by the distinctive modes of life and cultural expressions corresponding to them that draws class apart from class, gives cohesion to each class and stratifies a whole society".

Secondly, the membership of social classes depends on the personal achievements of the individual. People doing honourable work are included in higher classes while people doing menial work are rated in lower classes. Unlike caste membership the class membership is not based on birth. It is based on wealth, power and social position, all of which can be achieved by individual efforts. In class system nothing is pre-ordained and every thing is the result of human creation.

Thirdly, the members of each social class constitute something of an in group. They recognize one another as social equals and distinguish in a variety of ways between themselves and the members of other classes. They usually associate with the members of their own class and live together and apart from other classes. They have their own distinctive ways of life. In a sense, each social class is a society within a society. But it is not complete and independent society. Referring to this fact Maciver writes, "The consideration of the class as a status group renders it possible to apply it to any society which has many strata wherever a status group has a particular position in hierarchy of ascent and descent, the status groups can be called social classes. This not only separates the members of social status groups manifestly but the sense of social status separates them even mentally."

Fourthly, the class membership is not rigid and it is subject to alterations. It is so because class status is achieved rather than ascribed status. It permits social mobility and it is not very essential that persons born in low classes are bound to remain low for all times. They may rise in life and become the members of higher classes if they have the will and the capacity for that.

Fifthly, class system represents an open society. There are no social barriers restricting or prohibiting the social intercourse among different class groups. There is no fixity of occupations, nor is there any ban on matrimoinal relations. In this system people even enjoy freedom of food, dress and other social ways. For asserting their high prestige or for making a show of their superior place the members of certain classes may frame and follow rigid and specific codes of social behaviour. Otherwise in normal course of things the class-system is an open and free social system. Thus, in all these ways the social classes maintain their distinctive character and they differ from castes. It may also be noted here that from time to time the social classes have been changing and unlike class groups they have not remained ever the same.

Criteria of Class Distinctions

1t is a matter of common observation that society has been divided into different classes at different times. Now the question arises what principles are involved in the various modes of social classification. Different bases have been adopted from time to time for determining the status of persons. We place a person higher or lower in a status scale according to whether or not he has the given characteristics. But when we compare different societies, we find that people respond differently to different characteristics. In fact any characteristic such as occupation, wealth, birth, race, religion, education, speech, etiquette may become the basis for social ranking. Sometimes two or more characteristics combine to determine the status. Here, we shall examine the basis of birth and wealth that occupy the most important place in present day class distinctions.

Criterion of Birth. In feudal and early medieval times status was fixed by birth. Thus, there were the slaves and slave master, the noble and serf, the gentry and the commonalty. When status is determined by birth, the class structure becomes rigid and integrated. Social mobility is impossible. The attitude of members of each class tends to become habitual and quasi-automatic.

Creterion of Wealth. Birth continued for a long time to serve as the basis of class division. In the middle ages the feudal system was largely related to the criterion of birth. But with the fall of feudalism the criterion of wealth became more preminent. If was the "middle class", which were historically responsible for revolutionizing the feudal class system and secured a new definition of social status in terms of wealth. Under the feudal system the principal form of wealth was the land. In fact the whole system of feudal relationship was based on land ownership, which was the elemental fact in the feudal structure. With the rise of industrial age wealth has become the most important factor of class division. Land has been subordinated to other forms of wealth. Now hereditary ownership is regarded as inferior to wealth earned by enterprise. The classes are formed on the basis of holding of wealth. It is an open social order where in by virtue of their individual achievements people can rise in life. In society where wealth is the main basis of class divisions, due importance is given to initiative. In class system the class division is not rigid and it is apt to change with the changing times. In the new mobile capitalistic society wealth has taken on a more determinative role. In modern societies there is a fairly close relation between economic and social status. The traditional class demarcations have been blurred and a new social structure has taken birth. In it the workers and the capitalist alike strive to keep up with the Jonesses. Wealth has now penetrated all social divisions and has provided a universal and significant basis for social stratification. Those classes have been demarcated as-upper class, a middle class and a lower class. In the present time it is the criterion of wealth, which is more in use than the criterion of birth. It is true to the spirit of secular society and free enterprises sometimes occupation also play a vital role in the making of social classes.

The term Class-Consciouness. Some kind or degree of class-consciousness is almost universal in society class-consciousness is "the sentiment that characterizes the relations of men toward the members of their own and other classes. It consists in the realization of a similarity of attitude and behaviour with members of other classes. According to Mannheim, "Class-consciousness is the awareness of the similarity of social chances, the arising of a notion about similarity of interests, the growth of an emotional tie connected with this similarity of experiences and of a common striving towards a common social goal. Class-consciousness is the means by which the spiritual integration of persons possessing a similarity of social position and of life chances is transformed into a common group activity. Workers are said to possess class-consciousness when they feel that their interests as workers are common and since the interests are common they must exhibit class solidarity among themselves and common attitudes towards their enemy class—the capitalists. Karl Marx laid great emphasis on class-consciousness among the working classes. It was his endeavor to accentuate in the working classes the consciousness of their corporate capacity. Hence, his exhortation in the Communist Manifesto, "Workers of the world unite." But class-consciousness alone does not bring ab0ut an acting class; it is only the soil for an easier growth of similar activities, a favourable soil for the development of social movements. There must arise a certain organ of the class, which may transform this consciousness into activity. The most important organ is the political party. This is why Lenin added the idea of a party in Marxism to prepare the workers for revolution.

Conditions of Consciousness. It is agreed on all hands that there are some conditions which tend to make members of a class conscious of their membership. Ginsberg has mentioned three conditions, which are helpful in generating class-consciousness. *Firstly,* it is the case and amount of social mobility. If movement up and down is easy and rapid, differences in mode of life disappear; if it is impossible the attitudes of member of different classes to each other becomes habitual and *Quasi* automatic; if it is possible but not easy, the consciousness of differences is heightened. The second condition of class consciousness is rivalry and conflict. When the members of a class possess common interests, this possession is brought in consciousness by the need of defence against the common enemy. *For example,* workers possessing common interests have class-consciousness because they have to defend themselves against a common enemy, the capitalists. Their class is associational in character. The third factor is the growth of a common tradition embodying common standards of value and common traditions and they have common experiences. When the members come to possess common traditions and they have common experiences, it leads to the rise of class-consciousness among them. The existence of race prejudices and caste barriers serves as a powerful factor in the promotion of class-consciousness in the society. Absence of social mobility and the continuance of class struggle are some other factors helpful in the growth of class-consciousness, Caste-system and racial groups are regarded as the extreme examples of class-consciousness. The present day industrial society has given further impetus to the sentiment of class consciousness and the constant conflict between the capitalist and working classes bears ample testimony to its lasting nature.

Corporate Class Consciousness Vs. Competitive Class Feeling. Maciver draws a distinction between corporate class-consciousness and competitive class feeling. "Corporate class consciousness is a sentiment uniting a whole group sharing a similar social status. The working class exhibits most clearly corporate class-consciousness which has developed under the spur of strong economic incentives and gained more strength in the struggle to maintain or destroy the pre-determined status" Karl Marx laid great emphasis upon the need of corporate class consciousness among the working class. His aim was to develop solidarity and organization of the whole class of proletariat—the property less wage-earners.

But, on the other hand, competitive class feeling is characteristic of the competitive system that developed in modern society. It is a personal form of class sentiment that often determines the conduct of individuals toward one another without involving on their part any express recognition of whole groups to which they respectively belong. When Mr. A. blackballs, Mr. B. from membership in his club it does not mean that he thereby necessarily uphold the standards or the interest of a whole class or when Mr. A. patronizes Mr. B. nor does it mean that he necessarily feels solidarity with a whole order of superiors of Mr. B. In such cases the conduct of A. is specific, personalized, an expression of competitive class feeling.

Social Implications of Class Sentiment. Class consciousness tends to be stronger or weaker according to the degree in which the element of caste is present. When social conditions and customs fix rigidly a man's status in life, he identifies himself with the fellows living under the same conditions. In a caste-ridden society, *for example*, Indian society the class sentiment is stronger as it is among to Harijans. So when the mores of an authoritative religion hold sway, the members of the group lowly and reverently order themselves to all their superiors. But if the mores break, there comes a great social change. The members of the low class rise up higher in the social scale according to their individual efforts and enterprise. If the belief prevails that status is not rigidly determined and that higher status can be individually acquired, the class solidarity tends to be broken and the class-consciousness weakened. In this connection Maciver has aptly observed in these words, "Class sentiment takes a different range as well as quality according to the degree in which the element of caste is present. When a man's lot in life is fixed by anterior social conditions he more readily identifies himself with the whole group of his fellows subject to the same conditions. If the mores of an authoritative religion hold sway, so that the members of the group accept; in the language of the English Book of Common Prayer the duty to order themselves lowly and reverently to all their betters then the class-consciousness of the subject class is a conservative influence. If the old mores break, as they do in the process of industrialization and urbanization, this class consciousness becomes a powerful engine of social change." In either event the solidarity of class-consciousness depends on the sense of a sharp cleavage and on the recognition of an un-surmountable barrier under existing conditions.

SOCIAL MOBILITY

Social stratification is a characteristic of all societies. In a stratified society classes and individuals are rated high or low on the basis of characteristics possessed by them according to the social value-scale. Any change in the value scale or any change in the characteristics results in a change in the status of different degrees of esteem in different socities or within the same society at different times. The members of the priestly class were at one time rated higher than the members of the other classes in India. But today it is not so. A doctor or engineer enjoys greater prestige than a priest. In the same way if a person becomes a minister from an ordinary businessman his status is enhanced. But on the other hand, when a minister loses his post and comes back to his old business, he also comes to lose his high status and position. Thus, it is clear that people in society continue to move up and down the status scale. This movement is called social mobility. Mobility is to distinguished from migration which is movement in the geographical speed.

Inevitability of Social Mobility. The critics, in general, agree on the point that an absolute class system or caste-system is an impossibility social change is a natural phenomenon and the movement there is social change, there is also social mobility. Probably no society absolutely forbids social mobility and, no society is immobile. There is always the difference of degree with regard to the operation of the element of social mobility in different societies. For instance a class-ridden society is more mobile than a caste-ridden society. But it cannot be taken to mean that a caste-ridden society is absolutely immobile. In the present day democratic society the rate of social mobility has grown faster than was the case in earlier times.

Factors Helpful in the Process of Social Mobility. Now having made sure that some degree of social mobility is inevitable in every society, it remains to be known as to what factors prove more helpful in this process. Among the factors that make some amount of mobility inevitable in any society, Henry M. Johnson lists the following ones as important:

(i) Social prestige ultimately depends upon the accepted value system. If certain qualities or achievements are socially valued some people will strive for them.

(ii) At varying rates of speed, changes are always occurring in the demand for different kinds of skill.

(iii) The birth-rate of each class never exactly fills all the positions in the class.

(iv) Birth in upper classes sometimes fosters complacency in many persons.

(v) There is no constant tendency for intelligence and other kinds of native capacity to be confined to upper classes. It has not been uncommon for the sons of farmers and labourers to rise to the highest position in society.

Thus, we may infer that despite the hindering factors of inequality of opportunity in society a great deal of mobility occurs in every society.

On this issue Ogburn and Nimkoff have observed in these words," One of the two big questions about social stratification is the amount of social inequality existing in society. The other big question is the degree of opportunity. Opportunity means chance for changing and improving one's social status. Opportunity is related to social mobility or change its social status, although mobility may be downward as well as upward. Moreover, mobility does not necessaily lessen inequality. This is a point of some importance, since it is commonly and erroneously assumed in our democracy that if we give equal opportunity to everybody, social differences will be lessened. We sometimes see great differences in social achievements and social status among members of the same family because of differences in talents or luck, where the members of the family initially shared the same status and had comparable opportunities."

Need for Social Mobility

If the organization and working of a social order is kept in view it becomes clear that no social order can remain static. There are some elements in every society which emphasize the need for social mobility and which more or less make it an unavoidable process.

Firstly, social mobility is in accordance with the law of nature. It is the law of Nature that some castes expand in population while others contract. For those that expand, some new occupation must be found while for those who contract, replacements from other castes must be had. Thus, differences in population increase or decrease of various castes make social immobility impossible.

Secondly, geographical adaptations require social adaptations. There is a constant change in the physical setting of a society. As population grows, forests are depleted and fields eroded to provide more housing accommodation. New calamities and diseases appear. New economic and political developments take place. Naturally the social system must adjust itself to the changing physical conditions and such adjustment inevitably entails a certain amount of social mobility.

Lastely, every society allows some scope for personal ambition. Had it not be so, there would have been no progress every system there are different awards for different achievements and man makes an effort for that kind of achievement that is most rewarded. The belief that individuals can get ahead legitimately by their own effort is a basis for social progress. The social scale is related to and based on a scale of values. Any group that improves its standards, will also improve its social, status and inevitably some groups will strive to improve themselves. Thus, the very system of different values for different characteristics itself induce people to move up the scale of social status.

Amount of Mobility

It may be noted that mobility may be downward or upward. Downward mobility is permitted in every society. If a member of an upper class fails to live up to the class standards expected of him in his class. He will fall below the class status. In India a person may be excluded from his caste by marrying some one of another caste, especially a lower one. As regards upward mobility society absolutely forbids it but the amount and caste of upward mobility will depend upon certain factors. Among these the following ones may be noted:

1. Impact of Social Change. In general, the principal condition that favours or prevents mobility is the rate of social change. Conditions of rapid social change such as the Industrial Revolution or territorial expansion make for social mobility, while a period of very little technological or territorial change provides little opportunity for the individual to rise out of the status, which is ascribed to him. It may be noted that political, economic, religious or other revolutions may produce rapid social mobility so as to reduce the upper classes to the bottom of social scale and to elevate to the top classes formerly at the bottom.

2. Communication. Any system that limits communication between classes and restricts knowledge of the conditions of life to one's own class will also tend to discourage social mobility. Conversely a system through which members of all classes become familiar with the conditions of life in other classes facilitates mobility. Of course, the extent of mobility will be determined by the opportunities and needs that exist in different classes and the traditions against admitting members of another class.

3. Division of Labour. Finally, the amount of social mobility is influenced by the degree of division of labour that exists in a society. If the division of labour is very highly developed and if the degree of specialization and skilled training is very high it is correspondingly difficult for a person from one class to pass readily into other classes. Similarly, the sharply defined castes that have been assigned certain traditional functions, may retard social mobility despite the fact that other conditions are favourable for social movement.

***

13

Social Caste and Class-system

Caste-system is peculiarly an Indian institution. It is regarded as the steel-frame of Hindu society. The critics even go to the extent of describing Hinduism and caste-system as synonymous terms. There is no doubt that caste-system is prevalent in certain other countries also, but nevertheless India has been its strong-hold. It is in view of this fact that Maciver and Page say, "By far the most significant example of a caste-system is the one incorporated in Hindu society, Every Hindu necessarily belong to the came of his parents and in that caste he inevitably remains." The Indian society is a caste-ridden society because it is under great influence of religion and traditions. These two elements make a society, orthodox in outlook: And rigid in dealings. The caste-system although born of any factor or reason is now sustained by these two elements. This is why in the present day world when religion and traditions are losing their ground in India, the hold of caste-system is also on decline in due proportion.

Various definitions have been given of the word 'caste'.

The opinion of Lundberg is, "A caste is merely a rigid social class into which members are born and from which they can withdraw or escape only with extreme difficulty."

According to E. Blunt, "A caste is an endogamous group, or collection of endogamous groups bearing a common name, membership of which is hereditary; imposing on its members certain restrictions in the matter of social intercourse either following a common traditional occupation or claiming a common origin and generally regarded as forming a single homogeneous community."

Similarly Maciver opines, "When status is wholly predetermined, so that men are born to their lot without any hope of changing it then class takes the extreme form of caste".

C. H. Cooley says, "When a class is somewhat strictly hereditary, we may call it a caste".

In this connection S.V. Ketkar is of the opinion that a caste is a group having two characteristics in which membership is confined to those who are forbidden by an inexorable social law to marry outside the group.

In this way critics have differently defined the term caste. But as Ghurye states, "With all the labours of these students, however we, do not possess a real general definition of caste." The best way to understand the term caste is to examine the various factors underlying the caste-system. According to Megasthenese, "The two chief elements of caste-system are *(i)* there is no intermarriage and *(ii)* there can be no change of profession." But the best explanation of caste-system is given by A.W. Green in these words. "Caste is a system of stratification in which mobility movement up and down the status ladder at least ideally may not occur. A person's ascribed status is lifetime status. Birth determines one's occupation, place of residence, style of life, personal associates and the group from among whom one must find a mate. The caste-system is also protected by law and sanctified by religion." Thus, in short, caste may be defined as an endogamous group or collection of such groups bearing a common name, having the same traditional occupation, claiming descent from the same source and commonly regarded as forming single homogeneous community.

Main Features of Caste-System

The foregoing definitions of caste-system reveal that it is a distinct and rigid way of social life. It is marked by a number of characteristic features which are not found in any other social institution. The modern thinkers take note of these features in order to explain the meaning and nature of this social institution. *For example,* N. K. Dutt mentions these main features of caste-system which give it a distinctive status:

1. Members of a caste cannot wed outside their own caste.
2. For many castes the occupations are fixed.
3. There are similar but less strict laws governing the partaking of food with members of other groups.
4. Birth determines the caste of the individual for his entire life, so long as be is not extradited from it for violating its laws. There is no other possible way of transferring from one caste to another.
5. There are some accepted stratifications among the castes in which the brahmins have been accorded the best place at the top.
6. All occupations are based on the respect of the brahmins.

In view of all these features R.N. Mukerjee has beautifully remarked, "Based primarily on birth, caste is that dynamic system of social heirarchy and segmental division which enforces on its members more or less rigid restrictions in regard to eating and drinking, marriage, occupation and social intercourses."

Davis has also tried to enlist those common features and tendencies of the Indian caste-system, which distinguish it from other types of groups. He draws particular attention to these features of the Indian caste-system.

1. Membership in the caste is hereditary. The child at birth takes the rank of his parents.
2. Choice of marriage partners is strictly endogamous, for it must take place within the caste group.

3. This inherited membership is fixed for life because, except in the sense of being outcasted the individual cannot alter his caste by any effort of his own. He cannot change his status by good works, marriage, dissimulation or any other strategem.
4. Consciousness of caste membership is further emphasized by the caste name, by the individual's identification with his caste in the eyes of the community by his conformity to the peculiar customs of his caste.
5. The caste may be and in the past generally was united by a common traditional occupation, although it may be united in addition or instead by the brief in a common tribal or racial origin by adherence to a common religious sect, or by some other common peculiarity.
6. Contact with other groups is further limited by restrictions on touching, associating with dining with or eating food cooked by outsiders.
7. The relative prestige of the different castes in any locality is well established and jealously guarded.

Besides, these features there are some other features of the caste-system also. In fact the concept of the caste-system has been constantly undergoing changes and at different times its elements are also found changing. However, taking an overall view of the whole issue the following main features of the caste-system can be discussed in some what details:

1. Based on Birth. The society is divided into various castes with a well developed life of their own. The membership of different castes is determined by the consideration of birth. The status of a person does not depend on his wealth but on the traditional importance of the caste in which he had the fortune of being born. No amount of wealth and no amount of penance of prayer can change his caste status. Status is determined not by vocation but by birth. It is hereditary in nature and for this reason the caste status is ascribed status.

2. Social Hierarchy. A very important feature of caste-system is that it has got a definite scheme of social precedence. The whole society is divided into distinct classes with a concept of high and low. *For example,* Brahmins in India stand at the apex of the social ladder. In contrast to the high position enjoyed by Brahmins the Sudras are subjected to manifold disabilities and they are held to be the lowest in social status. Servitude is proclaimed to be a permanent condition of Sudras.

3. Endogamous in Nature. A very important element of caste-system is its endogamous nature. A person born in a caste remains in it for life and dies in it. Every caste is sub-divided in sub-castes, every one of which forbids its members to marry persons outside it. Thus, each sub-caste is endogamous. This principle of endogamy is so strict that one sociologist regards endogamy as the 'essence of the caste-system'.

4. Permanence of Caste Membership. Since the membership of caste is determined by birth. It is more or less permanent. A person remains the member of the caste into which he is born and his membership does not undergo any change even if changes in his status, occupation, education, wealth etc; take place. Referring to this fact Maciver and Page write thus, "Every Hindu necessarily belong to the caste of his parents and in that caste he inevitably remains. No accumulation of wealth and no exercise of talents can alter his caste status and marriage outside his caste is prohibited or severely discouraged. Although, there are some exceptions to the fixity of this order based on hereditary and exogamy und although whole castes sometimes shift position in the social structure, caste remains an almost complete barrier to individual mobility, except within the caste itself in principle there is an absolute and permanent stratification of the community".

4. Restriction on Food and Social Intercourse. Another element of caste is the complex of taboos by which the superior castes try to preserve their ceremonial purity. Thus, there are restrictions on feeding and social intercourse and minute rules are laid down with regard to the kind of food that can be acceptable by a person and from what castes. *For example,* Brahmin will accept 'Pakka food' *i.e.,* food prepared in ghee from any community, but he can accept 'kachcha food' at the hands of no other caste. The theory of pollution being communicated by some castes to members of the higher ones place severe restrictions on the extent of social intercourse.

6. Low Caste People Subjected to Disabilities. It is also a marked features of the caste-system society that in it the people of low castes are subjected to a good deal of social and religious disabilities. They are not treated at par with high caste people. The condition of untouchables in India stands a clear proof of this fact. Generally the impure castes are made to live on the outskrits of the city. In Southern India certain parts of the town or village are inaccessible to certain castes. All over India the impure castes were not permitted to draw water from wells used by the members of other castes. The public school did not admit the children of Sudras. The Sudras could not study the sacred literature and they could not even go to temples. It is only after independence that their condition has improved a bit as a result of the hard efforts of the Government on this issue. Maciver and Page write, "In India with the multitudlinous caste compartments in the Hindu system, the higher caste groups—at the top the Brahmin and next in order the Kshdtriya and Vaisya—are thought of as beings of different clay from the low caste group of the Sudras while still further beyond these are the "out caste" or "untouchables," whose very presence has been traditionally considered a defilement to the rest, who are still thought to pollute food and water by their touch and who in some regions are not permitted to approach the neighbourhood of the high caste-system and reveals most clearly how caste prevents common participation of the various groups in the communal life. While some of the more strict barriers have been relaxed in recent years in India, particularly the rules governing the former untouchables, the stratification system is so strongly imbedded in Indian life that only tremendous upheavals or the long processes of deep working technological and cultural change can greatly alter it." Thus, these are all the important features of caste-system. It is by the existence of many of them that the caste-system acquires the character of a distinct social institution.

7. Fixity of Occupation. Members of a particular caste are expected to follow the caste occupation. They cannot change to other occupation. The abandonment of hereditary occupation is not thought to be right. No caste would allow its members to take any occupation, which in its opinion was either degrading or impure. It was not only the moral restraint on the choice of one's caste-fellows that acted as a restraint on the choice of one's occupation, but also the restriction put by other castes where members did not allow members of the castes other than their own to follow their occupation. Thus, no one not born a Brahmin was allowed to function as a priest. According to Manu, "The functions of the Brahmin, Kshatriya, Vaishya and the Shudras were definite. The function of the Brahmin is to study, teach, to guide and perform religious rituals, give and receive aims; that of Kshatriya is to perform religious rituals, give alms, punish the evil and go to war; that of Vaishya is to study, perform religious ritual, give alms, work in agriculture, trade and animal husbandry; that of the Shudra is to do menial work for all the other Varnas. Having developed from Varna system the occupations in caste-system are definite. In Hindu society even today in most cases people adopt hereditary occupations. "

Origin of Caste-System in India

Caste-system is one of the deep-rooted and traditional social institution of human society. It has remained in force in some form or the other since the ancient times. The critics have tried to describe it in their own ways. According to Dr. V. A. Smith, "A caste may be defined as a group of families infernally united by peculiar rules for the observance of ceremonial purify, especially in the matter of diet and marriage." In the words of Sham Shastri, Caste means a social exclusiveness with reference to diet and marriage. Birth and rituals are secondary". When these definitions of caste-system are kept in view in the context of Indian social life, it becomes evident that caste-system is typically an Indian social institution. However, there is a difference of opinion among scholars with regard to the origin of the caste-system although it is admitted on all hands that it is a very ancient institution. According to Prof. Rapson, "The origin of caste-system is due to the distinction between white and dark complexion of the Aryans and the original residents." Originally, society was divided in two parts, the Aryans and the non-Aryans. According to Dr. Smith most of the misunderstanding on the subject of caste-system has arisen from the persistent mistranslation of Manu's term "varna" as caste, whereas it should be rendered class or order or by some equivalent term. The compiler of the institution of Manu was aware of the distinction between Varna and Jati. While he mentions about 50 castes, he refers only to four varnas."

Various theories have been propounded to explain the origin of caste-system and some of them may be discussed here.

1. Racial Theory. The racial theory is one of the oldest theories dealing with the issue of origin of caste-system. According to this theory castes are the product of racial differences of the people. Dr. Majumdar and Dr. Risely have been the powerful advocates of this theory. Even in the Rig-Vedic literature great support has been voiced for this theory. The caste-system took its birth after the arrival of Aryans in India. In order to maintain their separate existence the Indo-Aryans used for certain groups and orders of people the favourite word 'varna', colour. Thus, they spoke of the 'Dasavarna' not only in their colour but also in their speech, religious practices and physical features. While supporting this theory Dr. Gokhle writes, "The Indian terms used to describe the caste-system are varna and jati, complexion and birth. The former refers to racial difference and the latter means birth and descent." It was to mark off the racial difference between the Aryans and non-Aryans that the terms 'Arya-varna' and 'Das-varna' first came into use and they are used as such in the Rig Veda. When the Aryans came to India as invaders with radical differences in complexion, religion, customs and manners between them and the non-Aryan inhabitants, there came about the first broad grouping in the Aryan society.

2. Political Theory. According to this theory, caste-system is a clever device invented by the Brahmans in order to place themselves on the highest ladder of social hierarchy. This is why Dr. G Hurye states, "Caste is a Brahmanic child of Indo-Aryan culture cradled in the land of the Ganges and then transferred to other parts of India by Brahmin prospectors." The Brahmanic literature of the post-Vedic period mentions certain mixed classes and also a group of out-caste classes. Among the four varnas the old distinction of Arya and Sudra now appears as 'Dvija' and Sudra. The first three classes are called Dvijas because they have to go through the initiation ceremony, which is symbolic of rebirth. The Sudra was called 'ekajati'. The pre-eminence of the Brahman had secured him many social privileges sanctioned by the law-givers. The statement that God created the Sudra to be the slave of all is repeated and he is given the name of 'Padaja'.

3. Occupational Theory. Occupational theory is another important theory seeking the origin of caste-system. Among its exponents the name of Nesfield is pre-eminent. According to this theory, the origin of caste-system can be found in the nature and quality of social work performed by the various groups of people. Those professions, which were regarded as better and respectable made the persons who performed them superior to those who were engaged in dirty professions.

According to Nesfield, "Function and function alone is responsible for the origin of caste structure in India." With functional differentiation there came in occupational differentiation and numerous sub-castes. Thus, whatever be the root cause of the origin of caste-system in India but it is certain that occupational division has added to the number of castes and sub-castes.

4. Traditional Theory. According to this theory the caste-system is of divine origin. There comes in some references in the Vedic literature wherein it is said that castes were created by the Brahma—the supreme creator, so that human beings may harmoniously perform the various social functions essential for the maintenance of society. According to Dr. Majumdar, "If, however, we take the divine origin of the 'vamas' as an allegorical explanation of the functional division of society the theory assumes practical significance."

5. Evolutionary Theory. According to this theory, the caste-system did not come into origin all of a sudden or at a particular date. It is the result of a long process of social evolution. A number of factors played their part in the development of the present caste-system. Among these factors mention may be made of the following ones to understand this process fully :

(i) Hereditary occupations.

(ii) The unwillingness of rulers to enforce a uniform standard of law and custom and their readiness to recognize the varying customs of different groups as vaild.

(iii) The desire of the Brahmans to keep themselves pure.

(iv) Beliefs in re-incarnation and the doctrine of karma.

(v) Ideas of exclusive family, ancestor, worship and the sacramental meal.

(vi) The lack of rigid unitary control of the State.

(vii) Clash of races, colour, prejudices and conquest.

(viii) Clash of antagonistic cultures particularly of the patriarchal and the matriarchal systems.

(ix) Geographical isolation of the Indian Peninsula.

(x) Deliberate and economic and administrative policies followed by the various conquerors particularly by the British.

All these factors conspired to encourage the formation of small groups based on petty distinctions from time-to-time. Multiplicity of the groups and the thoroughness of the system are also due to the habit of the Hindu mind to create categories and to carry things to their logical end, a characteristic manifest in our literature, philosophy and religious creeds. It may, however, be noted that caste-system is not a monopoly of India. It existed and still exists in many parts of the world. The feudal system of medieval Europe was a species of caste-system. Certain ethnic groups such as Jews and Negroes are still treated as castes in many civilized countries including the United States.

Conditions Favouring Growth of Castes-System in India

It may not be possible to tell as to what was the exact factor, which accounted for the origin of caste-system in India. But it is certainly possible to tell the factors making India a strong-hold of caste-system. There is no doubt that in some other countries also caste-system exists, but in none of them it is found in as much completeness and force as in India. This is why like joint family system and rural community the caste-system is also regarded as a typically Indian institution. There are several factors, which have helped in strengthening the hold of caste-system in India and some of them may briefly be discussed here.

1. Geographical Isolation. The caste-system has flourished in India because of its geographical isolation in the ancient times. Orthodox institutions like caste-system grow fast in static and rigid societies. For this reason, the geographical isolation of India has a large part to play in rendering its society static and powerless. The absence of adequate means of transport have led to the geographical isolation, from other, of people who inhabit in distantly situated areas in this country. This fosters old customs, mores, traditions and superstitions all of which encourage the caste-system. India has remained a caste-ridden country because of its being a tradition-loving and custom-ridden land.

2. Rural Social Structure. The rural social structure is usually unchanging and static. Ancient traditions are better respected in it. As the rural structure weakens or in other words as urbanisation in the country increases, the caste also becomes progressively weaker. India has remained largely a country with rural population and in such a case it was quite natural for caste-system to make in this country much headway.

3. Static Society. Hindu society is a static society. There has never been any stupendous variation in its political situations and economic conditions. Its social mores customs and traditions have failed to change over the age, as times have marched along. But this does not mean that Hindu society does not change at all. To say that it is static or motionless is only to indicate the extremely slow rate at which variations and modifications are instituted in it. Generally speaking the caste-system was most acceptable in India in those days when the dynamic element was at allow ebb in the society.

4. Influence of Religion. The influence of religion is the most important factor contributing to the continuation of the caste-system. The Hindu caste-system is looked upon as a divine institution. People who violate it are considered sinners and it is believed that God will punish them. Due to this reason people do not have the courage to violate the laws of the caste-system.

5. Difference of Races. The existence of many races in the country leads to formulation of many strict laws concerning discrimination since each race endeavoured to maintain its purity. In the medieval period of Indian History stringent laws concerning caste were laid down to protect Hindu society from the Muslims.

6. Lack of Education. Lack of education occupies an important position among the factors, which have encouraged the existence of caste-system in Hindu society. An uneducated society is static and motionless. Superstitions, traditions and mores breed freely among uneducated people. In this way lack of education is a condition, which particularly favours the caste-system.

It is clear from the foregoing facts that the Indian caste-system is a complex social institution. Like all other institutions it is the product of evolution and not of creation. It is a growth rather than a make and in this process emphasis can be laid on a single factor. Thus, as Hutton remarks, "It is urged emphatically that the Indian caste-system is the natural result of the interaction of a number of geographical, social, political, religious and economic factors not elsewhere found in conjunction." It may also be mentioned here that the caste-system in India is confined to not only Hindus, but it also extends to the non-Hindu sections of the people. It seems that this institution is imbedded in the very soil of India. To quote Prof. Davis on this issue "Caste is extremely widespread and pervasive in India. It is present in all regions and affects nearly every person regardless of his religion". In the words of D. N. Majumdar, "The complex nature of the cast structure is evident from the fact that after a century of painstaking and meticulous research in the history and function of the social system, we do not possess yet a valid explanation of the circumstances that might have contributed to the formation and development of this unique system." But whatever the case may be now the time has come when the primacy of caste-system has been exposed to new perils and in times to come it may loosen the firm ground, which it has so far held in this country.

DISINTEGRATION OF CASTE-SYSTEM

India has been the earliest home of caste-systam. Not only this it is even the strong-hold of castes and one cannot think of Indian society without having the idea of caste-system. It is an all pervasive and universal social institution of Indian society that has held the sway on the life, habits and ways of the people since the ancient times. In order to emphasis the same fact Davis has remarked, "Caste is or was until recently, almost universal in India. The Hindus who are not members of some particular caste are few. Some reform groups such as Brahma Samaj and the Arya Samaj have professed to repudiate caste, but these have only tiny followings." It shows that people are very rigid about their caste affiliations. They follow the caste rules with regard to their food, occupation and social intercourse. But in the present time these caste barriers are fast whithering away. Now inter-caste marriages have become quite frequent and even in the choice of professions people do not pay much attention to the restrictions imposed by caste considerations. The fact is that the caste-ridden society of the by-gone ages is giving place to the casteless society of the times ahead. There are several factors, which have accounted for the disintegration of caste-system and the most important of these may be mentioned here:

1. Work of Socio-Religious Reform Movements. In the 19th and early 20th century there started in India some socio-relious reform movements. They also helped a lot in telling upon the strong hold of caste-system. Mention in this connection may be made of the work done by Brahmo Samaj and Samaj. The ideal of Brahmo Samaj was to establish a brotherhood wherein man shall not be divided from man on account of caste. Swami Dayanand preached for the substitution of four-fold division of Hindu society in place of the present manifold ramifications and started an association 'Arya Samaj' for reviving the ancient purity of the Vedic society. The chief centre of Arya Samaj was in Punjab. Mahatma Gandhi the Father of the Nation made the problem of the removal of untouchability a national one. His name will always be remembered in history of its abolition. Thus, the social reformers like Raja Ram Mohan Roy, Rabindra Nath

Tagore and Swami Dayanand in the 19th century and Mahatma Gandhi, in the present century played a vital role in hitting hard at the base of caste-system.

2. Impact of Western Education. The first important factor nibbing at the root of the caste-system was the spread of western education. The British brought with them to India a casteless culture and a literature full of thoughts on individual liberty. The Indians who studied this literature could not but be impressed with the progressive ideas of English writers. The educated Indians became liberal in outlook and they came to despise the orthodox and illogical ways of society. They realised the futility of caste-system, which created unnatural social inequalities among the people. They began to value the dignity of man and laid stress on the brotherhood of mankind. All these things went against the sanctity of caste-system and it began to lose its ground. As the number of educated people increased the popular faith in caste-system began to slacken in some proportion. In place of social inequality religious disabilities and caste restrictions, the principles of liberty, equality and fraternity came in the lime-light. Thus, the ground was prepared where the castless society of the western type could take the place of caste-ridden society of India. It also prepared the ground for other factors to flourish and to weaken the hold of caste-system.

3. Impact of Industrialization. The Industrial Revolution in India has also gone a long way in disintegrating the caste-system. Caste-system in India to a very large extent related to village industries and handicrafts. The decay of village handcrafts and hereditary occupations, which is the inevitable result of industrialization, affects the social structure in a number of ways. The old occupations having disappeared new occupations have appeared wherein the Brahman and the Sudra freely meet and mix. There is much more freedom of choice of occupation today than under the old regime. At present many members of the Brahman caste are seen engaged in almost any of the occupations, which were previously thought to be the occupations of other castes. Many members of the various artisan castes are shopkeepers, bank clerks and teachers. Whatever restrictions caste imposed on the choice of occupation have now ceased to exist and guide the individuals. Thus, in all these ways the growth of industrialization, has helped in loosening the caste-barriers in the Indian society.

4. Effect of the Developed Means of Communication. Means of communication developed along with the progress of industnalisation. This put an end to geographical isolation of the people of various castes. The thoughts and customs of various places have started influencing each other. It became difficult to maintain the rigidity of caste in the whirlwind of communication set into motion by industrialisation. Referring to this fact Risley says, "On a platform where the train halts momentarily one does not enquire the caste of the seller when purchasing something from him."

5. Importance of Social Classes. New classes are appearing in the society and this fact has also gone against the existence of caste-system. These social classes are replacing the caste. The organization of castes was vertical that of classes is horizontal. As the class-consciousness is increasing caste-consciousness is decreasing.

6. Effect or Urbanization. In the present century the hold on caste-system has suffered a great setback because of one more factor and this factor is the growth of urbanisation in India. Industrialization leads to urbanisation of population. The village people who are much caste-ridden flock to the city. In the city the people are forced to put aside their orthodox ideas and have to eat articles of food prepared by non-caste fellows. Economic necessity drives people to seek employment in fields other than that of their age-old caste profession. In towns people of all castes and creeds work side by side in factories, offices and shops. Whether in the school or on the university campus there are students belonging to all castes and creeds. Trade unions and political parties are cutting across caste. There is no place for caste distinctions in urbanized society.

7. Increase in the Importance of Wealth. In the modern age, wealth is replacing caste as the basis of social prestige. Now-a-days a person adopts that occupation which appears to him to be the most profitable. The consideration in the choice of a profession is no longer caste but individual capability and the facility in earning wealth. A wealthy Shudra is more respected than a poor Brahmin. For this reason, the ties of the caste are being loosened in the frantic race after wealth.

8. Change in the General Social Institutions. There has been occurring a general change in the social institutions. In this wave the caste-system has not remained unaffected. There has occurred changes in some of those institutions which have been working as the pillars of caste-system. Caste distinctions must go if democratic values have to gain ground. The joint family one of the main props of caste-system is disintegrating. Some of the other things connected with caste the purda system, child marriage and monopoly of the Brahmin to officiate in religious cere nonies are gradually disappearing. Thus, under this over all pressure of transformation of society caste-system could not remain static. Caste-system being based on orthodox elements pre-supposes a static society. But the modern society is a dynamic society where the rate of change is very fast to make room for democratic values. The caste-system being all institution of bygone age cannot fit in with the modern democratic set-up and so it must undergo a change.

9. Work of Legislation. During the British rule several legislations were passed from time to time to reform the Indian society. These legislations along with the activities of Reform Movements attacked the caste-system and sought to weaken its influence. The British rulers wanted to impose their own culture on India and in doing so they indirectly came into conflict with the institution of caste-system. By the establishment of British courts and administering a uniform criminal law, they removed from the hands of the caste Panchayats many matters that used to be erstwhile adjudicated by them. After it the British administrators tackled civil matters. In 1856 the Widow Remarriage Act was passed which contained clauses practically violating the customs of the lower castes. In 1876 the High Court of Bombay ruled that Courts of law will not recognize the authority of a caste to declare a marriage void or to give permission to a woman to remarry. Later on, it was ruled by the various High Courts that the people could engage any priest they liked and were not at all bound to call for the services of the hereditary priest. It led to the abolishing of the only bond of holding together the various castes *i.e.,* the employment of common priesthood. The caste Disabilities Removal Act of 1850 gave another blow to the caste integrity. The Act facilitated conversion to another religion or admission into another caste without affecting the property rights of the person. Then the Special Marriage Act was passed in 1872, which made it possible for an Indian of whatever caste or creed to enter into a valid marriage with a person belonging to any caste or creed provided the parties registered the contract of marriage declaring interalea that they did not belong to any religion. This clause was repealed by the Amending Act of 1923 which applies only to Hindus including Jains, Sikhs and Brahamos. The British Government took a further step for removing some of the civil disabilities of the untouchables. They recognised the rights of the untouchables to be properly educated and to be given all social, economic and political benefits. Government scholarships and concessions in fees were awarded to the students of the depressed classes.

10. Attack by Indian Constitution. The most systematic and severe attack on the caste, system has been recently made by the Constitution of India. It is mentioned in its preamble that the people of India have constituted themselves into a sovereign Democratic Republic. The aim is to secure to all its citizens justice, social, economic and political, liberty of thought, expression, belief, faith and worship; equality of status and opportunity and to promote among them all fraternity assuring the dignity of the individual. Equality, thus, guaranteed is not only of opportunity but also of status. Definite measures have been put in the Constitution to eradicate the evil of caste-system from Indian soil in this connection both positive and negative means have been adopted in the constitutional framework of free India. It is stated in the Article is of the Constitution that the State shall not discriminate against any citizen on grounds only of religion, race, caste, sex, place of birth or any of them. No citizen shall, on grounds only of religion race, caste, sex, place of birth or any of them be subject to any disability, liability, restriction or condition with regard to the enjoyment of general facilities and amenties of life. Articles 16 guarantees equality of opportunity to all citizens in matters relating to employment or appointment to any office under the State irrespective of religion, race, caste, sex, descent, place of birth, residence or any of them. Article 17 has abolished untouchability and its practice in any form is thereby forbidden. The right of freedom under Article, 19 guarantees among other things, the freedom of any lawful calling without restriction. The Constitution may thus, be said to have abolished caste and its lingering coercive practices. It is a solemn promise that the legislature will do every thing possible to create a society in which inequality of status does not exist.

It is clear from the foregoing facts that in India caste-system is on the decline under the pressure of these measures. But it has not vanished completely nor is it possible that it will lose its ground in India altogether. The only change that has occurred in it in the recent years is that its shackles have been loosened a great deal. Formerly the inter-caste marriages could not be even thought of, whereas now they have become possible. Even in the fields of social intercourse the people are not as rigid as before.

EFFECT OF CASTE-SYSTEM ON INDIAN LIFE

Caste-system has been one of the pillars of Indian society. It is among the oldest and the traditional social institutions. For good or for evil caste has played a very important role as a primary group of Hindu society. In fact caste and Joint family have been the most basic institutions of the Hindus through the ages. But on the whole it has proved to be a mixed blessings for India. According to R.P. Masani, "Class-consciousness is good but when it kills national consciousness, it becomes a serious drawback. Caste loyality is a virtue but when it degenerates into passive disloyality to the State, it is a passive crime. Caste restrictions on actions likely to undermine the foundations of the social, structure are wholesome but when such restrictions lead to disabling inequalities and denial of social justice, as in the case of the untouchables now mercifully called Harijans, they are a curse." In the words of A. R. Desai, "It is the caste that rigidly determines the place of its member in the religious life of the people."

In view of these observations we can examine the effects of caste-system on Indian society in the following way.

Good Effects or Merits of Caste-system

It is customary to attack caste-system vehemently and to aspire for its abolition root and branch. But despite all this it has survived through ages. The very fact that it continues in spite of these attacks as before goes to prove that the system is not so bad a, it is thought to be. It is definitely endowed with some virtues and it has left a good deal of wholesome effect on Indian society. To quote J.S. Furnivall, "The caste-system has afforded a place in society into which any community, be it racial, social, occupational or religious can be fitted as a co-operating part of the social whole, while retaining its own distinctive character and its separate individual life." In short, mention may be made of its following good points.

1. Helpful in the Preservation of Hindu Religion and Culture. The first service of caste-system has been that it has protected Hinduism against all kinds of odds. It is the caste-system that has been largely responsible for the preservation of Hindu religion and culture. The caste brotherhoods, on account of their policy of exclusiveness did not mix with the foreigners. So Greeks, Huns, or Muslims could not conquer Hindu Culture, On the contrary most of these foreigners were themselves absorbed into the Hindu fold.

2. Sound Basis for Division of Labour. The caste-system is based on the sound economic principle of division of labour, which ensures efficiency of production. A person from his birth knew what profession he was to follow later on. So from the start he devoted all his energy to the one profession of his forefathers it was because of this reason that in every period of Indian history, there was no dearth of highly skilled workers and scholar". In the words of Dr. Majumdar, "In sum, caste is one's mainline of defence in so far as it provides social-economic security within a permanent milieu which is not based on changing individual caprices."

3. Helpful in Fostering the Spirit of Co-operation. It has fostered the spirit of co-operation and fellow-feeling among members of the same caste. By helping the poor and needy, it has avoided the necessity of the State supporting the poor. It minimises envy and unhappiness and thereby promotes social harmony among the people. Dr. Majumdar is of the opinion that it has been found that inbreeding leads to a preponderance of males and by prescribing endogamy the caste-system has soothed the minds of thousands of generations of Hindus.

4. Provides for Various Functions. Caste-system provides for the various functions necessary to social life. It divides society in different functional division ensuring the efficient performance of all kinds of functions. People of different castes perform their assigned functions and none of them ever seeks to deviate from their inborn functions whether high or low. Consequently, all the functions in society ranging from respectable functions of priesthood down to the low function of sweeping the dirt are performed efficiently and automatically.

5. Influence on Intellectual mike-up of the Individuals. It influences the intellectual make-up of an individual. Since the caste dictates to each member customs to be observed in the manner of diet, the observance of ceremonies and whether he may marry a widow, his views on the social and political matters are bound to be influenced by his caste customs. This fosters the spirit of equality within the groups.

6. Means of Social Insurance. The caste provided a means of social insurance and promoted social-service activities. It made the individual learn the lesson of self-sacrifice and of subordinating the individual will to the collective will. Along with the guilds the castes enforced social and economic discipline among their members. Explaining this social function of the caste Hutton writes, "He is provided in this way with a permanent body of association which controls almost all his behaviour and contacts. His caste canalizes his choice in marriage, acts as his trade union, his friendly or benefit-society, his State-club and his orphanage, it takes place for him of health insurance and if need he, provides for this funeral."

7. Development of Country's Integration. It develops class-consciousness without breeding class struggle. It has created an efficient organization of Hindu society without giving any chance to class frictions and factions. It was the best device organised within one society people of different castes with different cultural levels. It prevented the country from splitting up in to warring racial units. It integrated Indian society into one vast and variegated community whereby a stable and orderly organization of society could be possible. Commenting on this fact Hutten has said, "It will be understood then that one important function of caste, perhaps the most important of all its functions and the one which above all other makes caste in India an unique institution is or has been to integrate Indian society, to weld into one community the various competing, if not incompetible groups composing it."

8. Helpful in Preserving Racial Purity. It has preserved the racial purity of the higher castes by for biding indiscriminate inter-marriages. It has also greatly fostered the habits of cleanliness by insisting on ritual purity. There is no wonder that the caste-system has been responsible for preserving the purity of blood among the various groups of Hindus even up to this day. Each caste made rigid rules for marriages. Inter-caste marriages were forbidden and in this way India was able to preserve racial purity to a large extent.

DEMERITS OF CASTE-SYSTEM

It is belived that the caste-system and particularly, the caste-system as it stands today has done more harm than good. Sir Henry Maine describes the caste-system, "as the most disasfrous and blighting of human institutions." It has in fact given rise to a number of evils and there by it has rendered great disservices to Hindu society. This fact will become explicitely clear from the following arguments.

1. Social Division Based on the Principle of Birth Undesirable. A caste-system based on the principle of birth is undesirable. The social divisions, according to Gita, should be based on "Guna and Karma", *i.e.,* character and functions. The present grouping of Indian castes is based on birth and so it makes no provision for low born talents to rise and high born incompetents to occupy a low position. In this way, it is also open to grave genuine criticism.

2. Impediment to Co-operation between Indians and Foreigners. According V.A. Smith, one of its chief defects is that "it shuts off Indians from Fee association with foreigners."

Thus, making it difficult for Indians to understand them. The upper caste particularly the Brahmanas would not mix with foreigners and consequently created innumerable difficulties and often hindered hearty co-operation between the Indians and foreigners during the various periods of Indian history.

3. An Anti-National Institution. The fundamental draw-back of caste-system is that it has proved to be an anti-national institution. Caste prejudices and caste feuds have always dominated our history. At the time of grave foreign dangers, only a section of the people, the Kashatriyas fought against the enemy. Other castes, being ignorant of fighting, stayed away in their home. This led to many great disasters. Caste rivalries were also responsible for many troubles in the days of the Rajputs and the Marathas. Rawlinson remarks, "By splitting the people into a number of water-tight compartments, the caste-system rendered the growth of a national spirit almost possible and it was one of the reasons why India for centuries was at the mercy of foreign conquerors."

4. Responsible for Stagnation in Society. Some critics are opposed to caste-system on the ground 'that it has denied mobility of labour. Since the individual must follow the caste occupation and cannot change it according to his likes or dislikes he cannot progress in life according to his capacity and desire. This leads to stagnation in society. It is in view of this fact that Dr. Radha Krishnan Mukerjee says, "Unfortunately this device to prevent the social organization from decay ultimately prevented it from growing."

5. Obstacle to National Unity. It has proved an obstacle to the growth of national unity in the country. The lower classes feel discontented at the behaviour meted out to them in society. As Dr. G. S. Ghurye states, "It is the spirit of caste-patriotism which engenders opposition to other castes and creates an unhealthy atmosphere for the growth of national-consciousness." E. Schmidt also pointed out that one of the most tragic consequences of he caste-system is that it prevents the development with the population of a general national consciousness."

6. Cause of Narrow Outlook Among Indians. The caste-system has been responsible for the narrow outlook and caste exclusiveness. Till recently, the Indians lived according to caste customs and never bothered about the general affairs of the country. Castes hindered the growth of nationalism. On account of these reasons an average Indian is conservative and stay-at-home.

7. Wrongful Placement of People Possible. The caste-system often· results in putting man on wrong occupation. There is no guarantee that a priest's son would also like to be a priest or would possess the qualities for a successful priest. Under the caste-system he cannot take up any other profession even though he may possess the skill and liking for that. It does not utilise fully the talents and capabilities of the population and is, therefore, a barrier to optimum productivity.

8. Obstacle to Social Progress. It is a great obstacle to the social and economic progress of the nation. Since the people believe in the theory of 'Karma', they become conservative. Again because their economic position is fixed, they are led to inertia killing their initiative and enterprise.

9. Opposed to the Spirit of Democracy. Caste-system is anti-democratic and denies equal rights to all. A man cannot join any profession or calling. Nor does every man, high low, enjoys the same privileges. Nor can he marry the woman of is own choice. All these are opposed to the spirit of democracy. It is quite unfortunate that social barriers are erected specially in the way of lower class individuals who are not provided with opportunities for their physical and mental development. The low caste people enjoy no freedom of any kind and they have to lead very hard and restricted life. It is not in keeping with the present day democratic set-up of society and this is why with the dawn of democracy in India caste-system is fast losing ground.

10. Root Cause of Untouchability. The caste-system has led to the evil of untouchability. In a caste-ridden society the low caste people are treated as untouchables and the high caste people do not like to have any sort of social intercourse with them. This problem is more particularly prevalent in India and has been eating into the vitals of Indian society. The Govt. of India has been forced to take special measures to eradicate this evil. According to Mahatma Gandhi, "It is the hatefullest expression of caste." Large sections of people are reduced to the state of virtual slavery.

A close study of the foregoing facts shows that the demerits of caste-system outweigh its merits. The caste-system has broken the solidarity of Hindu society, supressed the liberty of individuals and has become the instrument of oppression. It is millstone round the neck of the Hindus and is dragging them with a rapid speed towards political and social decline. The caste-system has outlived its utility. It is difficult to live according the caste-rules and prejudices in modern times. According to S. K. Sharma, "Caste-system is like a bad coin we should melt it and remint the same for our modern use."

CLASS VS. CASTE

There are two well-defined bases of social stratification. They are the basis of birth and that of wealth. These basis are applied to stratify human-societies in the way they suit the customs and habits of the people. The social divisions based on birth are given the name of castes and the social divisions based on wealth are called classes. The Indian society is an extreme example of caste-system while Western society is the representative of class-system. A caste-ridden society is called closed society while a class dominated society is viewed as an open society. The two types of social orders, are at variance with each other on several points. While explaining this fact Maciver has aptly remarked in these words, "Whereas in eastern civilization the chief determinant of a class and status· was birth, in the western civilization of today wealth is a class-determinant of equal or perhaps greater importance and wealth is a less rigid determinant than birth; it is more concrete and thus, its claims are more easily challenged; itself a matter of degree, it is less apt to create distinctions of kind alienable, acquirable and transferable, it draws no such permanent lines of cleavage as does birth."

Quite a similar opinion is held by Ogburn and Nimkoff. They write, "In some societies it is not uncommon for individuals to move up or down the social ladder. Where this is the case the society is said to have "open" classes. Elsewhere there is little shifting, individuals remaining through a life time in the class into which they chance to be born. Such classes are "closed" and if, extremely differentiated constitute a caste-system. According to C. H. Cooley, "When a class is somewhat strictly hereditary we may call it a caste." To quote Senart, "Castes were grafted on to ancient "classes"—those of the Vedic age and the original united Aryans. However, there is difference of opinion between class and caste. Class "serves political ambition," while caste "obeys strict scruples, traditional customs, at the very most certain local influences, which usually have no connection with class interests. The two institutions may, by the Reaction of systems on facts have become incorporated; but in essence they are independent." If the "existing system of castes was fitted into old divisions of race and class which were drawn (or that purposes; it was under the influence of properly Indian conditions." In view of these observations it may be said that the castes and social classes are the two-fold broad divisions of human society. If the first is based on heredity, the second is based on human creation.

Points of Similarity between the Two. It is clear from the foregoing facts that class and caste are two types of social stratification. They have some points in common. *Firstly,* there is some similarity in their origin, development and functions. Both of them are permanent, segments of society to which heirachical positions are assigned *Secondly,* members of a caste and a class regard themselves as equals and superior or inferior to members of other castes and classes. It is on the basis of their social feelings about the members of other caste and class groups that they decide their social relationship. In so far as possible people have relationship and social intercourse with the people of equal status. Therefore the question of superior and inferior people exists in all societies. *Thirdly,* both class and caste develop a consciousness of their own. This consciousness is based on the peculiar way of life and the peculiar privileges of a particular class or a caste. Fourthly, both he kinds of social divisions are more or less universal in their existence. This is to say neither caste-system nor class-system is confined to anyone country or to a single age. They are the symbols of social disparities and since these disparities exist in most countries, they cannot be free from such kinds of social groupings for instance, if India is regarded as the stronghold of caste-system, it is by no means absent from such other countries like America where colour bars and racial barriers exists on a large scale. Thus, it is obvious that class and caste groups exist in most countries of the world and they form the essential basis of social stratification in the societies.

Difference between Class and Caste

Castes and classes are two important elements of human society. From the organizational point of view they constitute essential bases of social stratification. In several societies caste and social class exist side by side. But it cannot be taken to mean from this that they are at one with each other. There are some clear cut differences between these two types of social organization and the more important of them can be discussed in the following manner.

1. Caste Stands for Closed Social order while Class Represents Open Society. To begin with, it may be said that class is more open than caste. In this connection Hiller writes, "A class-system an open system of rating levels... if a hierarchy becomes closed against vertical mobility, it ceases to he class-system and becomes a caste-system." Caste-system is a closed system in the sense that under it the status of the individual remains static He cannot alter it even with hardest efforts.

But class-system is an open system because it is dynamic. With his individual efforts a man may improve upon his original social status. A caste is thus, a closed class. The individuals status is determined by the class status of his parents, so that what an individual does has little bearing upon his status. On the other hand the membership of a class does not depend upon hereditary basis, it rather depends on the worldly achievements of an individual. So, in short, class-system is an open and flexible system while caste-system is a closed and rigid system.

2. Caste-System Places Restrictions on the People while Class-System Leaves them Free. Caste-system is a closed system and places many restrictions in the conduct of its members. These restrictions are meant to keep the solidarity of a particular class and at the same time the nature of the restrictions act as distinguishing features of that caste. Free association of different castes is checked. A class does not place restrictions on the conduct of its individual members. They enjoy the freedom of association and the freedom in general conduct whatsoever restrictions operate under a class-system are self-imposed restrictions and they do not carry any binding force.

3. Caste-System is Divine while Class-System is Secular. These two types of social divisions also differ on the point that caste-system is believed to be of divine origin while class-system is secular in nature. The caste-system is believed to have been divinely ordained. On this issue Maciver writes, "The rigid demacration of caste could scarcely be maintained were it not for strong religious persuasions. The hold of religious belief, with its super-natural explanations of caste itself is essential to the continuance of the system. The Hindu caste structure may have arisen out of the subjection or enslavement incidental or conquest and perhaps also out of the subordination of one endogamous community to another. But the power, prestige and pride of race thus, engendered could rise to a caste-system with it social separation of groups that are not in fact set apart by any clear social signs, only as the resulting situation were rationalised and made eternal by religious myths."

It is everybody's religious duty to fulfil his caste duties in accordance with his 'dhrama.' In the Bhagvatgita the creator is said to have apportioned the duties and functions of the four castes. An individual must do the duty proper to his caste. Failure to act according to one's caste duties meant birth in a lower caste and finally spiritual annihilation. Men of the lower castes are reborn in higher castes if they have fulfilled their duties. On the contrary there is nothing sacred or, of divine origin in the class stratification of society. Classes are secular in origin. They are not founded on religious dogmas.

4. Class-System having Greater Amount of Social Mobility than Caste-system. A very important difference between these two types of social divisions is that class-system contains greater amount of social mobility than is the case with caste-system. Since class is open and elastic, social mobility becomes easier. A man can by his enterprise and initiative change his class and thereby rise in social status. If a man is born in a labouring class, it is not necessary for him to live in the same class for life and die in it. He can strive for money and success in life and with wealth he can change his social status implied in the class distinction. But in case of caste-system it is Impossible to change one's caste status, once a man is born in a caste he remains in it for his life time and makes his children suffer the same fate. Thus, the caste groups allow no social mobility to its members whereas class groups do not make such kind of heavy claims upon the people. This point has been beautifully explained by N.D. Humphrey in these words, "A class is a social grouping in which members possess roughly equivalent and culturally valued attributes. A class is 'open' in the sense that one can escape from a class or fall into it or climb into it by acquiring attributes comparable to those already in it. A caste, on the other hand, is a closed matter with limitations to status clearly demarcated. One is born into a caste, marries in it and has benefits and handicaps to status determined by the fact of birth."

5. Caste-System was Related to Occupation but Class-System is not so. The caste in the past was generally associated with common traditional mode of occupation and hence, the occupational opportunities in caste-system are limited. Class allows its members to adopt the occupation of their likings. The real difference in this connection between the two is that while under caste-system it is the caste that determines the occupations of its members, under the class-system it is occupation that determines the class of the people. In caste-system there is no occupational mobility and the members of a caste generally adopt their ancestral occupations. But in class-system there is and can be occupational mobility and the people adopt occupation at their will.

6. Caste-System is Endogamous while Class-System is not so. The choice of marriage partners in caste-system is strictly endogamous. Members have to marry within their own groups. If an individual marries outside his own group or caste, he is treated as out-caste. No such restrictions exist in class-system, at least in their rigid form. A wealthy person may generally order to marry in a wealthy family but he may without being out-casted from the wealthy class can marry with a poor partner. Thus, caste-system imposes strictly marriage regulations on its members, which they cannot normally violate, but under class-system there are no such restrictions and the people enjoy freedom of mate choice.

***

14

Nature and Aims of Democratic Education

The Education Commission (1964-66), said that the development of values such as a scientific temper of mind, tolerance, respect for the culture or other national groups, etc., will enable us to adopt democracy, not only as a form of Government, but also as a way of life. This clearly shows that in a democratic country like India the first and the foremost goal of education should be development of democratic values. Indian democracy is made by the people who profess different religions, speak different languages, belong to different races, castes, classes and communities. keeping in mind these and several other characteristics of Indian democracy following should be the most appropriate goals of education:

1. National Integration. It means harmonizing religions, language, caste, class and community differences as they exist in India causing social tensions. It is essential that the people of India in spite of these differences live peacefully and co-operatively and utilize their varied talents for the enrichment of the national life as a whole. Education through various programmes and tailored curricula should make efforts to develop in the people such attitudes and values. It is difficult but possible. These changes include realizing the importance of knowledge and education, learning various social skills, developing scientific attitude, computer literacy considering science and technology important and so on. The Commission (1964) said that, "The most important tool in the process of modernization is education based on science and technology." But, the Commission, further said "Modernization, if it is to a living force must derive its strength from the strength to spirit."

The Secondary Education Commission (1952-53), has formulated three social or national aims of education. These are:

(a) Development of democratic citizenship.

(b) Improvement of vocational efficiency.

(c) Development of leadership which means training pupils for discharging their duties efficiently.

Ishwar Bhai Patel Committee (1977), also reiterated the importance of development of citizenship as a social or national goal of education.

The Adiseshiah Committee Report (1978) formulated the following goals to be achieved through education:

(a) Removal of unemployment.

(b) Removal of destitution, *i.e.,* poverty.

(c) Rural Development.

(d) Adult literacy.

All these foregoing aims are social or national objectives to be achieved through education. They are the tasks completion of which is imperative for strengthening the society. These aims have been discussed here with special reference to India. Hence, they may be considered national goals of education or ducational aims of national development.

Our schools should develop a strong tradition of striving to generate a sense of national unity and national consciousness, in the pupils. This can be achieved as suggested by the National Commission on Education (1964-66), by *(i)* making pupils understand and revaluate our cultural heritage and *(ii)* by the creation of a strong driving faith in the future towards which we aspire. The first may be promoted by well-organized teaching of the language and literature, philosophy, religion and history of India as well as by introducing the students to Indian architecture, sculpture, painting, music, dance and drams. Faith in future would involve an attempt to bring home to the students the principles of the Constitution, the great human values contained in preamble of the Constitution.

2. Development of Democratic Values in the People. These values apart from those given above include a spirit of large-hearted tolerance, of mutual give and take, of the appreciation of the ways in which people differ from one another. No education is worthwhile if an educated man does not translate these values in his behaviour and no democracy in that case can survive for long. Hence, education has to make deliberate and planned effort on development of these values in the people.

3. Development of Physical Resources through the modernization of agriculture and rapid industrialization should also be an important aim of education in a democracy like India. To achieve this purpose education should be linked with productivity, science should be made a basic component of education, work-experience should be considered important, vocational education should be expanded, scientific and technical education should be improved.

4. Development of Human Resources should be considered still more crucial an aim of education in Indian democracy. This aim implies changes in the knowledge, skils, interests and values of the people as a whole. In a democracy the individual is an end in himself and the primary purpose of education should be to provide him with the widest opportunity to develop his protentialities to the full, through social reorganization and empahsis on social perspectives. Cultivation of essential values in the people, development of dedicated and competent leadership and educated electorate are essential for strengthening democracy. Education, therefore, must develop such human resources needed for the defence of Indian democracy.

5. Development of Social, Moral and Spiritual Values. In a democratic country like India it is inevitable to inculcate social, moral and spiritual values in the people. Knowledge in the absence of essential values may be dangerous. The success of democracy, its strength and stability are contingent upon people's developed sense of social reponsibility and a keener appreciation of moral and spiritual values. Hence, education must make efforts on developing these values in the people. Nehru in his Azad Memorial Lectures (ICCR, 1962) said "Material riches without toleration and compassion and wisdom may well turn to dust and ashes."

DEMOCRATIZATION OF EDUCATION

It is only in recent times that democratic principles and values have entered the field of education. The credit of this revolutionary change goes to the American educationist Johy Dewey. He emphasized that in a democratic society, educational planning should be done in such a way that each individual member is made capable to shoulder social responsibilities efficiently and discharge them effectively and profitably. According to him, edcation should inculcate in the individuals the sense to welcome needful changes in the social structure and reoriented one's behaviour smoothly to the ever changing social milieu. The impact of this philosophy has brought about revolutionary changes in the thinking about educational planning and schemes of public education have begun to emphasize the provisions of the education of the masses so that general people become conscious about their rights and duties, about their individual and social responsibilities and about their National and International obligation. As the democratic rule is by the people for the people, they should be made to understand their obligations and to discharge their duties intelligently. Hence, in all democratically ruled countries, more and more emphasis is being laid upon free, compulsory and universal education.

Impact of Democracy on Education

The impact of democratic tendency on education is evident on the working of the following elements:

1. Provision of Equal Oportunities and Recognition of Individual Differences. In a democratic set-up, each child is a sacred and valuable entity of society. As such, equal opportunities are made available to one and all for their fullest development. In this connection the principle of individual differences is given proper recognition and therefore each child receive proper support according to his interests, aptitudes and capacities to develop his individuality to the fullest extent.

2. Free Education. The principle of universal and compulsory education involves free education to all irrespective of their social or monetary status. Hence, education is now regarded as the birth right of each child irrespective of colour, caste, creed and sex. In almost all democratic countries, education has been made free up to a certain standard. In addition, education of the physically and mentally handicapped is also receiving proper and increasingly effective attention.

3. Universal and Compulsory Education. In democracy, the reigns of Government remain in the hands of the people. Hence, common people must be so educated that they develop themselves as responsible and dynamic citizens conscious of their rights and duties, fully conversant with their National and International obligations, well aware with the Government procedures anti-administration processes.

4. Provision of Adult Education. Under the influence of democratic tendency, in different countries, emphasis is being laid upon adult education, women education and education of the mentally retorted and physically handicapped.

Schemes are under operation in our country also for the effective education of the adults who constitute a bulk of our entire population. Night-schools, short-term courses, one day schools and the schemes are being launched to solve this stupendous problem.

5. Methods of Teaching. Under the impact of democratic tendency, method of teaching are undergoing revolutionary changes. Old, traditional and mass education methods are being gradually replaced by individual attention methods. Nothing is now enforce or thrust in by force. Self-learning devices are encouraged and such methods are promoted which motivate children to pay attention and learn by their own efforts. Such wholesome and welcome environment is created wherein children search for truth, gain knowledge by their own efforts and learn by their own experience.

6. Social Activities. Bookish and academic activities are not over-emphasized in schools now-a-days. Proper attention is paid to social, cultural and co-curricular activities, so that children develop in a wholesome way and gain more and more social experience.

7. Child Centred Education. Democratic way of thinking emphasizes the importance of each child as sacred individuality. Hence, educational schemes and plans are so structured that each child receives full attention and full facilities to develop his individuality to the fullest extent.

8. Importance of Individual Attention. As discussed above, each child receives individual attention. His family background, his own interests, likes and dislikes, his needs and capacities are fully taken care off in all plans of educational development, the purpose being to achieve the maximum development of personality.

9. School Administration. To inculcate in children the sense of self-discipline and self-administration, their association with school administration is being welcomed. Such schemes are being formulated in various institutions where student participation in actual educational and school administration is a fact.

10. Respect of Teacher's Personality. Democratic philosophy respects teacher as a very dynamic and effective agency of social change for social progress. Thus, teachers are now made to participate more and more in curriculum construction and educational planning. Side by side, they are allowed to experiment freely in respect to methods, techniques and devices of teaching as well as materials which aid teaching prcedures and processes. Not only this, more and more plans are being laid and worked out for increasing the professional competency of teachers.

11. Student Unions. Student unions and student welfare associations are formed in institutions to promote student welfare in all spheres with the aim of achieving balanced, dynamic, efficient and socially motivated personalities.

12. Intelligence Tests. Schemes of intelligence tests are under operation in various institutions all over the world to evaluate the mental capacity, growth and achievement of children. Diagnostic tests are proving very useful for this purpose.

13. Physical Health of Children. To promote physical well-being of children, facilities for games and sports, gymanzia, medical tests and medical help are being provided freely and on an increasing scale. Medical check up, advice and medicines are now provided to the needy.

14. School. School is now regarded as a centre of promoting national consciousness and international understanding. Education for dynamic citizenship is associated with education for National and International understanding, amity and fellow-feeling. Thus, school is now regarded as a miniature of society.

15. Co-operation between all Agencies of Education. In a democratic set-up, all the agencies of education co-operate actively for the development of children. Hence, under the influence of democratic tendency, schemes are being formulated now-a-days to establish co-operation between all the agencies of education namely—family, school, community, church and state.

CONSTITUTION

A Constitution is a fundamental legal document according to which the Government of a country functions. It is the basic law which defines and delimits the main organs of Government and their jurisdiction as well as the basic rights of the citizens. A Constitution, thus, is superior to all other laws of the country and no law can be enacted which is not in conformity with the Constitution.

A Government looks after law and order in a society. It does so by making laws and maintaining order. But a Government cannot make laws and administer a country according to its own whims and forces. Every Government has to function in conformity with basic law of the land. The Constitution contains those laws which act as the source according to which the rules and regulations of governing a country are framed.

A democratic Government is one in which the citizens participate in the functioning of the Government, directly or indirectly. It is a Government in which the Government's powers are limited and clearly spelt out. Conversely, it is also a Government under which citizen's rights are also given clearly. Now, how are these limits placed on the activity of the Government? This is done by what is called a Constitution.

A Constitution is considered the source of powers and authority of Government. It lays down precisely what the powers of a particular Government agency are, what this it can, or cannot do. The idea is to minimize confusion and conflict of operation between the various organs of the Government. A Constitution is concerned with two aspects—the relation between different organs of Government; and between the Government and the citizens. More than anything else a Constitution is an instrument of controlling the abuse of power by the Government. That is why the Constitution is a very important document.

Preamble. "We, the people of India, having solemnly resolved to constitute India into a Sovereign Socialist Secular Democratic Republic and to secure to all its citizens: Justice, Social, Economic and Political; Liberty of thought, expression, belief, faith and worship; Equality of status and of opportunity; and to promote among them all Fraternity assuring the dignity of the individual and unity and integrity of the Nation; in our Constituent Assembly this twenty-sixth day of November, 1949, do hereby adopt, enact and give to ourselves this Constitution".

The Preamble sets out what the objectives of Indian Government the kind of value system the Constitution wishes to set-up in India. It declares India a sovereign state. Sovereignty means absolute independence, a Government which is not controlled by any other power. When India was under British rule, it could not be called a sovereign country. Besides, the Constitution provides for democratic society in India. Here every citizen enjoys equal political rights. The country is governed by the elected representatives of the people. There is no state religion of India. The state does not favour people of any particular religion. The citizens are free to follow and practise the religion of their own choice. The Constitution also declares socialism to be one of the objectives. The ideal of equality remains incomplete if it is restricted only to the political sphere. It must extend to social and economic life too. The Preamble declares India to be a Republic. It means that the haed of the state is not a monarch, but a president indirectly elected by the people.

Secular Government. The Government under the Indian Constitution has to be secular. This means that the Government must not formulate policies which discriminate between various religious communities which live in India.

Universal Adult Franchise. Indian Constitution establishes a system of universal adult franchise. Under this system, every Indian citizen above the age of 18 years has the right to vote and participate in choosing the Government.

Building a Just Society. Indian Constitution has one part dealing with the fundamental rights and fundamental duties of the citizens. Another part contains provisions which are called directive principles of the state policy. These are instructions which the Constitution gives to the States (the Government at both the central and the state level) for achieving a just society in India. Indian Constitution, also, has several provisions which seek to protect the interets of those people who have been traditionally poor and socially deprived, the Scheduled Castes and Scheduled Tribes and Other Backward Classes of Citizen (OBCs).

Emergency Provisions. Finally, Indian Constitution also foresaw that there could be situations of danger when Government could not be run as in ordinary times. To cope with these difficult times, it lays down some emergency provisions. In case of national emergency fundamental right can be restricted.

Fundamental Rights. The Indian Constitution mentions some of the most important rights of the citizens. These are called fundamental rights. These rights, are fundamental in two different ways. *First,* the Constitution gives us these rights. and guarantees them because it believes that the rights are necessary if citizens are to act properly and live democratically. *Secondly,* effective procedures for the enforcement of these Fundamental Rights have been guaranteed in the Constitution itself. A citizen has the right to go to the court of law if he/she is denied these rights. The Constitution is their guarantee.

This Constitution guarantees to six fundamental rights. Apart from these rights, the Constitution also mentions some

'Directive Principles of State Policy' and a list of fundamental duties of Indian citizens.

To understand the fundamental rights it is necessary to know about the directive principles and the fundamental duties.

Indian Constitution guarantees to Indian citizens six fundamental rights. These are:

(i) Right to equality.

(ii) Right to freedom.

(iii) Right against exploitation.

(iv) Right to freedom of religion.

(v) Cultural and educational rights.

(vi) Right to Constitutional remedies.

Directive Principles of State Policy

The name Directive Principles of State Policy, shows that these are actually directions given by the Constitution of the state to adopt policies, which would help to establish a just society in India. The aim of these instructions is to create proper economic and social conditions in which citizens of India can lead a good life. The idea of democracy need not be only a political idea. It can also be exended to the social and economic life of the people. Some of the principles are in the form of social and economic rights, *for example,* the right to work, the right to free and compulsory education of children up to the age of 14, right to equal wages for equal work; or the right to an adequate livelihood. These rights are not fully enjoyed by all Indian citizens today. The Government has to try to provide conditions under which these can become legal rights of citizens. Unlike fundamental rights the rights mentioned in this part are not justiciable. The Constitution, however, tells the state, *i.e.,* whoever runs the Government that it must not forget these long term aims and it should try to achieve them in reality. If the Government makes a law to enforce any of these principles it cannot be questioned in a court of law on the grounds that it violates any of the guaranteed fundamental rights. Indian Constitution mentions that the state should strive to give the right of work, right to education, right to assistance from the Government in case a citizen is unemployed, sick, retired, or disabled. It should try to give free legal aid to poor people; so that poor people, who suffer greater injustices in society, can also go to courts and defend their rights.

All the Directive Principles, however, are not concerning social and political rights. Some of them are instructions to Government in other matters. For instance, the Constitution says that state should try to prevent concentration of wealth, it should ensure that workers in factories can have a share in decision-making. It instructs the state to promote and look after the interests of Scheduled Castes and Tribes. The state is asked to promote cottage industries. It is instructed to protect forests, the wildlife of the country and ancient moments.

Fundamental Rights and Directive Principles

Fundamental Rights are justiciable. They can be enforced by courts. The Government cannot take away these rights. But the provisions of Directive Principles are not ineffaceable by courts of law. If a citizen is out of work, he cannot get a writ from the courts of law. If a citizen is out of work, he cannot get a writ from the courts of law. If a citizen is out of work, he cannot get a writ from the Courts directing the state to give him work. But if he is jailed by the policy without reason, he can go to the courts. And the courts will direct the Government to free him. The Government must obey courts' order.

Fundamental Duties

Fundamental Duties have been incorporated by the forty-second Amendment of the Constitution, with the purpose of making citizens partriotic, help them to follow a code of conduct that would strengthen the nation, protect its sovereignty and integrity of India.

(i) To defend the country and render national service when required.

(ii) To value and preserve the rich heritage of the nation's composite character.

(iii) To promote the common brotherhood of all people in India and renounce any practice derogatory to the dignity of women.

(iv) To develop scientific temper, humanism and spirit of inquiry.

(v) To protect and improve natural environment and have compassion for living creatures.

(vi) To strive for excellence in all spheres of individual and collective activity.

(vii) To safeguard public property and abjure volence.

IMPACT OF DEMOCRACY ON VARIOUS ASPECTS OF EDUCATION

In the following lines we are throwing light on the various aspects of education in a democratic set-up:

Democracy and Aims of Education. In a democracy, the aims of education are as under:

1. Development of Democratic Values. The success of democracy does not depend upon Legislative buildings and massive structures of Parliament houses, but it rests upon the quality of the citizens devoted to democratic values. As such, the prime aim of democratic education is to promote in children a sense of devotion to democratic values. No book teaching can achieve this aim unless children are provided with opportunities to practise democratic norms and standards of behaviour. In fact, a child learns to live democratically by living democratically.

2. Development of Vocational Efficiency. For the success of a democratic set-up, economic contentment of citizens is a must. An indigent and poor person can be a victim of all kinds of allurements, inducements and exploitation by the resourceful and the powerful. Hence, the third aim of democratic education is to develop vocational efficiency in children, so that they are able to become self-reliant and serve the nation as much as possible.

3. Development of Interests in Children. The third aim of democratic education is to develop useful and worthy interests in children. Interests form character and enrich a child's life. Hence, the famous educationist, Herbart has insisted upon the fullest development of diverse interests. To achieve this aim, children should be provided with various and varied opportunities to participate in diverse activities and programmes in all fields of human life. If a large number of worthy interests are developed in children, they will be happy, well-balanced and efficient as citizens.

4. Development of Thinking Power. The fourth aim of democratic education is to develop thinking power of children. In fact, children of today are citizens of tomorrow when they will be confronted with all kinds of problems in political, social and economic fields. Education should develop in children the capacity to think clearly and take decisions confidently.

5. Development of Social Outlook. Development of social outlook is the sixth important aim of democratic education. This aim emphasizes upon the fact that children should be imbued with the sense that they are the integral parts of society, the welfare of which should be their ideal. Not only this, they should learn to live and die for the nation. Education should develop this sense of service and sacrifice making them learn the sacredness of obligations and duties for the welfare of the nation to which they belong.

6. Development of National and International Feelings. For the success of democracy, the ninth aim of democratic education is to develop in children the sense of ardent nationalism and devotion to international brotherhood. It may be noted that the two are not contradictory. On the other hand, they are mutually complementary and supplementary. In fact a nation cannot exist in isolation. All the nations of the world are mutually inter-dependent. Hence, education should foster the sense of inter-dependence, international good-will and fellow-feeling.

7. Development of Leadership. The seventh aim of democrat education is to develop leadership qualities in children. For this, education should instil in children the leadership qualities from the very beginning. They are the future citizens who will have to shoulder the multifarious duties and reponsibilities of their nation in all areas. Their character, strength of will, insight, courage of convictions, clarity of thinking and decision-making will be the foundations on which the national edifice will go up and up.

8. Development of Sound Habits. The fifth aim of democratic education is to develop sound habits in children. Habits are the sources of good or bad conduct. Hence, education should develop good habits in children from the very beginning to make democracy a successful venture.

9. Development of Harmonious Personality—The eighth aim of democratic education is to develop the individuality of a child into balanced and harmonious personality. In the modern world of strife, stress and strain a balance and harmonious personality can only seek and find adjustment with the surroundings. Hence, education should develop character, dynamism ans social outlook for this purpose.

10. Training for Citizenship. Democratic education should impart of children training in dynamic and healthy citizenship. For this, education should instil in children:

(a) Capacity to understand and solve the diverse problems of the country.

(b) Capacity to distinguish between propaganda and reality.

(c) Capacity to think and decide about issues.

(d) Economic efficiency.

(e) Consciousness of one's rights and duties.

(f) Capacity to shoulder responsibility.

(g) Development of diverse interests.

(h) Sense of service and sacrifice, *(9)* Good use of leisure hour.

(i) Development of human qualities as love, sympathy, fellow feeling, co-operation, sense of nationalism and internationalism.

(j) Healthy and dynamic outlook about problems, good behaviour and respect for moral values.

Curriculum

In a democratic country curriculum construction is done with the purpose of realizing democratic values. Hence, those subjects, activities and programmes are included in the curriculum which instil and promote healthy attitudes, dynamic habits, insight and understanding so that children are able to lead successful lives as happy citizens. The bases of such a curriculum are as under:

1. Diversified. Democratic curriculum is divisively to suit the needs of all children with basic differences of interests and aptitudes. Class room activities, games, sports and other co-curricular activities bear an imprint of variety to suit various needs of children.

2. Achievement of Social Aims. While constructing a democratic curriculum emphasis is laid upon social aims and values. In other words, development of social sense in children is kept in view. As such, student activities, associations, corporate programmes and fellowship programes are liberally provided.

3. Emphasis on Local Needs. Democratic curriculum is constructed on the basis of local needs and available resources. It may be changed according to the needs of time, place and local requirements.

4. Flexibility. Democratic curriculum is flexible to accommodate various needs and requirements which are in a state of constant change. A portion of it is made compulsory in the form of co-curriculum and diversified subjects are made optional for children to choose according to their interests and aptitudes.

5. Emphasis of Activity. Democratic curriculum is laid on the foundation of an important principle known as learning by doing. It is through practical work and activities that development of mind and intelligence is fostered. Instead of enforcing and compelling cut and dried readymade concepts into the minds of children, they are allowed to search for truth through their own experiments and experiences. This is real learning. It develops confidence, foresight and far-sight, the three important ingredients of wisdom.

6. Place for Leisure Hour Activities. Democratic curriculum also contains such relevant and useful activities in which an individual can profitable indulge leisure time. Thus, it ensures the total development of personality.

7. Provision of Vocational Needs. Democratic curriculum very well meets the needs of vocations, professions and economic requirements of a region or the whole country. This enplanes the country to develop economically.

Discipline

Discipline is the corner-stone of democracy. But democratic discipline does not believe in respiration or compulsion. It advocates self-discipline. In schools where democratic set-up is in vogue, the following ideas are emphasized for fostering and developing self-discipline:

1. In democratic schools the headmasters, the teachers and the administrators are not despots or police officers. Instead, they are friends, philosophers and guides. Through their friendly and affectionate behaviour, they mould the behaviour of children and thus, promote self-discipline by creating a congenial and cordial atmosphere.
2. In democratic schools full freedom is given and opportunities provided for each child to develop his individuality to the fullest extent. Hence, no problem of indiscipline arises at any time.
3. In democratic schools, such activities and programmes are structured which cater to the interests and needs of children. This develops self-discipline among children.
4. In the administration of a democratic school, children participate actively, discuss problems and decide them freely. They, thus, feel their integral and intimate relationship with the school and feel internal kinship with its progress and development.
5. In democratic schools, the sense of rights and duties is instilled in children. They, thus, learn self-control through social service and social consciousness. Nothing is imposed on them from above. They discuss, decide and carry out the decision with perfect co-operation and cordiality.
6. In democratic schools, students unions, students parliaments and all kinds of student organizations are encouraged for the benefit and development of children. They learn self-Government, co-operation, fellow-feeling and other human qualities together with qualities of self-discipline and leadership.

Teacher

In a democratic set-up a teacher is a friend, philosopher and guide. He often works as a social reformer. Such teachers process the following qualities:

1. The teacher is devoted whole hearted to the ideals and values of democracy. Hence, he tries to impart the same faith to children through gently persuasion and affectionate rapport.
2. In a democratic set-up, a teacher lays greater stress upon environment rather than on heredity. Hence, he tries to structure such a wholesome environment for the child that fullest development is naturally achieved.
3. The teacher regards every child as a sacred legacy to society. Hence, believing in the principle of individual differences he allows every child to develop his individuality to the fullest extent according to his interests, aptitudes and capacities.
4. The teacher tries to solicit maximum co-operation from the guardians, parents and other social agencies for the greatest possible development of children as dynamic and socially oriented citizens of the future.
5. In a democratic set-up, each teacher is fully conscious of his rights and duties towards society. Hence, he tries to instil the same sense of responsibility in children and also to make them capable and intelligent citizens of tomorrow.
6. Each teacher is well-versed in knowledge of his subject and has full academic competency to make children develop physically, mentally, morally and spiritually so that they are able to shoulder national and even international responsibilities in times to come.

❋❋❋

15

Religion in Education

The most developed period from the view point of religion has been the Vedic period when religion was considered as a basis for human life and source of inspiration for virtuous conduct. Since then religion has been inspiring people to follow the right path, improve their conduct and imbibe human virtues. It is possible that certain superstitutions, conservation, frustrations, fears and doubts might have crept into religion due to some ignorance. Self-confidence has always been with man in the form of religion. Religion by adding to the human qualities, has made man capable of self-confidence, self-reform, self-realization, self-discipline, self-reliance and self-development.

Meaning of Religion

Vedas are the oldest books. Vedas are the repository of all knowledge. Here, in religion has been described in its wider perspective. According to the Vedas, the efforts, which inspire man for various conduct and develop human qualities, fall in the category of religion. Hence, than in characteristic of religion is inspiration for virtuous conduct. The modern word 'Religion' can not be a synonym for 'Dharm', bacause 'Dharm' has been considered as all-pervading in Indian scriptures. All activities from rising in the morning to sleeping a night and death and actions after death are all included in 'Dharm'. In fact, whatever qualities a person acquires are his Dharm. Here, qualities mean human qualities which are universal.

In Islam 'mazhab' is a way of imparting education for virtuous conduct. According to the philosophy of this religion, 'namaz', 'Roja' and 'Haj' are considered, a method for creating universal love and feeling of neighbourhood. To give some benefit to the society or social service are considered as a part of this religion.

Religion and Sects (Belief)

Some narrow minded people evince unnecessary opposition by equaling religion with sects. We should clearly understand the meaning of religion and sects. Religion is taken in the wider sense which means spiritual development of human society through the welfare of mankind. In other words; religion means human religion which every society is prepared to accept. A sect (belief) is a specific religious view point of a group of persons. That is the individual belief of the persons of that group, based on the wider values of religion. It is not necessary for other sects to accept that belief. Hindu religion accepts the opinion of Vedas, Islam that of the Quran and Christians of Bible. Hindu Dharm has been divided into Buddha sect, Jains, Sikh, Vedic (Sanatan and Arya Samaj) according to the different methods to philosophers and thinkers of these sects, although all these sects are parts of Hindu Dharm. Some agitators and diplomats propagated it as different religions in order to create faction in Hindu Dharm. The idea behind this propaganda was to cut of the organization and unity of Hindu Dharm. It is amazing that some Hindus also accepted the sects as different religions.

Islam Dharm has its original form the word 'Salm'. 'Salm' means peace which has been interpreted as knowing God peacefully and surrendering the self before Him. This is the true nature of Islam. Whenever some one seeks the shelter of God, forgetting his vanity and pride, he attain all-round development and divinity is rediated from his personality. In Christian religion, christianity was formed from the word 'christos' which means 'bathed in Divine wisdom'. Thus, christian religion extends that divine wisdom which creates brotherhood, love, sympathy and tolerance in the human society.

Vedic religion, is based on Vedas, 'Ved' means knowledge. Hence, Vedic Dharm means that scientific knowledge which by recognising the existence of 'Inner self' and 'Supreme self' *i.e.,* 'Antaratma' and 'Parmatma', develops human qualities like, non-violence, truth, humanism, love and compassion, etc.

Thus, religion is a source of morality. Science can be of great help in this direction, but science devoid of religion is meaningless. Religion is all-pervading and Universal. So it should be included in education.

Mis-use of Religion and Violence

Due to ignorance and superstitutions some universe followers of religions have strangulated humanity and have committed great atrocities. The reason for such violent attitude is misinterpretation of religion. These religions hypocrises of violent nature committed so many atrocities on humanity that man began to hate religion. These committing oppressions in the name of religion were non-vedic (unwise) and selfish. Religious reformers born from time to time led the people to the right path and presented the true nature of religion. Buddha, Mahavir, Shankaracharya, Dayanand, etc., were such great personalities. In the Western countries Rousseau and Locke suggested to save education from wrongly interpreted religion. Corrupt practice, in various religious bodies in the name of religion created hatred for religion.

Relation between Religion and Education

Religion and Education are closely associated with each other both are of spiritual tendencies. Spiritual, material or physical urge are dealt with by religion as well as by the education. "Both seek to emancipate man, not from contract with his environment, but from slavery to it." As has already been discussed, *education creates certain values of life and help in the modification of behaviour.* It gives certain mouldings to the life, while religion beautifies the life by cultivation of truthful heart with the moral and spiritual values.

In this way religion and education have different ways but the same aim of achieving God through cultivating three absolutes truth and goodness.

Religion must be given a suitable places in the curriculum because it is the core of our culture and 'heritage'. Gentle given a fine statement in regard to the place of religion in the curriculum.

He Writes. "National cultures have never been more conscious than now of the higher needs of the mind, needs that are not only aesthetic and abstractly intellectual but also ethical and religious. For a school without an ethical and religious constant is an absurdity." Thus, religion should find a suitable and proper place in the sphere of education. Education, according to Pestalozzi, is aimed at "natural harmonious and progressive development of man's innate powers." Wider education mean an education which broadens the outlook, awakens the inner powers and teaches us to respect all the religions. In this manner, a teacher should enable the pupils to cultivate religious attitude and mentality through education. Religion, in this sense does not mean merely a bundle of rites and of dogmas followed by symbols and emotions but it is applied to all that what noble. Religion and education with this collective and mutual efforts lead a person towards self-realization and self-understanding. Rousseau and Wordsworth believed in nature and education on the lane; of nature. The essence of their philosophy was to worship nature in practical way. In other words, we should obey natural laws and must follow the path traced by her.

Truly speaking, religious education does not mean something separable but pure, honest and beneficial. Education is nothing but religion, because both the religion and the education aim at harmonising the person to the ultimate truth. Religion is the pure form of education.

Education has been defined as "a process of development in which consists the passage of human being from infancy, to Maturity, the process by which he adopts himself gradually in various ways to his physical and spiritual environment." In this definition the ability of social adaptation means the development of the social qualities like co-operation, co-ordination among social groups and communities. This ability of the adaptation is religious, because religion in a wider sense says clearly that all are one. We are brothers and sisters borne of the same father. The same ideology of co-operation is found in this interpretation alike education. Therefore, curriculum construction should be based on the principle that education and religion are not the separate entities but they are one in nature and consequence.

What is man and what is God? These are the main problems dealt with by religion. These are the truth of a vital significance and are at the basis "of the whole structure of knowledge whether of fact or value and deprived of them education as well as life is radically defective, without centre, balance or proper sub-ordination of part to part."

The aim of education is all-round development of man. The same is the aim of religion. So because use of this common aim the corelation of education and religion quite natural. Now to include the various forms of religion in education, is a great problem. Some people due to their ignorance of the true nature of religion, do not and to give any place to religion in education, whereas some people want to give it an important place. Since earliest times in India, education and religion have been related to each other. With the break of this relation, indiscipline, violence and immorality have increased. According to Dr. Sarvapalli Radhakrishnan the reason for all vices and troubles pervading the world is want of morality which has been created due to education being not corelated to religion. Here, in India there were those centres of education in which people from all parts of the world came to receive education. In Western countries also Movements were started for, educational organization by correlating religion and education. Sunday School Movement, Religious Education Movement were some such movements in which the demand for integration of education and religion was asserted. The world has witnessed the evil effects of materalism. Hence, it has rightly realised that humanity cannot be saved without relating education to religion. Now, the need for education integrated with religion is being felt throughout the world. Some politicians and economic groups do not think it proper to give a place to religion in education. In fact, if religion is treated as 'human religion' a revolution can be brought out in the improvement of education. Peace can be established in the world through a religion integrated education based on thinking of universal peace, universal-brotherhood and universal-good.

CAUTIONS IN THE TEACHING OF RELIGION

An evaluation of advantages and limitations of religious education leads us to be conclusion that religion should be given a place in education. But religion should be included in such a way that the above mentioned defects religious education may be avoided. One of the objectives of religious education is self-realisation and to inspite virtuous conduct. It is necessary to make efforts in this direction. Self-realisation and virtuous conduct are inner-impulses. They cannot be imposed on anyone. Sermons and instructions alone will not achieve religious aims. Moral development and virtuous conduct through religion is possible only when opportunities are provided for such behaviour. A religious atmosphere in schools can make it possible. The incidents are greatly influenced by the ideal behaviour of teachers. So the teachers themselves should present examples of ideal behaviour by leading a religious, moral and virtuous life. The teacher religion alone cannot create a religious atmosphere in schools. All teachers should cooperate in this process.

Religious education should be kept away from narrow mindedness. It will be better to give religious eduction based on logic, analysis and criticism, otherwise it may lead to superstitions fanatics, jealousy and narrow-mentality.

In schools, religion should not be taken as an end in itself. It is simply a means for all-round development of the individual. The schools are not to be made temples, mosques, or churches by titling religious education to a particular sect. Schools are not to fulfil the functions of religious institutions other the religious institutions should work as schools. If religious institutions make an attempt for the all-round development of children through spiritual development, they will certainly lessen the burden of schools. It is, therefore, necessary for the religious bodies to take the form of educational obligations to the extent possible.

Educational Functions of Religion

A man is attracted towards religion only when he is mentally, healthy and a sound mind are sides in a sound body. So it is the function of religion to co-operate in the physical development of children. In vedic religions behaviour the ideal of celibacy is for the sake of physical development. The child who observes restraint up to maturity and takes physical exercises for the development of body makes himself sturdy. This restorative power prepares him for household life and his regulated behaviour keeps him healthy till death. Some religious people think that good physical health creates a liking or worldly pleasures and happiness. So a person desirous of religious knowledge should not pay any attention to physical development. This is their fanaticise. Religion should first of all educate the individual for his physical and mental development. Body, mind and senses are means of inhibiting religion.

Religion should always mean performing of duties. To think only of the next world (Parlok) through religious knowledge and to forget this world (Ih-lok) is not fair. The first field of performing duties is this world Karma-Kshetra (the field of action) is another name for Dham-Kshetra (fields of religious). The man who succeeds in the Karma-Kshetra of this world is entitled to reach the other world (Parlok). Therefore, religion should prepare man for the Karma-Kshetra (field of action). The field of action of the individual is determined on the basis of his aptitudes. So religion should inculcate in the child the ability to choose his field of action according to his interest and aptitude and to get success engaging himself in it.

The basis of religion is knowledge. An ignorant person can not be religious. A person may be familiar with religion and religious behaviour after he has attained knowledge. The basis of religion are logic, analysis, observation, contemplation and freedom of thought. So the child should be provided opportunities for independent thinking, logic, meditation, analysis and observation with an open mind. The doubt of some persons that the child does not believe in religious facts on the basis of arguments, analysis, observation etc. is baseless. The permanent religious feeling is always based on perception. To have faith in religion without independent thinking, logic and analysis will be blind-faith and fanaticism.

Some people consider aesthetic sense and artistic sense as hinderance to religion. But this is not true. Satyam, Shivam, Sundaram (Truth, Bliss and Beautiful) and the bases for artistic and aesthetic senses. Satyam and Shivam are the bases of religion. A thing which is not true or for happiness cannot be beautiful. The carving of Jain idols in Ellora caves and Jatak stories connected with the life of Lord Buddha and their carving in Ajanta, the poetry of Sur, Tulsi and Mira and all considered unique for propagation of religious feelings. So religion should diffuse an aesthetic sense also.

Although it is true function of schools to develop the moral and character of the child, but religious institutions can bring about better moral and character development, if they pay attention in this direction. The very meaning of religion is to inspire virtuous conduct and virtuous conduct develops moral and ethical qualities. Today the country needs able and noble citizens. The religious institutions can fulfil their national duties by giving education virtuous conduct.

Arguments in Favour and Aganist Religious Education

Those who want to separate religion and education, argue in the following way:

1. To give place to religion in education is not practicable, because children of all religions come to receive education in schools. In such a situation which religion is to be taught in a school? If one particular religion is taught in the school, the followers of other religions will not accept this position. It will lead to mutual ill-will quarrel and disturbance.
2. Doubts and mental conflicts are created in children as they cannot understand the abstract processes of sin virtue, reward and punishment as explained in religious educational schools.
3. Religion education is generally based on preaching. So long as desired changes are not brought about in the environment and ideal examples are not presented till then good conduct cannot be spread through religious education. Hence, mere teaching of religious doctrines in schools will not achieve the goal of education.
4. Religious education emphasises, religious sermons and religious knowledge. But life is not conducted according to these sermons. Man cannot become virtuous simply by getting knowledge of religion.

He become virtuous only when he puts the same into practice. This is not done in schools.

5. It is not possible for the modern teacher to analyse religious knowledge dispassionately because he may be faithful only to one particular religion. Consequently, the students will be incapable of understanding the true and obscure meaning of religion. It willl be better to analyse religion with the help of science but the teachers will not accept it because science may injure the personal beliefs. In fact, it will be difficult to get able and suitable teachers for religious education. It is a difficult task to correlate education and true human religion. Every teacher may not be capable of this.
6. Man imbibes 'religion' through self-realization. Self-realization is individualistic. Hence, inclusion of personal elements in religious conduct is natural. In the school environment, collective and social tendencies are found. So personal view point of religion cannot be given importance. This view point may be suitable to those children who agree with that line of thinking but not to others who follow other view point.
7. We have already observed that religion means human religion through which human qualities should be developed. But history bears testimony to the fact that humanity has been oppressed in the name of religion and in place of love, compassion, sympathy and co-operation, the feelings of enmity, hatred, jealously and opposition have grown. Such examples in the history of religion may create irreligious feelings in children.

Argument in Favour of Religious Education

There may be some strength in the above arguments. But this strength will be there only to the extent to which education is imparted on the basis one particular religions without understanding the true meaning of religion. Religion is universal, omnipresent and eternal. It is necessary to present its universal form. The following arguments may be presented in favour of religious education:

1. "All-round development of man is not possible only through physical, mental and intellectual development, as this requires, spiritual development also. Physical comforts alone do not provide real pleasure and peace. The more a man is absorbed in wordly pleasures, the more he is attached towards them. He tries to get the physical comforts of this material world through all possible means (even though in human action). He becomes prepared to commit atrocities and cruel actions. This disturbs world peace. Various subjects such as geography, science etc., lead to physical, mental and intellectual development, but they do not develop him spiritually. For spiritual development religion oriented education is needed. Only then the goal of an all-round development of the individual may be achieved.
2. We have said earlier that religious education becomes defective only when religion is teated in its narrow form. Religion is not be identified with any sect or opinion. The essence of all sects, is the true religion. This religion alone can be named as human religion. If it is taught through education, the follower of any religion will not be ignored. It will be worthwhile to provide education in high human ideals which are adored by people of every religion instead of giving place to the rituals of different sects.
3. Lack of religious faith in man is the cause of his troubles. All the vices of the world are due to irreligiousness and materialistic tendencies.

Selfishness is the outcome of materialism which creates vices like enmity, jealousy and intolerance. Hence, religious education is necessary in order to get rid of inhuman tendencies.

4. In such countries which are mainly religious, the religious education will be useful from educational point of view. Education based on religion will be easily understandable and interesting in such countries. India is one such country. But religion should not be taken into its narrow form. By adopting essence of all the sects, religious education should be given in its wider perspective.
5. The aim of education is all-round development of the individual in which development of character is the main aim. Religious education is the best source for character development. Today education being devoid of religion, the character of many of our youths is not what it should be. Evidently, religion is to be given due place in education for the sake of character development.

✹✹✹

16

Women Education in Society

The women not only played an important role in the home, they also played a very, significant role in the last fight for freedom. They rubbed shoulders with men in the past and are doing so even now. They are adopting their own careers and fighting vigorously for eradication of hunger, poverty, ignorance and ill-health.

Once we realise the importance of the roles a woman plays in the home and outside, the urgency of the need for educating her becomes distinctly clear. The role of woman outside the home is becoming an important aspect of the social and economic life of the country. In the coming future that role will assume far greater significance.

Problems of Women's Education

In the past no importance was attached to the education of girls. In the beginning of the present century the percentage of literate women was only 0.8. The enrolment in the primary schools was 12 for every 100 boys and that in the secondary schools it was 4 for every 100. The total enrolment in the colleges was 26,474.

The two problems of women's education that attracted the attention of educational commissions were :

(a) Backwardness.

(b) Slow progress.

As early as 1882 the Hunter Commission said that the female education in the country had been till then in a very backward condition and recommended for an over-all improvement in the condition. It recommended that more grants should be given to girls schools and that moneys should be spent in equitable proportion on girls and boys schools.

To encourage girls education the commission recommended for a liberal scheme of scholarships to girls, a provision of facilities for their professional training and opening of secondary schools.

In spite of valuable recommendations made by commissions and committees on female education, at the biginning of the present century there was hardly any provision for the formal schooling of girls. It was only after 1901 when women came out of homes to shoulder responsibility in the struggle for freedom, that we see a progress in the field of the education of girls.

During the first half of this century much faster progress was made. The education for women expended enormously. Their status in the society got raised. A few aspects of the phenomenal growth in female education are given below :

1. The rate of expansion of female education was higher than that among the boys.
2. The enrolment at the primary stage increased from 12 for 100 boys in 1901 to 39 for 100 in 1950.
2. The education in mixed schools was more in the primary classes than in the secondary classes.
4. The enrolment at the secondary stage increased from 4 for 100 boys in 1901 to 15 for 100 in 1950.
5. The enrolment in the university rose from 264 in 1901 to 40,000 in 1950.

But there was still a very wide gulf between the education for boys and that for the girls. It was specially hinted at by the National Committee on Education of Women under the chairmanship of Smt. Durgabai Deshmukh (1958-59). The Committee pointed out that the Government did not realise even as late as 1958 that the problem of female education was a special one and as such it failed to provide necessary funds for the rapid development of women's education for which a suggestion had been given as early as 1882.

The National Committee on Women Education suggested that the education of women should be regarded as a major programme in education for some years to come and that special schemes should be prepared for this purpose and funds needed to work them out should be provided on a priority basis. The committee also suggested the setting-up of a special machinery at the state as well as at the Central level to look after the education of women.

The problem of wide disparity between the education of boys and girls at all stages and in all sectors of education is really one that claims urgent solution. The Education Commission has stressed the need for solving this problem at an early date. It remarked that had the problem been given due attention right from the beginning the need for special programmes as suggested by the Durgabai Deshmukh Committee would have not arisen at all. We must therefore try to bridge the gulf between the education of boys and girls at all stages primary, secondary and higher and in all sectors of education.

The next Committee for the development of female education was the one which was headed by, Hansa Mehta. The Committee discussed the problem of differentiation of curriculum between boys and girls. The Hunter Commission had recommended in 1882 that curriculum for girls should be different from what it is for boys as the instruction which is useful fer a boy may not be useful for a girl. The Committee under the Chairmanhip of Hansa Mehta made the following recommendation.

(a) There should be no need to differentiate curricula on the basis of sex in a democratic socialistic society.

(b) In the transitional period we should accept certain psychological differences between the two sexes and we may build curricula in such a way that these differences are given due importance but care should be exercised not to perpetuate them.

The problem of differentiation of curricula for boys and girls has been already discussed under Section 12.9 in detail and hence, need not be repeated here.

There has been appointed one more committee which studied the problem of women's education in 6 states under the chairmanship of Shri M. Bhaktvatsalam. It had surveyed the education of girls and of concluded that the education has been very poorly developed so far.

Three aspects of female education stand out as follows :

(a) Problem concerning expansion of women's education.

(b) Problem of higher education of girls.

(c) Problem of professional education of girls and married women.

The problem concerning expansion has been very carefully examined by the National Committee on Women's Education (1958-59). So far as the expansion of primary education is concerned, the number of girls enrolled for every 100 boys is about 50 now. At the middle school stage the gap is still wider. The Constitutional Directive could not be fulfilled even by the end of 1980 even we if proceeded at a faster rate in the field of expansion of women's education. We will have to educate public opinion to overcome traditional prejudices against girls education. We will have to encourage girls education by providing free textbooks, writing materials and even clothing. We would have to make mixed schools popular at the primary stage and shall have to open separate schools for girls at the middle and secondary school stage wherever they are needed and it is possible to open them. Girls are more useful than boys at home.

Hence, they tend to be withdrawn earlier. Public opinion is still not in favour of extending education among girls to higher stages. Hence, a large portion of girls have to leave school early. For girls who leave the primary stage at about the age 14 and get married, it is proposed that part-time or full-time course should be organised in homescience or the household industries like tailoring arts and crafts, poultry and dairying so that they may prepare themselves better for their future life as housewives and mothers.

At the secondary stage, special programmes will have to be initiated for girls who intend to join secondary schools. In 1950-51 the proportion of the enrolment of the girls to that of the boys was about 1 : 6 in middle and 1 : 6.5 in higher secondary schools. By 1980 it had been raised to 1 : 2 in middle schools and 1 : 3 in higher secondary ones. Special efforts shall have to be still made to achieve targets set. Either more separate schools will have to be opened or where it is not possible to do so, women teachers will have to be kept on the staff. Women's Hostels or subsidised transport shall have to be provided. Encouragement shall have to be given in the form of scholarships and free education.

Problem of Training and Employment

The Indian society is undergoing a change. Woman is adopting her own career. Her age of marriage is rising. Her role outside the home is becoming an important aspect of the social and economic life of the country. The role of woman outside the home will assume still larger significance in time to come. There is a problem of unemployment among educated girls. It is therefore necessary to pay special attention to the problems of training and employment.

The 1961 Census showed that about a million young educated women above the age of 24, though matriculates, were working simply as housewives. The 1971 Census presented even more dismal picture. How horrible is it to lay waste their powers which could be profitably used for national reconstruction and development! There is a need for training and employing them in nation-building activities.

As the marriage age among girls rises, the number of young unmarried women becomes larger. A suitable career has to be singled out for pursuit before a girl gets married. Then again after marriage, when she becomes almost free from home-making activities and when her children reach a school going age, she needs some employment. The time at her disposal before she is married is to be used in some part-time job and the time after marriage when she is free has to be used in full-time work. Teaching, nursing and social service are some of the areas in which part or full-time jobs can be secured for women. Hence, there is a need for training girls for these services. Other fields of work will have to be surveyed and avenues for employment will have to be found out.

Women Polytechnics : Industrial

In all polytechnics courses of special interest to girls should be developed. A few such courses that have been started for women in 17 polytechnics spread all over the country are courses in :

(a) Architecture.

(b) Commercial art.

(c) Dress making.

(d) Electronics and radio technology.

(e) Pharmacy.

(f) Instrument technology.

(g) Interior decoration.

(h) Library science.

(i) Medical laboratory technology.

(j) Secretarial practice.

These courses are being offered at certificate are levels. Efforts should be made to attract into them girls who have just passed the middle or high school examination. More women polytechnics need opening. It is suggested that if guidance services are amply provided to school leavers at the high school stage and if the Principals of women polytechnics associate themselves with the headmistresses and Principals of higher secondary schools more girls may be attracted to these careers.

Women Polytechnics : Agricultural

A large number of girls in rural areas may be attracted to supporting services needed by a farmer. There are many trades which are based upon agriculture. At the post-matriculation stage, opportunities for giving vocational education in agriculture may be provided on a sufficiently large scale. Courses of special interest to girls will have to be devised and developed in agricultural polytechnics. *For example*; courses in applied nutrition, dairying, animal husbandry, poultry farming are most suitable for matriculate girls. Besides, there is an urgent need for such Courses in the country; for instance, in the present circumstances, we have to change our dietary habits and such Courses may help a great deal in meeting food shortage. Women in rural households can safely manage these affairs. A network of agricultural polytechnics may be set-up to provide girls vocational education in courses referred to above.

Higher Education for Women

We do not subscribe to the opinion that it is no longer necessary to give a special attention to higher education of women since they are taking its advantage fully. To begin with, it must be emphasised that there exists an acute shortage of educated women to shoulder directional and organisational responsibilities in many professions and occupations. *For example*, there is a great demand of highly educated women workers in a series of occupational fields, such as nutrition, dietetics, institutional management, etc. Specially vigorous efforts have yet to be made to expand women's education at the university level.

Considering the changing needs of the Indian society and the requirements of national development, a still greater expansion of higher education has becop1e imperative. During the decade 1950-1960 the proportion of women students in colleges and universities to the total enrolment was raised from 13 percent to 21. In the following decade it came about 30 percent : but there is an urgent need to raise it up to 40 percent at least. For the healthy growth of higher education among womenfolk the following programmes have been suggested by the Education Commission :

1. A programme of financial assistance and scholarships to women students in colleges and universities on a liberal scale.
2. A programme of suitable but economical hostel facilities for women on a large scale.
3. A free access to courses in arts, humanities, sciences and technology.

The first two programmes are self explanatory. The National Council for Women's Education appointed a committee under the chairmanship of Smt. Hansa Mahta. The committee recommended that courses available for women should not be strictly compartmentalised, implying that women should not in any case be compelled to take up a particular course. The Committee gave a warning that if choice is restricted to women it shall be wrong in national interest. The Education Commission also did not like that girls should be forced to take up particular courses only. It suggested that the more academic type of girls with ambitions of pursuing careers of research or teaching at the college or university level or in professions such as medicine and technology should have all the opportunities and incentives for doing so.

The most popular professions for women are nursing and education. Facilities for higher education in these areas have to be strengthened. At the B.Sc. level in some universities Nursing has been introduced with a view to preparing qualified nursing staff. A scientific and professional course needs development so that it may have an academic value besides leading to a higher level of professional training in nursing. Similarly, there is a need to vitalise and upgrade the courses in Education at B.A. level which have been introduced in eleven universities. Women decide earlier whether they would adopt teaching as their profession or not. Hence, it is necessary that either the courses in Education at B.A. level be so prepared that women opting for them may be directly employable in teaching or concurrent integrated courses in general and professional teacher education may be given to them to enable them to join teaching at an earlier age.

Higher education for women must be linked up with avenues of employment because in the absense of employment their education will be wasted away. Hence, specific avenues will have to be searched out where their services may be utilised fruitfully. The services of highly educated women are needed in education, social work and nursing and similar professional fields. Their services are also required in nutrition, dietetics, institutional management and similar occupational areas. Home science has been recognised as an academic discipline in as many as 33 universities. A woman who takes up this subject at the university level should be so equipped that she may be able to work in professional fields of dietetics, food technology, family welfare work, extension work in community development and welfare Extension Projects. She must be able to take up research work in projects end schemes of I.C.M.R., I.C.A.R. and Council of Child Welfare.

Three or four universities may set-up women wings for giving high level training in business administration and management. A National Institute for Women may be established separately for this purpose.

CO-EDUCATION

Co-education is the education of boys and girls together in the same institution, admission being secured on equal terms and opportunities being offered for the mixing of both the sexes in all the activities cannected with the institution. It does not mean admission of boys and girls into each other's institutions with no opportunities of mutual contacts in connection with the school activities. Co-education therefore, means education of the children of both the sexes in the same institution with fuller freedom of mixing with each other freely.

Brief History

Much has been said on the vexed question of co-education without any body as yet saying the conclusive word on it. It has been as much a perplexing problem in the West as it is in India. Its history in india is of a recent origin. We do not come across any references from our ancient culture about education. Our ancestors were against this institution. But the practice of co-education in the West is quite old. There was co-education in ancient Greece and Rome. Pestalozzi considered it as quite useful. Even in France, it was found practicable. As a matter of convenience, as a measure of financial economy and as a result of the belief that boys and girls have much to gain, mixed schools have gradually gained importance and increased in number. Co-education in the real sense obtains in America and U.S.S.R. In England, Italy and Germany, co-education is mainly confined to the primary and college stages. There general opinion is against secondary stage. In India also, co-education of this nature is prevalent.

How Far is it Desirable

In India it has remained in the nature of a problem. In the other countries co-education is a favoured idea. Is co-education a really immoral institution, resulting in gross corruption and criminal sexual laxity, spoiling the students completely or is it one of the most beneficial institutions the crying need of our country, the panacea of all evil, the only psychologically sound method of imparting education and removing the false sexological complexes?

There is no doubt that much can be said in favour of co-education psychologically. It is true enough that the establishment of normal relationships between boys and girls and the growth or familiarity between them would make them develop more naturally and would remove much of false shyness, abnormal and unnatural behaviour and would lead to a better understanding between boys and girls. Greater contact between boys and girls will, no doubt, result in a sense of comradeship and after due course of time will be able to approach each other without giving that undue emphasis to the sexual aspect. Also the awkwardness that overtakes both sexes now on meeting would disappear.

Competition amongst boys and girls would lead to greater efficiency. This is supported by the results of examinations in the United States of America where full scope is given to co-education at all stages primary, secondary and university. Co-education also tones up the discipline of the institution because the presence of the opposite sex has a wholesome effect on their morals. Boys become less coarse and vulgar and girls less shy and morbid. An eminent educationist once said, "I would advise the education of sexes together. Segregation is unhealthy and stirs the sex urge. I can guarantee nothing in a school where there are girls alone." There is some truth in it.

Co-education would engender good social contacts between the two sexes. They would be relieved of mental strain and a better social development would take place. Both would develop natural and rational personalities.

Co-education would suit a poor country like ours. There shall be a good deal of saving. Duplication of buildings, staff and other establishment expenses would be avoided. Co-education would be economical.

Advantages of Co-education

Co-education is as much a fascinating problem as it is vexing. It has both advantages and disadvantages.

1. It is psychologically very sound. The repressed feelings of both sexes find healthy and congenial environments. It would remove false complexes of both boys and girls.
2. It is most economical. We cannot afford to have separate medical, industrial and technical institutions.
3. The mixing of the sexes is natural as the feminine mind gains from association with boys and *vica versa.*
4. Students can study the characteristics of the opposite sex. Pope has said, "The proper study of mankind is man."
5. Co-education will lead to greater literacy.
6. General morals and character are also built.
7. Well integrated personalities are developed.
8. Most of the marriages made after co-educational experience are successful.
9. It will bring about saner attitude for each other. The boys will learn to respect girls and vice-versa. Better understanding will take place.
10. Co-education will lead to healthy compelition in studies and co-curricular activities.
11. In view of the growing demand for general education and lack of separate institutions co-education is the only solution of the problem.
12. Co-education will reduce mental diseases. Dr. Freud believed that co-education alone could keep young people free from certain dieases of mind.
13. Better demestic life would be developed through co-education. Addition once said, "Female friendship is necessary for intellectual development."

Disadvantages of Education

Let us consider the other side of the medal as well. Every rose has thorns with it. Every smile is accompanied by a tear. Wherever co-education bas so many merits, it has demerits also.

1. In all cases of repression, whenever freedom is gained all of a sudden, the result is always riot which, though it lasts for a short while, can never be avoided.
2. Co-education would mean the same type of education for both men and women. And men and women are temperamentally different and education, therefore must in their cases be different from each other.
3. Mixing of sexes at the adolescent stage when sex urge is at its highest pitch, is not advisable. It distracts the attention of both boys and girls and hampers their progress in studies.
4. Their vocations in life are different and this points out to the need of totally different types of education for them. The task of propagation of the race, bringing up children and building the nation has to be done by women, while men will have to do the roughest business. To encourage co-education would be silly.
5. The result of the impact of each other's personality would be that girls will become masculine and boys effeminate.
6. There are some subjects which cannot be taught together especially biology and poetry.
7. Co-education institutions are difficult to organise and manage and there is a good deal of truth in it. It will create many problems of discipline.
8. Under a uniform code of discipline, girls are likely to suffer more.

9. The strongest objection to co-education is from the moral point of view. Emotional disturbances will take place. They are exposed to sex appeal and morals are at risk. Sex criminality will increase with co-education.

Weighing the pros and cons of the problem and considering the peculiar conditions of India, her social customs and traditions, her orthodoxy and conservativeness, it is rather difficult to introduce co-education at all stages. It can, however, be done in the primary classes where the mixing of sexes is healthy and harmless and at advanced university stage when boys and girls have developed a sense of responsibility and where it is expensive to provide separate institutions for them. At all the other stages, girls schools must be separate from boys.

Apart from these, the writer ventures to give the following suggestions :

(a) Under the prevailing social and economic conditions, there is no harm in introducing co-education.

(b) Equal opportunities should be offered to both boys and girls for self expression.

(c) Curriculum should be prepared in such a way that it caters to the interests, needs and aptitudes of both boys and girls.

(d) Co-currcular activities, particularly N.C.C., girl guiding and physical activities should be conducted separately for girls.

(e) Separate retiring places and sanitary arrangements should exist for the girl students.

(f) Co-educational institutions should possess congenial climate.

(g) Provision should be made for the teaching of subjects like Music, House-hold Accounts, Domestic

Arithmetic, Home craft and other subjects intended for girls.

(*h*) Teaching staff (mixed) should be extremely efficient.

Co-education at the Various Stages of Education

Co-education at all stages of education exists only in a few western countries like U.S.A. and U.S S.R. In others, it exists at the primary and university stages. Let us discuss its possibility at all levels.

1. Primary Stage. There are strong financial and educational reasons in favour of co-education at primary stage. At this there is absolutely no harm in having co-education especially in those areas where the number of boys and girls attending a school is too less. It becomes, rather necessary to have co-education. Separate boys and girls schools would be too expensive. It will not give rise to problems at all. The sex consciousness is absolutely dormant at this age. They are too innocent. Even from the point of view of curriculum also there is little need for differentiation. From organisational point of view, it is possible to reproduce the spirit, conditions and relations of home. At this stage, the psychological differences are not at all prominent. So no problems can possibly arise so as to pose danger. Therefore the desirability of co-education at the primary stage is generally accepted.

Staff for the Primary Stage. It need not be stressed that the youngsters can be best handled by women. Since the mother is an important factor in the life of a child, a woman teacher as "mother substitute" has great potentialities. The writer has seen this system working well even in boys' schools where the primary school children are taught by female teachers. Women teachers have manners, sweet temper and dutiful nature. They are less harsh. The children love them as they love their mothers. Since women know proper handling of young ones, they are most competent to look after their educational needs. In co-educational primary schools

schools, lady teachers are a necessity. They are better fitted to do the job. If for some reasons, lady teachers are not available in a large number, mixed staff is needed.

2. Secondary Stage. Co-education at this stage presents many difficulties. Boys and girls reach the adolescence stage and it is fraught with many dangers. The objections to co-education at this stage can be discussed under psychological, physiological and moral heads.

(a) ***Psychological.*** The emotional and temperamental differences, are noticeable at this stage. Girls attach greater importance to feelings; and sentiments and are more serious and hard working than boys. They have a greater sense of responsibility. The interests of boys and; girls are quite different and the two cannot be taught with the same methods of teaching. Co-education at this stage will lead to premature sex stimulation which is not conducive to normal growth.

(b) ***Moral.*** People oppose co-education from the moral point of view. Boys and girls are extremely susceptible to sex appeal and the morals are exposed to risks. People consider co-education a monstrously immoral institution, which will result in gross corruption and criminal sexual laxity, wrecking the students completely. This is, of course, an extreme view.

Let us consider the views of the supporters of co-education with regard to morals. The co-educationists argue that wisdom lies in meeting the special dangers of the age when they arise and in directing the impulses and energies into healthy and useful channels. To run away from the problems of education is to adopt an escapist attitude. We must come to grips with the problems that arise out of it. Sex consciousness is reduced by the constant social contact of sexes. The sex relations become unsentimental with no mystery about sex. There are fewer changes of sex strains, perversions and abnormalilies. Co-education trains boys and girls for participating in the civic life on equal terms. To accept all this as correct would amount to shutting the eyes to stark realities of co-education. Some complicated problems will crop up, but they can be faced.

(c) ***Physiological.*** Vast physiological changes start taking place amongst boys and girls. One of the most important changes is the development of sex characteristics. There are primary sex characteristics and secondary sex characteristics. Primary sex characteristics include the development of reproductive organs while secondary sex characteristics include the development of pubic hair, appearance of board, width of hips, development of breast etc. These changes lead to fear and restlessness. Both find it difficult to adjust to new bodily changes and take to day-dreaming and remain pre-occupied with sex. In view of these physical changes it would be harmful to put boys and girls together in the same school.

3. University Stage. Co-education is very much favoured at the University stage. The reasons are obvious. The students are comparatively mature and they can think of their future. By this age, they have sufficiently gained proper understanding of each other. They have also learnt to respect each other. Some of the misunderstandings about the opposite sexes, too, are properly removed. By this stage, boys and girls are supposed to have secured control over their sex impulses and to have acquired enough intelligence and discretion. The ideas and attitudes of boys and girls towards life also start taking a definite shape. This stage does not pose any problem at all.

❋❋❋

Index

N

O

P

Q

R

S

T

U

V

W

Y